Charles Burnett: Interviews

Conversations with Filmmakers Series
Gerald Peary, General Editor

Charles Burnett
INTERVIEWS

Edited by Robert E. Kapsis

University Press of Mississippi / Jackson

For Julia and Johanna

www.upress.state.ms.us

The University Press of Mississippi is a member of the Association of American University Presses.

Copyright © 2011 by University Press of Mississippi
All rights reserved

First printing 2011

∞

Library of Congress Cataloging-in-Publication Data

Charles Burnett : interviews / edited by Robert E. Kapsis.
    p. cm. — (Conversations with filmmakers series)
  Includes index.
  ISBN 978-1-60473-949-7 (cloth : alk. paper) — ISBN 978-1-60473-950-3 (ebook)
1. Burnett, Charles—Interviews. 2. Motion picture producers and directors—United States—Interviews. I. Kapsis, Robert E.
  PN1998.3.B865A5 2011
  791.4302'33092—dc22
    [B]   2010037703

British Library Cataloging-in-Publication Data available

Contents

Introduction   ix

Chronology   xxvii

Filmography   xxxi

Black Independent American Cinema: Charles Burnett   3
    Corine McMullin/1980

An Artisan of Daily Life: Charles Burnett   5
    Catherine Arnaud and Yann Lardau/1981

Life Drawings: Charles Burnett's Realism   10
    Monona Wali/1988

The House of Spirits   25
    Samir Hachem/1989

The Long-Distance Runner: Charles Burnett's Quiet Revolution   28
    Lynell George/1990

The Black Familiar   38
    Lisa Kennedy/1990

Interview with Charles Burnett   42
    Michel Cieutat and Michel Ciment/1990

An Interview with Charles Burnett   53
    Bérénice Reynaud/1991

One on One: Charles Burnett and Charles Lane   65
    Charles Burnett and Charles Lane/1991

The House I Live In: An Interview with Charles Burnett   75
    Aida A. Hozic/1994

An Explorer of the Black Mind Looks Back, but Not in Anger   95
    Michael Sragow/1995

Burnett Looks Back   100
    Amy Taubin/1995

Violence Sells: So They're Telling Charles Burnett   103
    Wolf Schneider/1995

Above It All: Charles Burnett Puts Black Power in Subtle Films   106
    Gary Dauphin/1997

Talking with Charles Burnett   109
    Sojin Kim and R. Mark Livengood/1998

Invisible Man   118
    Terrence Rafferty/2001

Set This House on Fire: Nat Turner's Second Coming   126
    Gerald Peary/2001

Warming by the Devil's Fire: Director Interview   130
    Charles Burnett/2003

Charles Burnett   134
    Doug Cummings/2003

Independent Lens: Charles Burnett   138
    Scott Foundas/2006

Shadows of Watts, in the Light   141
    Dave Kehr/2007

A Vision of Watts Still Frozen in Time   145
    Mary McNamara/2007

This Bitter Earth   150
    James Ponsoldt/2007

A Conversation with Charles Burnett   161
    David Lowery/2007

Charles Burnett's *Namibia* Premieres at the 2007 LAFF   168
    Diane Sippl/2007

Charles Burnett Celebrates a Milestone   174
    Susan Gerhard/2007

Blues People   181
    James Bell/2008

Index   187

Introduction

Charles Burnett is a groundbreaking African American filmmaker and one of this country's greatest directors, yet he remains largely unknown. His films, most notably *Killer of Sheep* (1977) and *To Sleep with Anger* (1990), are considered classics, yet few filmgoers have seen them or heard of Burnett. The interviews in this volume explore this paradox and collectively shed light on the making of a rare film master whose work brings to the screen the texture and poetry of life in the black community.

As a supremely talented and fiercely independent film director, Burnett makes movies according to his own unique artistic vision and socially engaged viewpoint. His films' best qualities—rich characterizations, morally and emotionally complex narratives, and intricately observed tales of African American life "subtly layered with cultural references and mythic overtones"—are precisely what make his films such a "tough sell" in the mass marketplace (see Nelson Kim's profile of Burnett in *Senses of Cinema*, 2003; not included in this volume). Hollywood, as the interviews presented here reveal, has been largely inept in responding to the challenges of marketing Burnett's films. And no one is more aware of it than Burnett, who told Terrence Rafferty in 2001, "It just takes an extraordinary effort to keep going when everybody's saying to you, 'No one wants to see that kind of movie,' or 'There's no black audience.'"

Against the odds, Burnett did keep going. This book provides a window into three decades of his directorial career, during which he produced an extraordinary body of work. It focuses on his status as a true independent filmmaker and explores his motivation for involving himself in films that all chronicle some aspect of the black experience in America.

As a film student in UCLA's Graduate Program in Film and Television Production during the 1970s, Burnett, along with fellow students like

Julie Dash, Haile Gerima, and Billy Woodberry, set out to tell stories that rejected Hollywood stereotypes that depicted the black community in strictly negative terms—drug infested, violent, malevolent, and dysfunctional. Eventually this group of young filmmakers would come to be known as alternatively the "L.A. School of Black Filmmakers" and the "L.A. Rebellion." Burnett's student films included two shorts, *Several Friends* (1969) and *The Horse* (1973), and his feature-length MFA thesis film, *Killer of Sheep* (1977), an unusually complex and poetic vision of African American life set in the Watts section of Los Angeles. As Burnett saw it, these three films (and the rest that would follow) "offered insights" to black viewers about their own experiences growing up black in America. His films were in sharp contrast to the "action-packed dramas" produced by Hollywood that, according to Burnett, had reduced the black community to "drugs and mothers who prostitute themselves . . . I can sell a plot to a studio, I believe, about situations where a girl is on drugs, her brother is on drugs, their mother is on drugs, and their father disappeared and there is this white guy who is going to come and save the young boy or something like that" (*American Film*, 1991). "When I was in UCLA," recalls Burnett, "we were making independent films because we wanted to do something positive. Not necessarily to entertain" (*Boston Globe*, May 28, 1995; not included in this collection). "It was a period [the late 1960s and 1970s] when there was a lot of social activism [and] people were really using arts as a means to social change. Film was there, and I gravitated towards it" (*Sight and Sound*, 2008).

Burnett's first feature film, *Killer of Sheep* (1977), made the rounds at a number of European film festivals during the late seventies and early eighties, and went on to win the prestigious Critics Award at the 1981 Berlin Festival. Yet, as he reflected on this early phase of his career in an interview (Ponsoldt, 2007), Burnett recalled: "When *Killer of Sheep* won the Critics Award at the Berlin Film Festival it was in all the European newspapers but when I came back to the U.S., there was no press."

In fact, by the early 1980s, Burnett's work had begun to capture a glimmer of critical attention, principally in European film publications. This book opens with two interviews from that period published in France (McMullin, 1980; Arnaud and Lardau, 1981; see also "Black Independents: Interview with Charles Burnett" in *Skrien*, a film magazine from the Netherlands, April 1981, not included here).

Catherine Arnaud and Yann Lardau, writing in *La Revue du cinéma* in 1981, explore early influences that motivated Burnett to become a filmmaker and how those influences helped shape his approach to the medium. We learn that in film school at UCLA Burnett took a course from the British documentary filmmaker Basil Wright, who, says Burnett, "made me understand that the cinema was something serious, capable of expressing the nature and the dignity of man. He also made me understand the value of the documentary, the importance of not imposing your own values on the topics you film . . . He brought a certain humanism to my way of seeing things." In the same interview, we learn how Burnett would put Wright's ideas into practice. "I live in the community in which and about which I make my movies . . . The people I know are out of work . . . stuck in the insoluble problems they're obliged to endure [and] take out their frustrations in a very violent manner . . . I tried . . . to look at my community in a way that allowed me to find elements inside their own lives, and to construct a theme that would be seen and lived from their point of view."

Many of the people who acted in Burnett's early films were not professionals. "They're people I know who are part of the community of Watts. And so I have a particular responsibility with regard to them. I have to be very attentive to their way of seeing things . . . In *Killer of Sheep*, I tried to give a sense of the reality that they live with every day. I tried to construct a theme that captures something of their life in the most objective way possible."

In this interview, Burnett also explains the strong presence of children in the film: "In my community, the most important thing is to survive . . . and children are taught that they have to support their brother or their family no matter what they do, as the father says at the beginning of *Killer of Sheep*." We learn that throughout this film, Burnett treats the children as witnesses, particularly attentive to their parents' actions. From this the children will develop their moral sense—their sense of right and wrong. If the world of their parents revolves mostly around issues of survival, the children, according to Burnett, will not develop an emotionally rich inner life.

Monona Wali's interview with Burnett, the first to appear in an American film publication (*The Independent*, October 1988), gives the reader a profound sense of what it was like for Burnett and other black Americans of his generation growing up in the South Central section of Los Angeles during the 1950s and 1960s. "I was a product of that [period just before the] civil rights movement. You really felt your limitations. Your reality was a few square blocks. You felt this was your only world, and the only way to get out of it was to join the service." Burnett, instead, chose college (his way, we will learn in later interviews, to avoid the draft) and "began to see another world—that there's something more to life than thinking that by the time you're twenty you're going to be dead . . . And then I saw all these other people who seemed healthier—enjoying life—particularly when I went to UCLA."

The interview includes an insightful discussion of *Killer of Sheep*. We learn that at UCLA Burnett had seen a number of films about working-class life but could not relate to them in terms of his own experiences growing up in South Central Los Angles. In these films, according to Burnett, "issues were idealized, and . . . conflicts . . . reduced to problems between management and labor." Management exploits the workers, the union calls a strike, and the workers are saved. These were films, says Burnett, with a built-in resolution. By contrast, the issues in Burnett's neighborhood, as he saw them, were completely different. "What was essential was finding a job, working, making enough money, and then, at the end of the day, coming home and still trying to show signs of life." In fact, according to Burnett, that was what *Killer of Sheep* was really all about: "It's about how Stan, the main character, loses his sensitivity and still tries to maintain a certain kind of dignity. You can see at the very beginning [a child] traumatized by a fact of life. The father tells the little boy, 'If you see your brother's in a fight, you help him, whether your brother's right or wrong. You don't stand and watch. You go and help your brother.' Which is okay, but you can imagine what effect this has if you have a conscience and are developing a moral concept. It was that kind of conflict that I was interested in trying to portray. How do you work in this environment? How do you maintain a certain amount of dignity? I wanted to show what price it takes to survive. How you survive is a personal choice. I don't think a film should tell you A happens, and then B, and then C will necessarily follow. Life isn't necessarily that simple. Films have a tendency to generalize, to reduce complex issues."

In this interview, Burnett also discusses his second feature film, *My Brother's Wedding* (1983), and how it differed in both subject matter and style from *Killer of Sheep*. More striking, however, is what these two films have in common, namely, Burnett attempting "something . . . very difficult—mak[ing] sense out of life." This search would continue with his third feature, *To Sleep with Anger*, which, at the time of Wali's interview, was in its planning stage.

The release and critical reception of *To Sleep with Anger* (1990) mark an important turning point in Burnett's career. Tackling the fractured struggles between good and evil within a middle-class black Angelino family, the film appeared at a number of film festivals (including Sundance, Cannes, Toronto, and New York), winning a special jury prize at Sundance. It opened to mostly enthusiastic reviews, and went on to win Independent Spirit Awards for Best Director and Best Screenplay and special awards from the Los Angeles Film Critics Association and the American Film Institute. Not surprisingly, a number of interviews with Burnett were published around this time and several are included in this volume. Particularly newsworthy for this period are the Burnett profiles published in the *Village Voice* (August 22, 1989, and October 16, 1990), *LA Weekly* (October 12, 1990), the *Los Angeles Times* (August 12, 1989, and October 24, 1990), and the *New York Amsterdam News* (November 3, 1990)—among the first media to introduce and, in some cases, actively champion Burnett's career in the United States. (*The Village Voice* and *LA Weekly* profiles are included in this volume.) It would be several years before detailed profiles of Burnett start appearing in influential dailies like the *New York Times*, the *Washington Post*, and the *Boston Globe*.

The two *Village Voice* profiles from 1989 and 1990 deserve special comment. The 1989 profile by Samir Hachem focuses almost entirely on *To Sleep with Anger*, which was in production at the time of the interview. We learn from Burnett that the film is about "three generations in a middle-class black family wrestling with its own values and those of a new culture," and what happens when a character patterned after the folkloric characters found in southern black myths pays the family an unexpected visit. "He's a [trickster]," says Burnett, "that comes to steal your soul, and you have to out-trick him. You can bargain with him. But you have to be more clever than he is." We also learn that Burnett's own skills as a storyteller, according to Hachem, can be largely "attributed to his grandmother, a solid Mississippi woman who taught him his first lessons and tall tales." The rest of the piece is more of a production story that, among other things, reveals some of the frustrations Burnett had to deal with as a result of making his first film with "Hollywood money" where the emphasis is on "getting it done [that is, on time], not how." This pressure was especially palpable given that the interview took place on the set of *To Sleep with Anger* with only three shooting days remaining. Problems associated with making an all-black film also surfaced during the interview. The Corporation for Public Broadcasting had initially backed the script development but eventually pulled out because, according to Burnett, "they didn't like the [folklore] elements in it." By the time the picture was ready to go into production, it had accumulated six producers. The experience of making *To Sleep with Anger*, admits Burnett, was "an eye-opener."

Lisa Kennedy's 1990 profile of Burnett appeared in the *Village Voice* less than two weeks after *To Sleep with Anger* opened in Manhattan. Kennedy, who is African American, was the *Voice*'s senior film and arts editor at the time of the interview. Clearly this is a self-initiated assignment and one Kennedy felt strongly about doing, as she presents to her readers the strongest case possible for viewing Burnett as a major visionary artist: "*To Sleep with Anger* is not artful docudrama, not comedy," asserts Kennedy, "but the work of a visual novelist. The company Burnett keeps is not with his would-be peers—[Spike] Lee or the Hudlins [Reginald and Warrington] or the Wayans [Marlon and Shawn]—but with Toni Morrison or playwright August Wilson; being a filmmaker though, this makes him hard to pigeonhole and harder to market." According to Kennedy, Burnett is a master at revealing (in both *To Sleep with Anger* and *Killer of Sheep*) that African American lives "are symbolically rich." Other films, she acknowledges, have touched on this. What is unique about Burnett's films, argues Kennedy, is that they are black "without trying to explain blackness" to whites—"a subtle, important shift." Significantly, his films visualize the ambivalence that many northern blacks feel about their southern roots. Burnett was born in Mississippi but when he was a small child his family moved to South Central Los Angeles. "My mother hated the South," says Burnett. "My grandmother was always telling stories about it, my mother hated it, she never wanted to go back, never went back. My uncle's the same way. But I have a cousin who's a country preacher and when we go to visit him, you're in church all day. We've always had this love/hate thing in the family about the South. I think there was a kind of denial at work. I remember a time when being called 'country' was the worst thing that could be said about you." Elsewhere in the interview, Burnett admits his own ambivalence about his southern heritage. Growing up, he would on occasion posture about "hating the blues" (clarified during a personal exchange between Burnett and the editor, Los Angeles, March 2010), but his films, as Kennedy notes, are "buoyed" and "swayed" by them. "I couldn't understand," says Burnett, "how people liked [collard] greens." Then all of a sudden, as a teenager, he developed "a craving for greens." And now, as Kennedy informs us, "They're a staple in his movies." Adds Burnett, "You can only stay away from home so long."

The *LA Weekly* profile by Lynell George, appearing around the same time as Kennedy's piece, focuses less on Burnett's artistry and more on the special challenges he faced as the director of films like *To Sleep with Anger*, which are such a tough sell in the mass market place. The *LA Weekly* profile is also effective in uncovering clues to Burnett's character and sense of self. For example, his serious yet unassuming nature is captured in the following description: "The director prefers the low profile that has allowed him to traverse his neighborhood streets unnoticed . . . [I]f you 'take a meeting' with him on home ground, he'll suggest someplace low-key and convenient for both parties, Sizzler or I-Hop. He arrives—out of breath—casually dressed in a fresh white T-shirt, the factory creases still at sharp points, a warm-up jacket, and crisp blue jeans. Lowering himself into a booth, he politely requests coffee or a single glass of white wine that he'll nurse for three hours . . . 'Make sure you have Charles tell you a story,' an old school friend of his insists, '*any* story. Charles tells a great story.' That's clear from his new film which, like his conversations, is full of storytelling. Burnett tells stories with his hands, with dark serious eyes, continually tempering and reshaping them." What emerges from this interview and subsequent ones (see, e.g., Rafferty, 2001) is a portrait of Burnett as serious, fearlessly independent, hard-working, gentle, soft-spoken, unassuming, resilient, serene, and always bemused by the idiocies and cruelties of the human condition. Indeed, several interviewers observe that when Burnett "recounts battles with other producers and distributors," he does so "in a serene, matter-of-fact tone"—never voicing anger, outrage, or bitterness (see Rafferty, 2001).

European journalists and critics continued to respond enthusiastically to Burnett's work. In fact, the interview by Michel Cieutat and Michel Ciment published in *Positif* in November 1990 is one of the most detailed, comprehensive, and impassioned pieces included in this volume. Unlike most of the other interview/profiles appearing in the early 1990s, the *Positif* piece focuses as much on film technique, cinematic vocabulary, and style as on content. Especially engaging is Burnett's discussion of the importance of music in his films, where he states his preference for southern blues over more urban-based jazz. Another highlight of this interview is an unexpected discussion of Van Gogh's paintings in relation to Burnett's own allusive way of telling a story. The question that triggered his discussion of Van Gogh is reproduced below along with Burnett's response:

> **Positif:** You mentioned Russian literature. One could think in particular of Chekhov because your way of telling stories is very circuitous, in contrast to Spike Lee, who addresses himself directly to the public. Your own commentary on the society is just as strong, but you express it implicitly.
>
> **Charles Burnett:** I prefer to remain allusive, to proceed by metaphor. It gives more meaning and poetry to things you can't explain. I've never met a person who wasn't complicated. There are always several layers of meaning, several intentions in what people say. So it's necessary to be suggestive . . . I am a great admirer of Van Gogh. I love his paintings. I read the complete edition of his letters to his brother, and one of the most interesting things you find there is that according to him the essence of expression is situated in gestures. It's by gestures that you can express the exact temperature of a bath, the right shoes. That's the case in *The Potato Eaters*, where you can feel the heat escaping from the potatoes through the exaggerated expressions of the characters. It's better to capture the essence than to be limited to photographing reality.

Bérénice Reynaud, then the New York correspondent for *Cahiers du cinéma*, interviewed Burnett prior to the 1990 Cannes Film Festival, where *To Sleep with Anger* opened to mostly favorable reviews. An updated version of this interview appeared in the *Black American Literature Forum* (1991). One of its many revelations is Burnett's speculation that "a serious speech impediment" may have led him to become a filmmaker: "I always felt like an outsider—an observer—who wasn't able to participate because I couldn't speak very well. So this inability to communicate must have led me . . . to find some other means to express myself . . . I really liked a lot of the kids I grew up with. I felt an obligation to write something about them, to explain what went wrong with them. I think that's the reason I started to make these movies."

One of the most disturbing aspects about the whole *To Sleep with*

Anger phenomenon was that, despite all the rave reviews and prestigious awards, few people actually went to see the film. Even more puzzling, according to a marketing piece appearing in the *New York Times* a month or so after the film's release, was the fact that *To Sleep with Anger* typically performed five times as well in white neighborhoods as in black areas (*New York Times*, November 20, 1990; not included in this volume). The film's poor performance among blacks obviously upset Burnett, who told the *Times* that he thought this was due not to a lack of interest but rather to inept marketing on the part of the film's distributor, the Samuel Goldwyn Company. "It's not that the black community is not responding," says Burnett, "but that the film companies have not really tried very hard to communicate with black audiences." Goldwyn executives interviewed for the story claimed that they did work hard to get the black press interested in the film but that, with few exceptions, the effort failed. The *New York Amsterdam News* turned out to be almost the only leading black publication to interview Burnett about the film (November 3, 1990; not included in this collection). The lack of response from black publications, argues Burnett, is due to the fact that the Hollywood studios "just call [them] up out of the blue once every two years or so instead of having an ongoing relationship." According to Goldwyn's vice president for theatrical distribution, the film appealed primarily to the "middle and upper classes, both black and white, not blue-collar blacks [and blue-collar] whites." In other words, it was drawing the "classic art-house crowd." Still there were no signs that Burnett had abandoned his efforts to attract his target audience—working-class blacks—to the film. "People have been going around putting up posters in Washington and Chicago, and we've been going on [all black] radio stations," he said.

In 1991 *American Film*, the official magazine of the American Film Institute, published a scintillating conversation between Burnett and fellow African American director Charles Lane about the seemingly insurmountable challenges facing black directors (especially those like Burnett with an uncompromisingly independent predisposition) working in the white-dominated film business. From this exchange it becomes clear that Burnett continued to view himself as a political activist filmmaker who used the film medium to effect social change. Implicit in Burnett's critique of what's wrong with Hollywood is the desire for a more socially engaged cinema:

> Sometimes to make a film gives the impression that everything is fair and that whenever you depict the dominant culture, you have to show it in a good light. It's like a committee imposing on the structure. That's one of the reasons why we haven't made social progress. We just saw Rodney King get beaten to a pulp, and in Boston where this guy killed his wife and blamed it on the black community, the whole nation wanted to hang everybody there. You can't walk down Little Cicero or even drive through Beverly Hills now without being harassed. We don't use film as a means to confront real issues that over time will create a better society.

After *To Sleep with Anger*, Burnett co-directed a documentary about immigrants, *America Becoming*, which aired on public television in 1991. The ninety-minute film focused on how the U.S., a country that was becoming increasingly multicultural, was relating to new waves of migration from Asia, the Middle East, Africa, and Central and South America. Burnett told Aida Hozic (*Callaloo*, 1994) that the project fell far short of his expectations. "When we started filming," says Burnett, "I thought that we were supposed to be objective about what was going on in this country." PBS and the Ford Foundation, the sponsors of the project, saw things differently. According to Burnett, they wanted the film to "paint a rosy picture of American immigrants"—to show that the "melting pot [is] working, that immigrants do well, that they bring a lot of resources to this country." "What saddens me the most," said Burnett in this interview, is that the documentary "could have anticipated all these riots and problems that different ethnic groups are facing in America today—and we did not."

Burnett's collaborator on *America Becoming* was Korean American filmmaker Dai Sil Kim-Gibson, who produced, co-directed, and co-wrote the documentary. A *Korea Times* profile of the two filmmakers reported that they were working together on a new project, a feature drama about Korean-black relations (January 13, 1991; not included in this collection). "What we are trying to do," explained Burnett, is "make a story that not only deals with the conflict between blacks and Koreans," but also probes the differences between "Korean and black cultures." (The finished product, a short film titled *Olivia's Story*, was released in 1999.)

The next three interviews presented are from 1995—the year that *The Glass Shield*, a police procedural drama set in Los Angeles, opened in theaters. This film was Burnett's first feature since *To Sleep with Anger* in 1990. During this five-year period, his credentials as an "art house" director had solidified. Published pieces about him routinely mentioned his $275,000 "Genius Award" from the MacArthur Foundation, the acclaim his films received at international film festivals, his prestigious fellowships from the National Endowment for the Arts and from the Rockefeller and Guggenheim foundations, and, most recently, that his original screenplay for *To Sleep with Anger* had received the National Society of Film Critics Award for best screenplay of 1990. None of these accomplishments, however, helped his reputation with the Hollywood studios that, increasingly, viewed him as just another one of those "art house" directors not fit for the big time.

On the other hand, the *New York Times* and other upscale publications found Burnett's art house reputation attractive. In 1995, Michael Sragow's passionate and detailed profile of the director appeared in the Sunday Arts and Leisure section of the *Times*. It was the first extensive interview of Burnett to be published there. What precipitated the interview was news that the American Museum of the Moving Image (AMMI) was holding a two-day retrospective of Burnett's feature films and a preview of his fourth, *The Glass Shield* (see "A Pinewood Dialogue with Charles Burnett," 1995; not included in this volume). The profile fills in some of the specifics about the MacArthur genius award Burnett received in 1988. The award gave him $275,000 over five years. The prestige of the award helped launch *To Sleep with Anger*, while the generous stipend, distributed in equal amounts over the five year period (1988–93), enabled Burnett for the first time in his career to focus exclusively on making his own films. One learns that Burnett had experienced lean times before the award, "struggling to make his own films," explains Sragow, "while seeking grants and mowing lawns, doing cinematography and screen writing for friends and messenger work and script reading for a talent agency." Interestingly, Sragow erroneously classifies Burnett as essentially a director of art films. This surfaces while Sragow is describing what he believes was the motivation behind Burnett's latest feature film: "Like all of Mr. Burnett's movies," says Sragow, "*The Glass Shield* was done on the cheap; nevertheless, it tries to blend realism and flashy stylization. It marks a transition for the director. After two decades of making art films, Mr. Burnett is trying to appeal to a wider audience." Sprinkled throughout Sragow's profile of the director are direct references and allusions to famous artists whose concerns, apparently, Burnett shares, starting with William Faulkner who, says

Burnett, "was aware of . . . black psychology." "The right to exist, how to exist, [and] the power to endure," says Burnett, "were always part of his theme." Faulkner comes up again during a discussion of *The Glass Shield*, Burnett's police drama about how a black rookie cop, the first minority officer in an all-white L.A. County sheriff's office, is forced to deal with the blatant racism he experiences there. "Mr. Burnett was drawn to the plight of the black police officer," says Sragow, "because he—like . . . Joe Christmas in Faulkner's *Light in August*—exists 'in a white world and a black world at the same time.' Faulkner, says Mr. Burnett, understood how people with a foot in each world are forced to adjust, 'how it affects their speech when they're in one or the other.'" Other artists mentioned or alluded to in this piece include Ernest Hemingway, Albert Camus, Jean Renoir, Roman Polanski, and the black writers of the Harlem Renaissance.

Also on the occasion of AMMI's two-week retrospective, the *Voice* (January 10, 1995) featured a short profile on Burnett that was attuned to some of the problems he was having with *The Glass Shield*, particularly with Miramax, the distributor. Many of these problems are discussed more fully in an *LA Weekly* (June 2, 1995) profile that appeared in conjunction with the general release of the movie in theatres. One of Burnett's frustrations revolved around Miramax's fateful decision to pitch *The Glass Shield* as a *Boyz n the Hood* type of action film that would appeal mainly to black males aged fourteen to twenty-four, rather than treating it as a thoughtful and morally ambiguous police drama that might attract a broader audience. As a result, the film was test marketed in the South Bronx, where the youthful black audience thought they were going to see an action movie with rap music starring Ice Cube, who figured prominently in the ads and posters but who, in reality, played only a supporting role in the film. Despite the disastrous outcome of this decision, Burnett told me that it was not his greatest problem during production. He said that from the beginning, Miramax had been "upfront about how they wanted to market the film." "The major conflict," he says, "was with Pierre Rissient, who was representing CiBy 2000, the French company that produced the film. Pierre disagreed with the casting of the film and was never happy with it. He made life difficult from preproduction on. If we had given in to his demands, the film would have been a disaster" (interview with Burnett, Los Angeles, March 2010; cf. interview with *LA Weekly*, June 2, 1995).

Another problem had to do with the ending. The audience attending the special screening had reportedly screamed in protest at the original downbeat ending. As a result, Miramax decided that the ending needed to be changed, and Burnett, according to the *LA Weekly* piece, "reluctantly" agreed. When I spoke with Burnett about this in 2010, however, he stated categorically that the changes he eventually made were exactly what was required. "I needed to cut down on the crying of the main character at the end. I didn't have the material to make the scene shorter, so Miramax gave me the money to change the scene." The new ending, as he told the *LA Weekly* interviewer, suggests a more positive resolution. "It's more obviously upbeat," said Burnett, "rather than sort of ambiguous. More of a closure." In any event, and unfortunately for Burnett, Miramax's campaign to package *The Glass Shield* as a "hood" movie failed miserably, and the film, despite the many enthusiastic reviews it received from leading critics, never reached the more upscale audience that Miramax should have targeted.

After *The Glass Shield*, Burnett worked on two back-to-back film projects that created quite a stir among leading film critics such as Jonathan Rosenbaum, Armond White, and Terrence Rafferty. Chicago critic Jonathan Rosenbaum would characterize one of the projects, the twelve-minute jazz-inspired *When It Rains* (1995), as "one of those rare movies in which jazz forms directly influence film narrative" (*Chicago Reader*, November 13, 2003). In an interview by Susan Gerhard from 2007, we learn that the film came about because Burnett wanted to do something more personal. "We had the use of a camera, and a group of us just shot [*When It Rains*] over a couple of days. It was kind of therapeutic and refreshing." His other project, *Nightjohn* (1996), for the Disney Channel—his first feature for television—was about a slave who sacrifices his freedom in order to teach his fellow slaves how to read and write. In 1998, *Nightjohn*, based on a children's book by Gary Paulsen, would receive a special award from the National Society of Film Critics for a film "whose exceptional quality and originality challenge the strictures of the movie marketplace"—in other words, it is a TV movie made for children that is a masterpiece.

In 1997, the Film Society of Lincoln Center and the Human Rights Watch International Film Festival honored Burnett with a two-week retrospective of his films that showcased *Nightjohn* as the centerpiece of the series. For this occasion, both the *New York Times* and the *Village Voice* featured interviews with Burnett. While the *New York Times* profile (January 30, 1997; not included in this collection) chose not to mention *Nightjohn*, preferring instead to concentrate on Burnett's earlier masterworks and their limited mass appeal, the *Village Voice* interview by Gary Dauphin focused almost entirely on the Disney film (February 4, 1997). Taking his lead from critic Armond White, who once wrote that "[Burnett's] films not only depict black life but sustain it," Dauphin shows that "Burnett's vision comes through quite clearly in *Nightjohn*." Here was a case, according to Burnett, of "an ordinary event" (learning to read) turning "ordinary people into extraordinary ones." "Learning how to read was a dangerous, secretive thing for slaves," says Burnett; "it required quite a bit of courage. You can see that courage echoing in the later lives of great leaders and orators like Frederick Douglass, but also in the commitment to education that still exists in large numbers of people."

Also included in this volume is an atypical interview from this same period published in the *Journal of American Folklore* (1996) that explores how Burnett incorporates folkloric concepts such as "storytelling," "folkways," and "community" into his films. In another unorthodox conversation published that year that could not be included here, Burnett talked freely with cultural critic bell hooks about the challenges and frustrations of making serious films on a shoestring budget (see bell hooks, *Reel to Real: Race, Sex, and Class at the Movies*, Routledge, 1996, chapter 17).

Between 1998 and 2000, Burnett directed three television films: *Oprah Winfrey Presents: The Wedding* (1998), a two-part TV miniseries, adapted from Dorothy West's novel, that deals with issues of race and class in mid-twentieth century black society; *Selma, Lord, Selma* (1999), a TV docudrama about the civil rights movement of the 1960s that aired as part of "The Wonderful World of Disney"; and *Finding Buck McHenry* (2000), about a white Little Leaguer's fascination with a school janitor who may have been a legendary pitcher in the old Negro Baseball League, that aired on Showtime and received a Daytime Emmy for Outstanding Performer (Ossie Davis) in a Children's Special. None of the TV work mentioned above was based on material written by Burnett himself. In 2001, Terrence Rafferty asked Burnett how he felt about directing other people's work. "I'd love to do my own films," Burnett says, "but it takes so long [and] you have to pay the rent" (*GQ*, 2001).

As it happens, during this TV film-for-hire phase of his career, Burnett was also involved in more personal projects, such as *Nat Turner: A Troublesome Property*, about the 1831 slave rebellion in Southampton,

Virginia, led by the black slave, Nat Turner. Part documentary, part fictional re-creation, the completed film, which aired on PBS in 2003, doesn't present one definitive "Nat Turner" but instead, following a *Rashomon*-like narrative structure, re-creates episodes from Turner's life from six contradictory texts in which six different actors play him. In 2001, while the film was still in production, Burnett explained to Gerald Peary (*Village Voice*, September 2001) that his approach and that of his collaborators (Frank Christopher and Kenneth Greenberg) to the source material was to faithfully capture the essence of each of the six contradictory stories about Nat Turner that make up the core of the film—to "take the [various] stories we're given [about Turner] as almost etched in stone." "[Harriet Beecher] Stowe's Nat," says Burnett, "is a simple, angelic innocent, so we show him with a skunk and a mountain lion. In another story [William Styron's version], there's the murderous Nat, so this violent person emerges with a sword." When asked about his own Nat Turner, Burnett is unequivocal in his reply, "He's every man who'd fight for the liberation of others, who realized the evils of slavery and wanted his people to live in a normal way. Everyone has inalienable rights, and he, in a sense, was interpreting the Constitution. Nat Turner was more American than those whites who denied him."

During a lively discussion about the film that took place after a special screening at CalTech, Burnett spoke candidly about some of his own reservations about the finished product—the difficulty of securing funding for the project, how the final version was a compromise in length (initially conceived at two hours, the film now clocks in at fifty-eight minutes) and emphasis (too much time devoted to William Styron's suggestion that Turner was a psychologically disturbed murderer and not enough attention to Burnett's vision of him as a heroic warrior fighting to overthrow the horrific system of slavery). At this point in the discussion, we learn that several white college students begin to "openly question Burnett's perspective." Throughout, soft-spoken Burnett holds steadfast to his views. (The filmmaker's appearance at CalTech is reported by Doug Cummings in *Film Journey*, 2003).

Around the time of the Turner project, Burnett also became involved in another deeply personal assignment, joining forces with Martin Scorsese, Clint Eastwood, Mike Figgis, and other distinguished directors for the documentary miniseries *The Blues* that aired on PBS in 2003. In an interview that appeared on the series' website, Burnett describes what led him to *Warming by the Devil's Fire*, the semi-documentary that he came up with for the series. We learn that unlike the other contributors, Burnett decided to frame his documentary around a fictional story. "The story's told from the perspective of the narrator, [a] young kid," says Burnett, "who returns to Mississippi and becomes aware of the blues as an art form. It's through his eyes that we, the audience, meet the blues. It's through his ears that we listen to the blues and come to appreciate them. The film includes a wide range of music, from raw gutbucket blues to the more sophisticated R&B, and is representative of both male and female singers." As in earlier interviews, Burnett once again reveals how he uses the power of film to capture the rich legacy and poignancy of his southern roots, in this instance, showing how the blues "came out of the South . . . and it speaks to the [oppressive] circumstances for blacks of an earlier time."

In a 2007 *New York Times* profile, Dave Kehr focuses on Burnett's 1977 debut feature *Killer of Sheep* and the news that the film is about to have its first theatrical release after being "hidden in shadows for almost thirty years." For this story, Kehr interviews Burnett as well as other collaborators, such as colorist Kathy Thomson, who were involved in the process of transferring *Killer of Sheep* from film to video for its first DVD release (March 25, 2007). According to Burnett, *Killer of Sheep* "was never meant to be shown in public" and that, says Kehr, "is why he had never obtained permission to use the musical passages—marvelously apposite choices of blues, pop, and jazz—that accompany and accentuate his images." In April 2007, after the music rights for the film had been cleared, *Killer of Sheep* finally received its long-awaited debut theatrical release. Several interviews with Burnett appeared on the occasion of the film's release, and three are included here: McNamara, *Los Angeles Times*, 2007; Ponsoldt, *Filmmaker* (a magazine devoted to independent films), 2007; and Lowery, road-dog-productions.com (a filmmaker's blog), 2007. All focus almost exclusively on *Killer of Sheep*, exploring many different aspects of the film, especially interpretative issues, production history, and reception.

Understandably, the interviewers are preoccupied with questions having to do with change: What was it like returning to the film after so many years? Has your craft as a filmmaker changed between 1977 and 2007? Does *Killer of Sheep* remain as relevant today as when it first came out in 1977? Is the film business less racist now than when you first started? Overall, what is perhaps most striking about these interviews is how little Burnett's concerns and perception of the world had changed since his student days at UCLA. For example, according to Burnett, racism remains widespread in Hollywood, as succinctly conveyed in the following anecdote reported in the *Los Angeles Times* profile from this period. "[Burnett] tells a story to illustrate what he sees as the continuing arrogance, and racism, of the [film] industry. A film crew had set up in his neighborhood and Burnett, riding by on his bike, asked what was going on. 'This grip looks at me and says, "It's too difficult to explain,"' Burnett says with a smile that is truly amused. 'Too difficult to explain. To me.'"

Other post-2000 interviews include discussions of recent projects such as *Namibia: The Struggle for Liberation*, 2007 (see Sippl, 2007), older films like *When It Rains* (1995) issued for the first time on DVD (see, e.g., Gerhard, 2007), as well as more broadly conceived profiles looking back on Burnett's career from the vantage point of the first decade of the twenty-first century (see e.g., Rafferty, 2001; Foundas, 2006; and Bell, 2008, which are among the most insightful interviews in this collection).

In conclusion, I would like to add a few words about Burnett's unrealized film projects. In the mid-1990s, for instance, Burnett revealed in several interviews (such as Hozic, 1994) his ambition to make a film of epic proportions about the life of the great orator and abolitionist Frederick Douglass. However, as he told Hozic, he wanted to be in a position to do the film "the way I want it," without the limitations imposed by the marketplace and studio bureaucrats. Unfortunately, Burnett has yet to arrive at that position. In March 2010, he described to me a number of other films he had wanted to make or had begun development on (interview with Burnett, Los Angeles, March 2010). They include feature-length films about the lives of African American cultural icons Paul Robeson and W. E. B. Du Bois, and two projects set in New York City, "Man in a Basket," based on a Chester Himes crime novel about the Harlem cops Coffin Ed Johnson and Grave Digger Jones, and "145th Street," adapted from a collection of short stories for children by Walter Dean Myers. There were also two projects that touch on the extremes of the African American experience—"The William and Ellen Craft Story," about two slaves who escaped from Georgia in 1848, Ellen Craft, who disguised herself as a white man, and her husband William, who posed as her servant, and "Stanley Ann Dunham: A Most Generous Spirit," a documentary on the life of President Obama's mother that Burnett is currently seeking funding for. It remains to be seen whether Burnett's future holds the realization of some or all of these plans.

As with all books in the Conversations with Filmmakers series, the interviews are presented in chronological order and unedited (typographical errors and the like have been silently corrected).* The overtly repetitious aspects of these interviews reflect not only Burnett's recurring concerns but also his low public profile and, hence, the tendency of many of the interviewers, regardless of whether the interview took place early in Burnett's career or much later, to present Burnett anew—as a great find to share with readers who have never heard of him.

I would like to acknowledge Peter Brunette, former general editor of the Conversations with Filmmakers series, who passed away suddenly in 2010. Peter's dedication to the series over the years was invaluable, and I am grateful for his support on this project as well as my previous volumes: Jonathan Demme (2009), Woody Allen (2006), and Clint Eastwood (1999). I also thank Leila Salisbury, Walter Biggins, and Valerie Jones of the University Press of Mississippi, for their guidance and encouragement. Thanks also to Andrew Beveridge and Dean Elizabeth Hendrey of Queens College for providing much needed financial support, and to Charles Silver of the Museum of Modern Art and the staff of the Margaret Herrick Library of the Academy of Motion Picture Arts and Sciences for their help on this project. I am also grateful to Andrew Beveridge for creating the maps of Charles Burnett's Los Angeles. Special thanks are due to Kathie Coblentz, my translator and editorial assistant, and to Susan Kapsis, my editorial consultant and confidant, for their invaluable contributions. Finally, thanks to Charles Burnett for generously sharing his time and discussing his life in film with me.

REK

*The one exception is the 1990 *Positif* interview that contained a few rather lengthy passages that required extensive editing. For clarification, see the Editor's Note in that interview.

Chronology

1944–53   Charles Burnett is born in Vicksburg, Mississippi, in 1944. His family moves to Los Angeles in the late 1940s and settles in South Central (near Watts) circa 1953.

1949–60   Serviceman father and mother separate. Burnett and brother raised by grandmother while mother works. Burnett fondly recalls the African American community of his youth as "southern in culture."

1961–66   Majors in electronics at Los Angeles City College but discovers his calling in a creative writing course.

1967–77   Receives a bachelor's degree from the University of California (UCLA) in 1969. Enrolls in UCLA's Graduate Program in Film and Television Production. Along with fellow students such as Julie Dash, Haile Gerima, and Billy Woodberry, who come to be known as members of the Los Angeles School of Black Filmmakers, Burnett sets out to tell stories about African American life that reject the stereotypes of Hollywood commercial cinema. His student films include two shorts, *Several Friends* (1969) and *The Horse* (1973), and his first feature, his MFA thesis film *Killer of Sheep* (filmed in 1973–75), a neo-realist drama set in Watts.

1977–81   Receives his MFA from UCLA, 1977. His thesis film, *Killer of Sheep*, is shown sporadically in museum and university screenings and at festivals, including the first Festival of Three Continents in Nantes, France (1979).

1981   *Killer of Sheep* wins the FIPRESCI Prize at the Berlin Film Festival as well as other prizes on the film festival circuit.

1983–84   Writes and directs his second feature film ,*My Brother's Wedding*. Opens at the Toronto International Film Festival (1983) and the New Directors/New Films series sponsored by the Film Society of Lincoln Center and the Museum of Modern Art's Film Department (1984).

1988	Receives a "Genius Grant" from the MacArthur Foundation.
1990–91	Writes and directs his third feature, *To Sleep with Anger*, the story of a middle-class black family. It opens at a number of film festivals, including Sundance, Cannes, Toronto, and New York. The film wins a special jury prize at Sundance and goes on to win Independent Spirit Awards for Best Director and Best Screenplay and a National Society of Film Critics Award for Best Screenplay. Burnett wins a special award from the Los Angeles Film Critics Association and the Maya Deren Independent Film and Video Artists Award from the American Film Institute. Receives fellowships from the Guggenheim and Rockefeller foundations and from the National Endowment for the Arts.
1991	Co-writes and co-directs (with Dai Sil Kim-Gibson) *America Becoming*, a documentary about race relations for public television with support from the Ford Foundation.
1994–95	Writes and directs the police drama *The Glass Shield*. It is nominated for a Golden Leopard Award at the Locarno International Film Festival. The Museum of the Moving Image (Astoria, Queens, New York) honors Burnett with a complete retrospective of his films.
1995	Writes and directs the twelve-minute jazz parable *When It Rains*.
1996–98	Directs *Nightjohn* (1996), a feature-length film about slavery, for the Disney Channel. A number of distinguished critics, including Terrence Rafferty, Jonathan Rosenbaum, and Armond White, single it out as a masterpiece. In 1998 the film receives a special award from the National Society of Film Critics for a film "whose exceptional quality and originality challenge strictures of the movie marketplace."
1997	The Film Society of Lincoln Center and the Human Rights Watch International Film Festival honor Burnett with a two-week retrospective of his films.
1998	Directs *Oprah Winfrey Presents: The Wedding*, a two-part TV miniseries, adapted from Dorothy West's novel, that deals with issues of race and class in mid-twentieth-century black society.
1999	Directs *Selma, Lord, Selma*, a TV docudrama about the civil rights movement of the 1960s that aired as part of "The

	Wonderful World of Disney." Directs the romantic comedy *The Annihilation of Fish*. Premieres at the Toronto Film Festival.
2000	Directs the baseball drama *Finding Buck McHenry* for Showtime. It wins a Daytime Emmy Award for Outstanding Performer (Ossie Davis) in a Children's Special. The Harvard Film Archive of Harvard University honors Burnett with a retrospective of his films.
2003	Co-writes and directs the documentary *Nat Turner: A Troublesome Property* for PBS. Writes and directs *Warming by the Devil's Fire* for the documentary mini-series *The Blues* that aired on PBS in 2003.
2004	The Pacific Film Archive at the University of California, Berkeley, honors Burnett with a ten-day retrospective of his films.
2007	Burnett's 1977 debut feature *Killer of Sheep* (1977) receives its debut theatrical release after the music rights for the film are cleared. The film was restored by the UCLA Film & Television Archive. The film goes on to win a New York Film Critics Circle Special Award. Burnett's second feature *My Brother's Wedding* (1983/2007) has its theatrical premiere in a shortened "director's cut" version at the IFC Center in New York City. The film was restored by the Pacific Film Archive at the University of California, Berkeley. Directs *Namibia: The Struggle for Liberation*. Premieres at the Los Angeles Film Festival.
2008	The American Film Institute honors Burnett with a retrospective of his films. Receives a Lifetime Achievement Award from the 14th Annual Temecula Valley International Film and Music Festival.
2009	Directs *Relative Stranger*, a family drama for the Hallmark Channel.
2010	Directs Juliette Fairly in her one-woman show *Mulatto: A Never Ending Saga* in Sherman Oaks, California, and afterward in New York City.
2011	The Museum of Modern Art honors Burnett with a full retrospective of his films.

Filmography

As Director

1969
SEVERAL FRIENDS (student film)
Released by Milestone Film & Video, 2007
Producer: **Charles Burnett**
Director: **Charles Burnett**
Screenplay: **Charles Burnett**
Cinematography: Jim Watkins
Editing: **Charles Burnett**
Cast: Andy Burnett, Gene Cherry, Charles Bracy, Cassandra Wright, Donna Deitch, Deloras Robinson, James Miles, L. E. McGraw, Ernest Cox, E. R. Canan, Arthur Boot, Allen Jurgins
Black and white, 21 minutes

1973
THE HORSE (student film)
Released by Milestone Film & Video, 2007
Producer: **Charles Burnett**
Director: **Charles Burnett**
Screenplay: **Charles Burnett**
Cinematography: Ian Conner
Editing: **Charles Burnett**
Music: Samuel Barber, "Knoxville: Summer of 1915"
Cast: Gordon Houston (William), Maury Wright (Ray's Boy), Gary Morrin (Walter), Roger Collins (West), George Williams (Lee), Larry Clark (Ray)
Color, 13:50 minutes

1977
KILLER OF SHEEP (student film)
Released by Milestone Film & Video, 2007
Producer: **Charles Burnett**
Director: **Charles Burnett**
Screenplay: **Charles Burnett**
Cinematography: **Charles Burnett**
Editing: **Charles Burnett**
Music performed by Paul Robeson, Dinah Washington, and others
Cast: Henry Gayle Sanders (Stan), Kaycee Moore (Stan's wife), Charles Bracy (Bracy), Angela Burnett (Stan's daughter), Eugene Cherry (Eugene), Jack Drummond (Stan's son)
Black and white, 80 minutes

1983
MY BROTHER'S WEDDING (released in the U.S. in 1991; director's cut, 2007)
Charles Burnett Productions, Zweites Deutsches Fernsehen / Milestone Film & Video, 2007
Executive Producer: Gaye Shannon-Burnett
Producer: **Charles Burnett**
Associate Producer: Brigitte Kramer
Supervising Producer: Earl C. Williman Sr.
Director: **Charles Burnett**
Screenplay: **Charles Burnett**
Cinematography: **Charles Burnett**
Editing: Thomas M. Penick
Music includes traditional hymns, performed by Dr. Henry Gordon and others, and indigenous African music
Cast: Everette Silas (Pierce Mundy), Jessie Homes (Mrs. Mundy), Gaye Shannon-Burnett (Sonia Debois), Ronald E. Bell (Soldier), Dennis Kemper (Mr. Mundy), Sally Easter (Mrs. Richards), Hobert Durham Jr. (Mr. Richards), Angela Burnett (Angela)
Color, 118 minutes (director's cut: 81 minutes)

1990
TO SLEEP WITH ANGER
SVS Films / Samuel Goldwyn Company

Executive Producers: Edward R. Pressman, Danny Glover, Harris E. Tulchin
Producers: Caldecot Chubb, Thomas S. Byrnes, Darin Scott
Director: **Charles Burnett**
Screenplay: **Charles Burnett**
Cinematography: Walt Lloyd
Editing: Nancy Richardson
Production Design: Penny Barrett
Art Direction: Troy Myers
Music: Stephen James Taylor
Cast: Danny Glover (Harry), Paul Butler (Gideon), Mary Alice (Suzie), Carl Lumbly (Junior), Vonetta McGee (Pat), Richard Brooks (Babe Brother), Sheryl Lee Ralph (Linda), Ethel Ayler (Hattie), Julius Harris (Herman), Sy Richardson (Marsh), Davis Roberts (Okra Tate)
Color, 102 minutes

1991
AMERICA BECOMING (documentary)
Public Broadcasting Service
Producer: Dai Sil Kim-Gibson
Directors: **Charles Burnett**, Dai Sil Kim-Gibson
Screenplay: **Charles Burnett**, Dai Sil Kim-Gibson
Cinematography: **Charles Burnett**
Editing: Baylis Glascock, Judy Reidel
Narration: Meredith Vieira
90 minutes

1994
THE GLASS SHIELD
CiBy 2000 / Miramax
Executive Producer: Chet Walker
Producers: Thomas Byrnes, Carolyn Schroeder
Director: **Charles Burnett**
Screenplay: **Charles Burnett** (based in part on the screenplay "One of Us," by Ned Welsh)
Cinematography: Elliot Davis
Editing: Curtiss Clayton
Music: Stephen James Taylor

Cast: Erich Anderson (District Attorney Ira Korn), Richard Anderson (Watch Commander Clarence Massey), Michael Boatman (Deputy J. J. Johnson), Bernie Casey (James Locket), Wanda De Jesus (Carmen Munoz), Victoria Dillard (Barbara Simms), Elliott Gould (Greenspan), Don Harvey (Deputy Jack Bono), Tommy Hicks (Reverend Banks), Ice Cube (Teddy Woods), Michael Ironside (Detective Gene Baker), Natalija Nogulich (Judge Helen Lewis), Lori Petty (Deputy Deborah Fields), Sy Richardson (Mr. Taylor), M. Emmet Walsh (Detective Jesse Hall), Gary Wood (Sergeant Chuck Gilmore)
Color, 110 minutes

1995
WHEN IT RAINS
Leapfrog Productions / Milestone Film & Video, 2007
Producer: Chantal Bernheim
Line Producer: Jon Oh
Director: **Charles Burnett**
Screenplay: **Charles Burnett**
Cinematography: **Charles Burnett**
Editing: **Charles Burnett**
Music: Stephen James Taylor
Cast: Ayuko Babu, Florence Bracy, Kenny Merritt, Juno Lewis, Charles Bracy, Brittany Bracy, Soul, Billy Woodberry, R. Ray Barness, John Rier, Barbara Bayless, Jonathan Burnett, Steven Burnett, Brad Bracy, Damon Ray Ritchie, Sandy Shaw
Color, 13 minutes

1996
NIGHTJOHN (television)
RHI Entertainment, Disney Channel Productions, Sarabande Productions, Signboard Hill Productions / Disney Channel Productions, Hallmark Entertainment
Executive Producer: David Manson
Producer: Dennis Stuart Murphy
Co-Producers: John Landgraf, Bill Cain
Director: **Charles Burnett**
Teleplay: Bill Cain, based on the book by Gary Paulsen
Cinematography: Elliot Davis
Editing: Dorian Harris

Production Design: Naomi Shohan
Art Direction: Jim Hill
Music: Stephen James Taylor
Cast: Beau Bridges (Clel Waller), Carl Lumbly (John), Lorraine Toussaint (Dealey), Bill Cobbs (Old Man), Allison Jones (Sarny), Kathleen York (Callie Waller), Gabriel Casseus (Outlaw), Tom Nowicki (Dr. Chamberlaine), Joel Thomas Traywick (Jeffrey Waller), Monica Ford (Egypt), Robin McLamb-Vaughn (Sarny's Mother), Jordan Williams (James G. Waller)
Color, 96 minutes

1997
THE FINAL INSULT
Documenta X, Arte, ZDF
Producer: **Charles Burnett**
Director: **Charles Burnett**
Screenplay: **Charles Burnett**
Cinematography: **Charles Burnett**
Editing: **Charles Burnett**
Music: Stephen James Taylor
Cast: Ayuko Babu (Box Brown), Charles Bracy
Color, 70 minutes

1998
THE WEDDING (mini-series for television)
Hamdon Entertainment, Harpo Films / American Broadcasting Company
Executive Producers: Kate Forte, Oprah Winfrey
Producer: Doro Bachrach
Associate Producers: Daniel Schneider, Valeria Scoon
Director: **Charles Burnett**
Teleplay: Lisa Jones, after the novel by Dorothy West
Cinematography: Frederick Elmes
Editing: Dorian Harris
Art Direction: Geoffrey S. Grimsman
Music: Stephen James Taylor
Cast: Halle Berry (Shelby Coles), Eric Thal (Meade Howell), Lynn Whitfield (Corinne Coles), Carl Lumbly (Lute McNeil), Michael Warren (Clark Coles), Marianne Jean-Baptiste (Ellen Coles), Shirley Knight

(Gram), Cynda Williams (Liz Coles Odis)
Color, 180 minutes

DR. ENDESHA IDA MAE HOLLAND (documentary)
Director: **Charles Burnett**
Cinematography: **Charles Burnett**
Editing: **Charles Burnett**
Cast: Endesha Ida Mae Holland (Herself)
14 minutes

1999
THE ANNIHILATION OF FISH
American Sterling Productions / Regent Entertainment
Executive Producer: Kris Dodge
Producers: Paul Heller, William Lawrence Fabrizio, John Remark, Eric Mitchell
Line Producer: Arlene Albertson
Director: **Charles Burnett**
Screenplay: Anthony C. Winkler
Cinematography: John Ndiaga Demps
Editing: Nancy Richardson
Production Designer: Nina Ruscio
Music: Laura Karpman
Cast: Lynn Redgrave (Poinsettia), James Earl Jones (Fish), Margot Kidder (Mrs. Muldroone)
Color, 108 minutes

SELMA, LORD, SELMA (television)
Esparza/Katz Productions, Walt Disney Television / American Broadcasting Company
Executive Producers: Moctesuma Esparza, Robert Katz, Julian Fowles
Producer: Christopher Seitz
Director: **Charles Burnett**
Teleplay: Cynthia Whitcomb, after the book by Sheyann Webb and Rachel West Nelson, as told to Frank Sikora
Cinematography: John Simmons
Editing: Nancy Richardson
Production Designer: Naomi Shohan
Music: Stephen James Taylor

Cast: Mackenzie Astin (Jonathan Daniels), Jurnee Smollet (Sheyann Webb), Clifton Powell (Martin Luther King, Jr.), Ella Joyce (Betty Webb), Yolanda King (Miss Bright), Elizabeth Omilami (Amelia Boynton)
Color, 94 minutes

OLIVIA'S STORY
Producer: Dai Sil Kim-Gibson
Director: **Charles Burnett**
Screenplay: Dai Sil Kim-Gibson
Cinematography: Steve Schecter
Editing: **Charles Burnett**
Music: Stephen James Taylor
Cast: **Charles Burnett** (Umpire), Sungia Moon (Grandmother), Ilyon Woo (Olivia)
14 minutes

2000
FINDING BUCK MCHENRY (television)
Lin Oliver Productions / Showtime Networks
Executive Producers: Robert Halmi Jr., Lin Oliver, Bobby Heller
Line Producer: Stephen J. Turbull
Director: **Charles Burnett**
Teleplay: Alfred Slote, David Field, after the novel by Alfred Slote
Cinematography: John L. Demps Jr.
Editing: Dorian Harris
Production Design: Kathleen Climie
Art Direction: Marilyn Kiewiet
Music: Stephen James Taylor
Cast: Ossie David (Mr. Mack Henry), Ruby Dee (Mrs. Henry), Ernie Banks (Ollie Johnson), Michael Schiffman (Jason Ross), Duane McLaughlin (Aaron Henry), Megan Bower (Kim Axelrod), Kevin Jubinville (Chuck Axelrod)
Color, 94 minutes

2003
NAT TURNER: A TROUBLESOME PROPERTY (documentary)
Subpix, in association with KQED Public Television / ITVS, California Newsreel

Producer: Frank Christopher
Co-Producer: Kenneth S. Greenberg
Associate Producer: Cynthia Griffin
Director: **Charles Burnett**
Writers: **Charles Burnett**, Frank Christopher, Kenneth S. Greenberg
Cinematography: John Demps
Editing: Michael Colin, Frank Christopher
Production Design: Liba Daniels
Music: Todd Capps; additional music: Stephen James Taylor
Cast: Alfre Woodard (Narrator), Carl Lumbly (Nat Turner-Gray), Tom Nowicki (Thomas R. Gray), Tommy Hicks (Nat Turner-Edmonds), James Opher (Nat Turner-Styron), Megan Gallacher (Margaret Whitehead), Michael Lemelle (Nat Turner-Brown), Reshara Coleman (Lucinda), Mark Joy (Judge Jeremiah Cobb), Justin Dray (Thomas Moore), Michael Kennedy (James Trezevant), Harry Kollatz (Benjamin Phipps), Laurel Lyle (Harriet Beecher Stowe), Tony Miratti (Governor John Floyd), Billy Dye (Nat Turner), Patrick Waller (Nat Turner-Stowe), and with Herbert Aptheker, **Charles Burnett**, Ossie Davis, Henry Louis Gates, Eugene Genovese, Martha Minnow, William Styron, and others
Color, 58 minutes

WARMING BY THE DEVIL'S FIRE (episode 4 from the documentary series THE BLUES)
Road Movies Filmproduktion, Vulcan Productions / Public Broadcasting Service
Executive Producers of the Series: Martin Scorsese, Ulrich Felsberg
Episode Crew:
Executive Producer: Paul G. Allen
Producers: Margaret Bodde, Alex Gibney
Co-Producers: Wesley Jones, Mikaela Beardsley
Line Producer: Daphne McWilliams
Director: **Charles Burnett**
Writer: **Charles Burnett**
Cinematography: John N. Demps
Editing: Edwin Santiago
Production Designer: Liba Daniels
Original Score: Stephen James Taylor
Cast: Carl Lumbly (Narrator), Tommy Redmond Hicks (Uncle Buddy), Nathaniel Lee Jr. (Jr.), Susan McWilliams (Herself), Nathaniel Lee Sr.

(W.C. Handy), Sonny Boy Williamson (Himself); archival footage of: Son House, Sister Rosetta Tharpe, Mississippi John Hurt, Victoria Spivey, Willie Dixon, Muddy Waters, Ida Cox, Mamie Smith, Lightnin' Hopkins, Reverend Gary Davis, Big Bill Broonzy, Sonny Boy Williamson, Bessie Smith, Dinah Washington, Elizabeth Cotten
Color, 106 minutes

FOR REEL? (television)
Public Broadcasting Service
Producers: **Charles Burnett**, Skye Dent
Director: **Charles Burnett**
Writers: Bill Plympton, **Charles Burnett**, Skye Dent
Cinematography: John L. Demps Jr.

2007
NAMIBIA: THE STRUGGLE FOR LIBERATION
Namibia Film Commission, Pan Afrikan Center of Namibia
Executive Producer: Uazuva Kaumbi
Producers: Abius Akwaak, Steve Gukas
Associate Producer: Edwin Kanguatjivi
Line Producer: Antoinette Parkinson
Director: **Charles Burnett**
Screenplay: **Charles Burnett**
Cinematography: John L. Demps Jr.
Editing: Ed Santiago
Music: Stephen James Taylor
Cast: Carl Lumbly (Sam Nujoma), Danny Glover (Father Elias), Joel Haikali (Nujoma at 16), Chrisjan Appollus (Sam Hosea), Obed Emvula (Red)
Color, 161 minutes

QUIET AS KEPT
Milestone Film & Video
Producers: **Charles Burnett**, Jon Oh
Director: **Charles Burnett**
Screenplay: **Charles Burnett**
Editing: **Charles Burnett**
Cinematography: **Charles Burnett**
Cast: Nathaniel Lee Sr. (The Father), Sharial C. Lee (The Mother), Dan-

iel Curtis Lee (The Son); also credited: Nathaniel Lee Jr.
Color, 6 minutes

2009
RELATIVE STRANGER (television)
Larry Levinson Productions; LG Films / Hallmark Channel
Executive Producer: Larry Levinson
Co-Executive Producers: Randy Pope, Michael Moran
Producers: Erik Olson, Brian Martinez
Director: **Charles Burnett**
Teleplay: Eric Haywood
Editing: Craig Bassett
Cinematography: Todd Barron
Production Design: Laird Pulver
Music: Nathan Furst
Cast: Eriq La Salle (Walter Clemons), Michael Michele (Charlotte Clemons), Michael Beach (James Clemons), Dana Davis (Denise Clemons), Sherri Saum (Nicole Tate), Carlos McCullers II (Andy Clemons), Dan Castellaneta (Father Gary), Alan Fudge (William Kirkland), Jerry Hauck (Manager), Andre Kinney (Shawn Hughes), Cicely Tyson (Pearl)
Color, 88 minutes

Miscellaneous Credits

1975
WELCOME HOME BROTHER CHARLES
Bob-Bea Productions / Crown International Pictures
Production Executive: Robert L. Gordon Sr.
Producer: Jamaa Fanaka
Director: Jamaa Fanaka
Screenplay: Jamaa Fanaka
Editing: Jamaa Fanaka
Cinematography: James Babij
Camera Operator: **Charles Burnett**
Music Producer: William Anderson
Cast: Marlo Monte (Charles Murray), Reatha Grey (Carmen). Stan Kamber (Jim), Tiffany Peters (Christina Freeman), Jake Carter (N. D.)
Color, 91 minutes

1977
PASSING THROUGH
Mypheduh Films
Director: Larry Clark
Screenplay: Larry Clark, Ted Lange
Editing: Larry Clark
Cinematography: George Geddis, Roderick R. Young
Camera Operator: **Charles Burnett**
Cast: Cora Day (Oshun), Maria Gibbs, Pamela Jones (Maya), George Kramer, Clarence Muse, Horace Tapscott, Nathaniel Taylor (Warmack)
Color, 105 minutes

1979
BUSH MAMA
Mypheduh Films
Producer: Haile Gerima
Director: Haile Gerima
Screenplay: Haile Gerima
Editing: Haile Gerima
Cinematography: **Charles Burnett** (as Charles Burnette), Roderick Young
Music: Onaje Kareem Kenyatta
Cast: Barbara O. Jones (Dorothy), Johnny Weathers (T. C.), Susan Williams (Luann), Cora Lee Day (Molly), Simmi Ella Nelson (Simmi)
Black and white, 97 minutes

YOUR CHILDREN COME BACK TO YOU
Women Make Movies
Producer: Alile Sharon Larkin
Director: Alile Sharon Larkin
Screenplay: Alile Sharon Larkin
Cinematography: **Charles Burnett**
Black and white, 27 minutes

1982
A DIFFERENT IMAGE
Women Make Movies
Producer: Alile Sharon Larkin
Director: Alile Sharon Larkin

Screenplay: Alile Sharon Larkin
Editing: Alile Sharon Larkin
Cinematography: **Charles Burnett**
Music: Dankwa Khan, Munyungo Darryl Jackson
Cast: Michael Adisa Anderson (Vincent), Margot Saxton-Federella (Alana), Michael Bruce (Ralph), Leslie Speights (Diane), Mandisa Oliver (Alicia)
Color, 51 minutes

ILLUSIONS
Executive Producer: Brenda Y. Shockley
Producer: Julie Dash
Director: Julie Dash
Screenplay: Julie Dash
Editing: **Charles Burnett**, Julie Dash
Cinematography: Ahmed El Maanouni; additional photography, **Charles Burnett**
Music: Eugene Bohlmann
Cast: Lonette McKee (Mignon Dupree), Rosanne Katon (Esther), Ned Bellamy (LL), Jack Radar, Jack Lundi Faust (Janitor)
Black and white, 34 minutes

1984
BLESS THEIR LITTLE HEARTS
Independent Feature Project
Producer: Billy Woodberry
Director: Billy Woodberry
Screenplay: **Charles Burnett**
Editing: Billy Woodberry
Cinematography: **Charles Burnett**
Music: Little Esther Philips, Archie Shepp
Cast: Nate Hardman (Charles Banks), Kaycee Moore (Andais Banks), Angela Burnett (Banks Child), Ronald Burnett (Banks Child), Kimberly Burnett (Banks Child)
Black and white, 80 minutes

1986
CROCODILE CONSPIRACY
Mosaic Films, Third World Newsreel

Director: Zeinabu Irene Davis
Screenplay: Zeinabu Irene Davis
Editing: Zeinabu Irene Davis
Cinematography: **Charles Burnett**
Cast: John Jelks, Sandra Sealy
Color, 13 minutes

1989
GUESTS OF HOTEL ASTORIA
Take 7 / Melior Films, International Home Cinema
Executive Producer: Bijan Shamoradi
Producer: Rafigh Pooya
Associate Producer: Barbara Bryan
Director: Reza Allamehzadeh
Screenplay: Reza Allamehzadeh
Editing: Reza Allamehzadeh
Cinematography: **Charles Burnett**
Cast: Shohreh Aghdashloo (Pori Karemnia), Marshall Manesh (Dr. Parto), Mohsen Marzban (Mr. Karemnia)
Color, 124 minutes

1994
YOUNG AT HEARTS (documentary)
Don Campbell Projects / Outsider Pictures
Executive Producer: Thomas Byrnes
Producer: Don Campbell, Michael Lowe
Director: Don Campbell
Screenplay: Don Campbell
Editing: Jim Davis, Mary Morrisey
Cinematography: **Charles Burnett** and others
Music: Mario Grigorov
Cast: Edna Brenner, Ida Engel, Fay Fishman, Bernice Kotz, Freda Samuels, Gert Shapiro, Edna Star, Ray Stein
Color, 73 minutes

1999
SILENCE BROKEN: KOREAN COMFORT WOMEN (documentary)
Dai Sil Productions / Public Broadcasting Service
Producer: Dai Sil Kim-Gibson

Co-Producer: **Charles Burnett**
Director: Dai Sil Kim-Gibson
Screenplay: Dai Sil Kim-Gibson
Editing: **Charles Burnett**
Cinematography: **Charles Burnett**
Music: Donald Sur
Cast: Hwang Jin Kyung (Song Shin Do), Lee Kwang Sun (Yun Doo Ri)
Color, 88 minutes

2004
WET SAND: VOICES FROM L.A. TEN YEARS LATER (documentary)
Dai Sil Productions / Center for Asian-American Media
Producer: Dai Sil Kim-Gibson
Director: Dai Sil Kim-Gibson
Screenplay: Dai Sil Kim-Gibson
Editing: **Charles Burnett**, Richard Kim
Cinematography: **Charles Burnett**
Music: Stephen James Taylor
Color, 57 minutes

Charles Burnett: Interviews

Black Independent American Cinema: Charles Burnett

Corine McMullin/1980

Published in *Cinéma*, no. 264 (December 1980): 61.
Editor's note: In December 1979, Charles Burnett's *Killer of Sheep* was screened at the Festival of Three Continents in Nantes, France. The following year, in Paris, it was seen again, along with the short *The Horse*, as part of the retrospective "Black Independent American Cinema." *Cinéma* featured statements from four of the directors whose films were shown in this retrospective, William Greaves, Ben Caldwell, Charles Burnett, and Larry Clark. We present here Burnett's statement only.

Working on the Coast like Ben Caldwell is Charles Burnett, whose excellent *Killer of Sheep* was on view again, and whose short *The Horse* was seen for the first time. He develops here an entirely different concept.

"Can you call us a 'New Wave'? No. We're not a single school of filmmakers sharing the same ideas. We are very independent. The only points we have in common is that we are Black and we feel close to the Third World. What is relatively new is that Blacks in greater numbers have the possibility to make movies, but everyone goes in his own direction. Until now, it's always been very hard for minorities to break into the movies. It's true that there were some directors in the 1920s and 1930s, with Oscar Micheaux, but it was only in the '60s that Elyseo Taylor started a communications course at UCLA, which allowed minority students to enter the profession.

"At the time, I already had a degree in electronics, but I wanted to change fields. Since I had free time, I went to the movies. The problem was that I came from Watts where people didn't have much money, and I had never seen a movie with which I could identify, aside from *Nothing but a Man*, by Robert Young, which features a young man and his wife working hard to survive in a racist environment. The movie is full of anger but without hate.

"And then I saw *The Southerner*, by Renoir, made in the USA in 1941. It didn't have anything to do with Blacks, but since I'm from Mississippi, I remember Zachary Scott in the role of the poor man who worked on a farm. There was also a Black couple and the movie shows how they helped each other to survive in this miserable situation; it was man against nature and how much it costs whites as well as Blacks to survive.

"I greatly admire James Agee's concern in *Let Us Now Praise Famous Men*, to tell the truth as an outsider who doesn't want to exploit the people he describes, who searches for what the exact impact of his position as a journalist will be. I think people of the Third World and minorities should be inspired by it. Being Black doesn't necessarily mean you're close to the problems; you can also be foreign to the community you're from, especially if you don't live there anymore and you make yourself its spokesman.

"When I came back from college, which my friends hadn't gone to, I had an attitude entirely different from theirs. There's no way I could have called myself representative of Blacks and especially not those of my class. I had to be very careful not to take a position. I try to be objective and I know that, in certain situations, I express some Black values but I cannot speak of my movies as 'Black' movies. It is debatable. I tried to speak of the Black experience, as I perceived it.

"As for the style, I had read Georg Lukács. I was very influenced by what he wrote on his manner of perceiving the world and, when I made *Killer of Sheep*, I was very concerned with learning how to give an account of this world, and not just to find a plot or to reduce life to a simple situation where problems can be solved. *Killer of Sheep* was not supposed to entertain the spectators. The film had eighty-seven scenes, which I reduced to twenty-three while shooting. I wanted to shoot enough of reality to give the feeling of its existence. I wanted to preserve a manner of living that has been destroyed. I'm not trying to be romantic about the ghetto, but I wanted to remember how it was. It's changed a lot. There are things that I liked about Watts, that forged my character. I know all the more about it now that I've associated with people of the 'middle class.' Their way of perceiving is abstract."

(Translated from the French by Kathie Coblentz)

An Artisan of Daily Life: Charles Burnett

Catherine Arnaud and Yann Lardau/1981

Published in *La Revue du cinéma*, July–August 1981, 92–94. Reprinted by permission.

Born in the South of the United States (and profoundly marked by it), Charles Burnett grew up in Watts, the Los Angeles ghetto, which about ten years ago experienced violent disturbances, and he lives there still. A cameraman by training, he has directed *Several Friends* (1969), *Killer of Sheep* (1977), and a short, *The Horse* (1973), a prize winner at Oberhausen. He has also worked as cinematographer on many independent movies, such as *Your Children Come Back to You* by Alile Sharon Larkin, *Bless Their Little Hearts* by Billy Woodberry, and others.

Question: Your original training is in electronics. How and why did you choose the cinema?
Charles Burnett: I've always been interested in photography, even though I was never lucky enough to own a camera when I was a child. That was the first thing that attracted me to the movies.

I was working in Los Angeles, but I had a lot of free time and I spent my free hours going to the movies, to kill time! Gradually, I got caught up in it and I thought maybe I could work in this field. So I looked for a school and enrolled at UCLA, to learn film technique. There I discovered that what interested me wasn't only camera work, but also telling stories. So I changed sections to study film direction. I also took courses in screenwriting ("creative writing"), and I combined the two elements, writing and direction, which, for me, represented the most creative part of film work.

As a matter of fact, before entering UCLA, I was very illiterate about the cinema. I didn't know film history well at all, and I only gradually became interested in the work of directors and cinematographers and learned to recognize it. I was also impressed by old movies, especially the French films of Vigo, Renoir, and Bresson, and the old Hollywood movies as well.

At UCLA I had the great luck to take a course of Basil Wright's. When I enrolled in his course, I didn't know his name or his work (*Song of Ceylon*). He made me understand that the cinema was something serious, capable of expressing the nature and the dignity of man. He also made me understand the value of the documentary, the importance of not imposing your own values on the topics you film, particularly when you come from a different world. He brought a certain humanism to my way of seeing things.

Afterwards I looked at film in a different way, not only as entertainment, but as something that could become a part of change, something that could express my reality. Thanks to him, I have a lot of respect for the documentary, which sometimes goes farther than the fiction film, at least in spontaneity and the expression of a certain truth of the topic being filmed.

Q: You make your movies primarily for an African American audience. What ethical and aesthetic responsibilities follow from this choice?

CB: I live in the community in which, and about which, I make my movies. I look at the movies in a very different way, more concerned with the real feelings of people.

I've worked on (and seen) many movies about the working class that showed the exploitation, then the consciousness raising, the organization through unions, the victory, and so forth. But in reality, it doesn't happen like that. The people I know are out of work; the kind of movie where all the problems get solved can't be of any interest to them. Life is not an object lesson of the type $A + B = C \ldots$

After I'd seen a number of these movies, made by socially involved people who didn't have any real experience of the working class, I realized that their conception of the social movie came from their perception of the milieu that they were familiar with—the middle class. However, the people that I knew were out of work, they didn't have union experience, or a political consciousness, or time to become politicized. This type of film, where problems were solved for the spectator, couldn't have any relevance for them. I tried to work in another way, to look at my community in a way that allowed me to find elements inside their own lives, and to construct a theme that would be seen and lived from their point of view.

The people that act in my movies are not professionals, with the exception of Henry Sanders (Stan, the main character in *Killer of Sheep*). They're people I know who are a part of the Watts community. And so I have a particular responsibility with regard to them. I have to be very attentive to their way of seeing things.

In fact I am confronted by a number of contradictions. I live in this community, I am a product of it. I went to UCLA by accident, but during my studies, I changed. I know that there is a difference between the individual I was in the beginning and what I am today. Consequently, I can't say that I speak for the community, because my perception of things is very different. They are trapped in an extremely emotional situation, stuck in the insoluble problems they're obliged to endure. They take out their frustrations in a very violent manner. They and I don't have the same ideas, and we don't have the same limits. And so what interests me is to represent with honesty the way they live through a situation; and when I say that, I mean the working class and the underclass, since most of them are unemployed.

Because of these preoccupations, fiction films posed a serious problem for me, because fiction gives a filmmaker more of a chance to present his own problems, rather than the topic at hand. I've lived in the ghetto all my life, and I consider myself to be happy, because I accidentally went to school. I'd like to tell you two anecdotes to help you better understand the difference in points of view between myself and the people of my community. A friend of mine, Junior, was involved in a robbery and murder. He was facing capital punishment, and we were discussing it with his brothers. I expressed reservations about his attitude and my friends retorted that I was wrong: the man Junior was confronting had a gun, and so Junior had to protect himself. It's the law of the jungle, only the strongest survive. I can understand this reasoning, even though I think differently. People think in terms of survival . . .

Here's another anecdote to show you the contradictions I'm caught up in. A friend of mine had a brother in jail. Her other brother was killed in a car accident. So she was trying to borrow money to pay for his bail, so her brother could be released to attend the funeral. At that moment, I had just received the grant I needed to be able to make my movie, and I prayed that she wouldn't come to me to ask for money. I'm supposed to be a filmmaker who makes movies to help to change people's lives, and when I had the opportunity to do something, I thought that my film was more important.

When you're caught up in such contradictions, and you make a movie centered on the life of a certain social group, you have to be very attentive to the differences that exist between yourself and them. In *Killer of Sheep*, I tried to give a sense of the reality that they live with every day. I tried to construct a theme that captures something of their life, in the most objective way possible.

Q: In your two movies, there is a very strong presence of children, often in contradiction to the world of the adults.

CB: Without children, there is no survival. For me, growing up was a bad experience. I had to face a lot of contradictions that I wasn't prepared to face. In my community, the most important thing is to survive above all else, and children are taught that they have to support their brother, or their family, no matter what they do, as the father says in the beginning of *Killer of Sheep*.

When you're growing up, it poses some moral problems. You become more and more insensitive: the only thing that matters is survival. This callousness gradually alienates you, distances you from other people and complicates relations in a peculiar way—survival implies a great deal of mistrust—particularly relations between men and women. That's why I show these children in *Killer of Sheep*, always there, attentive to what their parents are doing, the witnesses of everyday drama. These children will grow up to be like Stan, the main character, insensitive, without a chance to experiment with their emotions and be honest with them, if they're lucky . . . Otherwise they will develop their individuality from the concept of what is right or wrong as it pertains to their personal survival. That leads to everything.

Q: In what conditions was *Killer of Sheep* filmed?

CB: At the beginning I wanted to use only non-professionals, people from the community. But the man I wanted to play the role of Stan was in prison, so I had to use an actor, Henry Sanders. The other characters are interpreted by people from the community, which forced us to film on the weekends. And when we were filming, we took up a primary part of people's lives, their leisure time. That's why I often needed to go to look for them at home, because they had no awareness of the time. It's also why I was obliged to dispense with the professionals (people from UCLA) who composed the technical team at the start. Professionals are impatient. Non-professionals don't really realize the importance of the movie, of time, and so forth. So I used other people for the technical team: myself, the actors and the children. They were very young, but they did the sound, helped with the lighting . . . 90 percent of the movie was made with children. But this way of working, on weekends, over a long period of time with non-professionals, affected the structure of the movie, more than I would have wanted it to. I wanted the film to have a rough, raw aspect, without light . . . I wanted the texture to be rough, as if the movie had been made by someone who didn't know how to make movies. I wanted this movie to seem like a work in which the filmmaker didn't try to manipulate things. But in fact, I got a result that surpassed in primitiveness what I had hoped for! My goal wasn't to entertain. I was concerned with the painting of a certain truth. That's what gives the rough appearance to the film. This movie was also made to preserve, to write down in the memory. In music, in the thirties and forties, we had blues; what I tried to do here is to preserve a certain form of life, to record it.

The very structure of the film comes from this preoccupation: how to represent life, the everyday crises.

Killer of Sheep is a fiction film, with a written script, but initially, I did a lot of research in order to accumulate the essential elements of what happened in people's daily lives, in their evolution. It's practically an ethnographic film. And at the same time, I didn't want to reduce the complexity of the real to a simple plot.

(Translated from the French by Kathie Coblentz)

Life Drawings: Charles Burnett's Realism

Monona Wali/1988

Published in the *Independent* 11, no. 8 (October 1988): 16–22. Reprinted by permission.

Charles Burnett, forty-four years old, is a fiercely independent Black filmmaker living in Los Angeles. His first feature film, *Killer of Sheep*, made while he was a student at UCLA in 1978 for ten thousand dollars, is a masterpiece of American neo-realism, a painfully humorous and tragic account of the daily life of a slaughterhouse worker in South Central L.A. *Killer of Sheep* won the Critics Prize at the Berlin Film Festival and received other awards in the U.S. and abroad. *My Brother's Wedding*, his second feature, made for eighty thousand dollars in 1983 and financed by the West German public television channel ZDF, tells the story of a young man caught in a morality play that opposes his loyalties to his family to those to his best friend. It is ironic that Burnett's films employing subtle realism are better known in Europe than in the United States. Since the completion of *My Brother's Wedding*, Burnett has been developing new projects and struggling to find financing for his next film. This July, he was awarded a prestigious John D. and Catherine T. MacArthur Foundation Fellowship, popularly known as the "Genius Grant," which will pay him an annual stipend for five years. The following interview took place in the fall of 1987. Burnett and I discussed his background, his experiences in South Central L.A., and how this influenced his work and his career, as well as some themes and directions in his filmmaking.

Monona Wali: When you were growing up, what did you think you were going to do?
Charles Burnett: I didn't know really. I thought I'd join the service, because my friend Bobby and other guys were going into the service.

MW: Why didn't you?
CB: We were forced to take a position against the war. Before I got out of high school, a recruiting officer came around. When I turned eighteen, I didn't go down and register immediately, even though they stress how if you don't do that you can get arrested. I didn't take it seriously. When I did go down to register, they gave me the third degree, and I was really angry. A lot of things began to gel. I was aware of institutionalized racism, because in school I became very aware of it—the way they wanted to shove us into shop class—the whole attitude of "well, you're not going to do anything anyway..."

When I did go to register at the draft board, there was this lady who noted every mark, like scars, for identification purposes. She was very rude, and I'm thinking I'm doing them a favor, right? She acted like they owned me. I was in school at the time they wanted to draft me, so I got a school deferment, but I had to go down to the draft board anyway. There were long lines—zigzagging up the stairs and in twos and fours. It was like a dream. And there were these guys hollering at you like you're already in the service. There was this blonde kid, typically collegiate American guy, walking up and down and cheering us on: "We've got to go fight for this country." And we were looking at him, thinking, "What is the matter with this guy?" It was one of the first times that someone pointed and said, "You're an American, and you have obligations." He was saying that you were supposed to support his way of life—freedom. I'm saying, "*What?* Freedom?" At the same time the police would call you "nigger" in a minute. You would walk down the street, and they would pull you over. It was rumored that the L.A. police recruited southern whites to dominate the Black community.

MW: Did you get your deferment?
CB: I got a deferment. But the whole Army business was a joke, because they would only take kids who didn't have any prison record or police record. They took the core—the potential—of the Black community. All these guys who were fighting each other and wanted to prove themselves physically went to jail. It was a double whammy.

I was in line at the store not too long ago behind this huge guy. I recognized some of his features. Then he turned around and said, "I know you." I said, "Yeah, you look familiar. Where do I know you from?" He said, "You don't recognize me. We went to school together, but I was really thin at the time. During the time I was drafted, I gained weight by eating a lot. I drank a lot of salt water to get high blood pressure, and then when I got huge I couldn't get my weight down." He was big as a door. And when I was at the Toronto Film Festival I ran into a guy I hadn't seen in a long time, and I said, "What in the hell are you doing way up here in Toronto?" And he said, "I came up here to dodge the draft and made a living and stayed."

MW: Was this during the sixties?

CB: Yes. I had just finished high school. I was a product of that pre–civil rights movement. You really felt your limitations. Your reality was a few square blocks. You felt this was your only world, and the only way to get out of it was to join the service. But that was when the war in Asia started to blossom, and the draft wiped out my whole neighborhood.

MW: Kids you grew up with?

CB: Kids who were friends died in the service, and I remember one particular case—actually two cases. One guy was killed and he had a twin brother. The troubling thing was I didn't know which twin was killed. And there was another kid who was one of these guys that detonated mines. One of the mines went off and blew him to nothing. When they brought his remains home, they didn't open the casket. That left an impression. That was after the Watts riot, and people had had enough police harassment.

MW: Was that 1964 or '65?

CB: The summer of '65. At the time of the riots I was at Los Angeles City College. I would catch the bus—looking for summer jobs—and come back towards South Central and see smoke columns—back to reality, right? It was very strange because the first night of the riot I didn't know what was going on. The riot started after the attempted arrest of Marquette Frye—we went to junior high school together.

MW: Where were you living during that time?

CB: In South Central—99th and Towne, off Avalon and Century. During the last stages of the riot I could see the National Guard stationed at the corner from my window. During the day I would observe the results of frustrated people, and at night I would go out in the street and witness the destruction.

MW: Did you participate?

CB: No. Actually, it was just a few people. There were more people standing around. It only takes a few people to do damage. It relieved a lot of pressure. It also hurt the community. It dispersed the community because before that there was a center. When those areas were destroyed all the stores were closed, and it took a long time for the businesses to move back in. But there was a migration of the middle class just before the civil rights movement. The Watts riots really speeded up the process, leaving a vacuum—moral, economic, political. Watts lost its center.

MW: You were going to college at the time? What were you studying?

CB: Electronics. I don't know why, but I became disenchanted with it. I was lucky though, because I had a writing class at LACC with Isabelle Ziegler—a really great person—and I became interested in storytelling. I also had a feeling of wanting to find out what went wrong when I was growing up. Some of the kids I grew up with disappeared—violently—or went to jail. It was a tightly knit community. When I went to college, I began to see another world—that there's something more to life than thinking that by the time you're twenty you're going to be dead. In the community, the only world is a few square miles. And then I saw all these other people who seemed healthier—enjoying life—particularly when I went to UCLA. Still, South Central was an interesting area. Most of the people were from the South—Texas, Arkansas, Mississippi, Alabama—mostly Mississippi and Arkansas.

MW: What about your family?

CB: They're from Mississippi. I was born there but my family moved to L.A. when I was just a child during the migration of people moving north and west because of the war. At the time, L.A. was very racist and segregated. It was like South Africa and still is in many ways. In the forties, you had to live east of Central Avenue. I was told there were areas you couldn't go.

The thing that influenced me when I was a kid was that everyone was working all the time—strenuous work—and there was a healthy attitude about it. My family and neighbors used to raise chickens and grow food. But one of the things that began to happen with my generation and continued to grow was a rejection of the kind of work the parents did, particularly domestic work. There was a stigma attached to what they did. Your parents worked hard and always said, "I don't want my kids to work hard like I do. I want something better." As a consequence, they sort of sheltered their kids. There was also a negative attitude about the past.

When I was growing up I used to work during the summer for a friend's father who was a carpenter. Everyone was a plasterer or carpenter, or something like that. I used to admire those guys in many ways. There was a man named Bland who had big arms with veins like ropes—I always wanted big veins—and big hands. I remember Bland keeping the cement mixer going, and I'd try to mix . . . forget it. That kind of work is bad on the heart. These guys were young and strong at one time, but later on they just crumbled from the strain. Bland died early. The drug scene wasn't as bad as it is today, and people had a sense of coming to terms with their lives much better than they do now. There wasn't anything like the random violence today. People would fight, but only on an extreme occasion were people killed. There was some sense of limitation.

MW: Did you get into a lot of fights?

CB: Everybody had to know how to box. You had to know how to protect yourself. You couldn't go around whining. It's how you carried yourself that got you through the day. And then, in the area I grew up, there were a lot of gangs. I lived right in the center of it, so I couldn't avoid taking sides. You had to identify with one group or another, even if you weren't part of it. The gangs weren't connected to drug trafficking, like they are today. It seemed then that the law was very hard on pushers. Alcohol was the thing.

MW: The worst?

CB: No. There were some pills like reds, fender benders, uppers and downers—I never took any of the junk. The reason they called it fender bender was because they would get in the car and bang into something.

A lot of the guys were sent to juvenile camp and got physically big, really muscular and exaggerated their physical strength. There was an emphasis on physique and physical prowess—being able to knock somebody out with one punch.

MW: Did this affect the way boys and girls got along—or didn't it?

CB: Relationships with women were strange then, very strange—lot of myths, false notions. There was really a dichotomy of sexes. When we were young, groups of boys would do things like going to the swamp—Devil's Dip.

MW: Where was that?

CB: L.A. had a lot of undeveloped areas that you could walk or ride a bicycle to. Devil's Dip was where Southwest College is now, which used to be an oil field. There were steep hills, and we'd go take our bikes and fly down the hills. There were metal shops in junior high school where you could make metal bows. So we'd go out with BB guns and bows into these swamps for the sheer adventure of it. Girls couldn't come along. We couldn't participate in their world and vice versa.

When we got older there was this notion of a rap—a way of talking to a girl. You talk her into dating, you talk her into going out with you—talking nonsense: "Oh baby, I love you" and this and that. The younger guys didn't know what was going on and would ask, "How'd you get that girl?" "Well man, you have to have a rap." "What do you mean, a rap?" "I can't tell because, hey, you might steal my woman." Then the older guys would say, "Your rap's not better than mine. I'll take your woman anytime." So there was a mystery. It was a difficult period for a lot of guys because, in a sense, nothing was real. All these obstacles were generated by myths, cultural myths that no one really stopped to analyze. You just had to live through it.

MW: What kind of family did you have?

CB: My mother worked all the time. She had a job at Good Samaritan Hospital as a nurse's aide. She left the house at four in the morning and sometimes didn't get back until the evening. So we grew up on our own somewhat, with the help of my grandmother. She had to quit work to help out.

MW: What about your father?

CB: He was in the service, so it was a one-parent family.

MW: He never came home?

CB: Except one or two occasions. That was it. He didn't have any impact at all.

MW: Did you go to church when you were a kid?

CB: Yeah.

MW: Was your mother religious?

CB: My grandmother was. If you can go to the movies you can go to church—that's how she thought. There was a strong moral sense of good and bad still in the air. My grandmother had a great influence.

MW: When did you start going to the movies?

CB: At an early age. They had these ten-cent shows during the summer where they showed old time black and white serials. It was a social thing. Invariably there would be a fight. First you'd see the movie. Then between that and the second show, you'd gather in the lobby or the bathroom with your friends. So would the guys from the other side. Then all hell would break loose. You'd go there to pose and posture.

MW: Was there any types of movies you preferred?

CB: I liked a lot of old Hollywood films. Most of the kids in the neighborhood were overwhelmed by scary movies like the original *Frankenstein* and *Werewolf*. Every time they screened everyone would go to the theater. I missed what they called "race movies"—by Oscar Micheaux,

Spencer Williams—films made by Blacks about Blacks. That was missing from my experience until later on.

MW: Did you think about the kinds of roles Blacks played in the movies you saw?

CB: They used to show Tarzan movies. And there was Tarzan who would pick up these Black guys, throw them across the river, and outrun them. He'd wipe out a whole village of Black warriors, and we'd cheer, "Yeah! Yeah!" We used to yell, "Get him, Tarzan! Yeah, get him, Tarzan!" Identity crisis, right?

You know what that reminds me of? *Hearts and Minds*. There is a Black guy in *Hearts and Minds* who's shot as a talking head—from the top up. He talks about a battle he was in against the North Vietnamese when they asked for air support. When the jets came, they hollered, "Yeah, jets! Yeah, jets!" But the jet dropped the canister with napalm on them instead of the Viet Cong. Then the camera reveals that he was burned and maimed by the napalm.

MW: How did you decide you wanted to make films?

CB: I always wanted to get involved in photography when I was in high school. I didn't have a camera, but this guy I knew had one—a regular eight home movie camera—and his was the first camera I ever looked through. Somehow it was there, in the back of my mind—something that wasn't really formed yet. And when I went to City College I worked in the main branch of the L.A. public library downtown. I worked in the evenings and usually had a couple of hours to kill, so I'd go to a movie. So it was that, combined with studying writing. At the time, the arts became very fashionable. So it was just a matter of finding the right medium. There a lot of people were involved in plays, and lots of people were writing poetry.

MW: Were your friends doing that, or was it mostly your friends in college?

CB: Mostly the friends in college. The Watts Writers Workshop was blooming. Until—it was rumored—an FBI informant burnt it down.

MW: Were you part of the Workshop?

CB: No, but people I knew were. It's hard to explain how things like Malcolm X had an influence on taking me in a certain direction or toward a form of expression, but somehow it did.

MW: Was he a hero for you?

CB: He made a strong impression. The mosque that the police attacked wasn't too far from where I lived. Across the street was the famous nightclub called the Five-Four Ballroom. The police and the media saw the Muslims' political positions as a threat. There was a shootout at the mosque. We used to go by and look at the bullet holes in the building. Years later, when I was in East Berlin, walking down the streets where you can still see bullet holes in the walls, the mosque in L.A. came to mind.

It was a time of choosing. Some people supported, some denounced Malcolm X. He was building self-confidence, because he'd demystify whiteness. I never start disliking people just because of race, so I never took on the hate aspect of the philosophy. But Malcolm X had a lot of presence, and there was an element in his character that you could borrow from. His story was incredible. He went through the same things as the man on the street. His story is a familiar one, like so many people who started the wrong way. However, his story departs from the familiar one because he took a negative experience and changed it into a positive force.

MW: He was one of the only voices speaking loudly and clearly.

CB: I found that people I knew gravitated toward Malcolm X, as opposed to Martin Luther King. I think he spoke about a different need. He said, "If some so and so spits in my face, he's not going to spit in nobody else's face." That's what people wanted to hear. Because you get tired of people kicking you. Particularly when the double standard was so apparent and second class citizenship was such a part of one's life.

MW: But were you ever part of any group?

CB: I've never been part of any group. There were a lot of guys that joined the Panthers because it offered a direction for young people and tried to give them a focus. You were like part of an army. You had a uniform—a black leather coat and tam. I couldn't take a lot of it seriously because I knew some of the guys who joined the Panthers, like this guy Jerry. We were in school together. He was a nice guy, in many ways, but he didn't have any direction. One day I ran into Jerry at Avalon and 97th. He was in his black leather jacket recruiting for the Panthers. I listened to his rhetoric and said to myself, "Here's this brother. You couldn't get him to sit still in class for two seconds." He was carrying Mao's *Little Red Book*. While we were talking the police drove by. The L.A. police were notorious for shooting people at the slightest provocation. They used to look for confrontation. So the police drove by, and Jerry made eye contact. He stopped talking like a pit bull seeing another pit bull, or like Japanese fighting fish in the same fish bowl.

I thought, "Let me get away from this fool." I used to run track, and I'd jog to the store to keep in shape. Later on that night I was running down the street, and all of sudden police cars raced out of the alley and surrounded me. The police jumped out of the cars with guns drawn but saw that I wasn't the person they were looking for, jumped back in the car, slammed the door and zoomed off. What happened was that Jerry and another Panther tried to shoot a policeman on Central Avenue. Jerry got killed during the exchange.

MW: When you went to UCLA, you already knew you wanted to make films?

CB: Yeah. But it's sort of strange, because I knew if I told people I wanted to be a filmmaker and make movies, they would think I was nuts. Even years later, whenever I told people what I was doing, I felt a little strange. If you said you wanted to be a lawyer, that's fine, a doctor, that's fine, but a filmmaker—what? That was *not* a Black man's job at that time, even though there were people like Bill Greaves and Carlton Moss, who had been around for a long time.

MW: What year did you go to UCLA?

CB: Around '67.

MW: So was going to UCLA a turning point in your life?

CB: The turning point, I think, was earlier. I used to think that UCLA was like the twilight zone. At LACC there were working class people, really practical people, pragmatists. They went to night class because they were working during the day. And it was cosmopolitan. There were all sorts of ethnic groups. UCLA was mostly white, and I noticed the liberty these people had. When I was in South Central, if the police drove down the street and smelled dope—marijuana, anything—he went through your pockets and dusted your pockets looking for evidence. If there were any seeds or any residue of any marijuana, you'd be picked up and taken away. When I went to UCLA, some students were doing it in the open and were not paranoid. I was paranoid. I said, "What are these guys doing? They must be crazy!" The security guard would go through the hallway, ignoring everything. His only interest was seeing if the doors were locked. I said, "Damn!"

MW: Who else was there then?

CB: As for other Blacks in the department—Bob Grant was there, John Henry, Don Blackwell.

MW: *Killer of Sheep* is one of the few realistic films about the Black community. What were you thinking about the films you were seeing at UCLA?

CB: I saw a lot of films concerning the working class. But the issues were idealized, and the conflicts were reduced to problems between management and labor. Management exploits the workers, and the union goes on strike. These films had a built-in resolution. Those weren't the kind of films I was interested in, because they didn't represent the experiences that I had gone through, the things I saw, or how I saw working people in my neighborhood. The issues are completely different. What was essential was finding a job, working, making enough money, and then, at the end of the day, coming home and still trying to show signs of life. How does that affect the family? What are the consequences of not having time to spend with the family?
MW: Isn't that what *Killer of Sheep* is about?
CB: It's about how Stan, the main character, loses his sensitivity and still tries to maintain a certain kind of dignity. You can see at the very beginning that this kid is traumatized by a fact of life. The father tells the little boy, "If you see your brother's in a fight, you help him, whether your brother's right or wrong. You don't stand and watch. You go and help your brother." Which is okay, but you can imagine what effect this has if you have a conscience and are developing a moral concept. It was that kind of conflict that I was interested in trying to portray: How do you work in this environment? How do you maintain a certain amount of dignity? I wanted to show what price it takes to survive. How you survive is a personal choice. I don't think a film should tell you A happens, and then B, and then C will necessarily follow. Life isn't necessarily that simple. Films have a tendency to generalize, to reduce complex issues.
MW: You've mentioned that in your own community people didn't feel that their stories were important.
CB: The perception of what stories are about generally comes from Hollywood or from something commercial. Ordinary things that have meaning are lost. Stories make it possible to reveal that we share a common fate.
MW: Do you perceive a shift between *My Brother's Wedding* and *Killer of Sheep*?
CB: There are obvious stylistic differences, but the concerns are the same. It portrays a different aspect of a problem that I was concerned with, and I think it demanded a certain style.
MW: How would you describe that style?
CB: First of all, it's about values. For example, the main character, Pierce, is not that emotionally mature. Philosophically, he looks at life

in terms of the haves and the have-nots and gets frustrated with people who don't care about poor people. He romanticizes the poor for the wrong reasons, and he hates the middle class for the wrong reasons. He sees things in black and white. His problem is not being able to formulate a realistic view of life. He vacillates and wavers at the wrong moment.

In *My Brother's Wedding*, three different things are going on at the same time: the wedding, his friend getting killed, and Pierce's promise to his mother. The conflict evolves: Pierce has got to be at his brother's wedding at the same time as his friend's funeral, and he can't decide which is most important. So, he's no help to anybody. It creates a conflict—a crisis—because he's not able to evaluate things. If he had made a decision and not made promises he couldn't keep, he wouldn't have created a sad situation. Whereas *Killer of Sheep* is about a guy who—in order to survive and to keep the family together—has to be focused. For Stan, every day is a crisis. Pierce is like an accident waiting to happen. That film is more satirical. You see what he's going through and what the problem is. It's plotted to lead to a definitive conclusion. *Killer of Sheep* wasn't, but drifts off into a comment about being born again and sticking to the struggle. *My Brother's Wedding* comes to an end by focusing on the necessity of making a decision.

MW: With that kind of resolution in *My Brother's Wedding*, I missed the open-ended structure of *Killer of Sheep*. I missed that lack of resolution. *My Brother's Wedding* seems to fit into a more standard conception of what a movie is. Was that intentional?

CB: No. It was made in 35, for a larger audience. But that wasn't why the two films end differently. *My Brother's Wedding* could only take that form. The story almost dictates it. *Killer of Sheep* is supposed to look like a documentary. And in *My Brother's Wedding*, my concern was to make it tense and claustrophobic, to make things seem in relief, up close. It's like rushing head on into a wall. The metaphor is running blindly—a man who refuses to take control of his life. These guys are rushing into life with limited knowledge. No, it's not so much knowledge they lack, it's wisdom.

MW: Pierce's brother and the girl he marries don't seem very wise either.

CB: They were the other extreme, with no soul, no morals or wisdom. *My Brother's Wedding*, I think, was more moralistic than *Killer of Sheep*. It is more didactic.

MW: It strikes me that *Killer of Sheep* is really a tragedy. There are some very funny moments, but, ultimately, there is a sense of utter hopelessness. Have you been criticized for that?

CB: It depends on the audience. It's not a film for everybody. It's not a film that entertains. It's more sociological. It's meant to provoke a discussion. There are people who live on the edge. Not only does Stan continue to struggle, but he does so without falling into an abyss or becoming a criminal or doing other anti-social things. When I was invited to talk at Harvard, some of the Black students were very concerned about getting good jobs and being productive citizens. For them, what's substantive is the illusion of progress. They are interested in how to arrive, and they thought images of struggle should be about that.

MW: That reminds me of Greek tragedy and how a community does not like to see their own circumstances as tragedy.

CB: But classical Greek tragedy is about conflict involving kings, not the common people, which limits how tragedy is considered.

Also, some Black people don't like to deal with the past. Slavery, for instance, is a sort of stigma. I wanted to do a story about slaves. I have a book of slave narratives. I happened to mention to some people that I was interested in that period, and the first thing they came out with was, "Why that? Forget about the past. Everyone knows about it." That's one of the fallacies—that people assume that everyone knows about history. But if you ask some people who Martin Luther King was, who Malcolm X was—it's recent history—they don't even know.

MW: Has there been any place that you thought you could live—other than L.A.? It seems to me that you have a lot of attachments here.

CB: True. If you live in a place where all your formative years take place, you sort of draw from that. But, I would like to live in a safer place. I don't think at this point my living in another place would be a problem. It could be a positive thing. For example, there were some Russian writers who wrote most of their good work in exile.

MW: What about living in Africa?

CB: Actually, I was talking to Haile [Gerima] about that. I haven't visited Africa, and I have a strange feeling about it.

MW: A lot of people draw their identity out of Africa and try to go there to find something unique.

CB: It's a very scary idea for me. I don't know how to describe it—like visiting a sacred ground. You want to go back, because those are your origins—but there's an eerie feeling of touching the soil.

MW: How do you support yourself?

CB: Until recently I had a nine-to-five job working at a talent agency. But I was doing a film at the same time, and it was very difficult.

MW: Tell me about the projects you've worked on since *My Brother's Wedding*.

CB: At one point CPB [the Corporation for Public Broadcasting] gave me eleven thousand dollars for script development for a film I wanted to do about the death of a girl, a true story.

MW: What was it called?

CB: It didn't have a title as such. It was based on a murder that happened here, and I wanted to make the girl a hero, because she stood up and did everything right and still got killed.

MW: Who killed her?

CB: Gang members. She saw the murder of a cab driver. The police came to her to testify, and she agreed. When the defense attorney learned of her existence as an eyewitness, he told his client, who was in jail. He called her from the jail and harassed her. But when the girl's family complained about the harassment, the police said their hands were tied: "We can't do anything until something physical happens." Finally, the guy in jail had his brother kill her.

I presented this story to CPB, and they accepted it. But when I started corresponding with them about it and got their comments, I saw they wanted to take it in another direction. I thought, "What the hell is this? All the guts are taken out. This wasn't the story we agreed on. Let's do another one." And I started writing another story. In the end, the same thing happened.

MW: Does the second project have a title?

CB: *To Sleep with Anger*.

MW: What is it about?

CB: It has to do with Black folklore being superimposed on a situation today. It's about a family. There's Gideon and his wife—about seventy years old—their kids and grandkids. He's retired, and his wife's a midwife. He worked at different jobs, laid track and things like that. They're from the South, they grow food, and they're a little old-fashioned, very moralistic. The sons went different roads. One son is a lot like the father. The other one is more materialistic or buppie kind of a guy. And there is some sibling rivalry between them. And then there is a grandkid who listens to his father tell animal stories.

There is a Georgia folk character named Hairy Man. An old friend Harry comes to visit. He's an evil spirit embodied in a human being. Gideon and he knew each other years back, but Harry admits that he's a stranger now. Still, Gideon invites him in. So Harry stays, and the family is continually disrupted. Gideon gets ill after a party, and Harry emerges as the center of the family. And while Gideon is still alive, Harry has a friend of his propose to Gideon's wife. Harry is also dominating Gideon's younger son—Babe Brother—the materialistic one, who adopts him as his spiritual father because he couldn't identify with his own father. Harry is everything: a gambler and maybe a murderer—he may have killed somebody in the past. Gideon's wife worries that maybe Harry is really bad, and she confronts him after this other guy proposes to her—it's like a satire—and he's very honest about the whole matter. He tells them, "I told you, I am not the person you knew. I intend to leave." But he wants to take Babe Brother. The two brothers fight about it, and the mother is injured, and they take her to the hospital. Gideon isn't part of this because he has become unconscious from his illness; he's gotten worse and worse since the party. When they come back from the hospital, Harry is waiting to get the son but ends up dying on the kitchen floor. And, they can't get rid of him *then*. *So* it's a continual battle to get rid of Harry.

MW: Is this a real character in Black folklore?

CB: Yes, it's a mythical character. What happens is that, in order to escape him, you have to out-trick him. I was trying to establish some sort of continuity between the present and the past by using contemporary situations, combined with this folklore character. I started doing that, but CPB didn't like the idea that I was combining fantasy and reality after seeing the first draft. Now I'm working with Cotty Chubb, who will produce the film.

MW: In this film, will you deal with conflicting philosophies like those in *My Brother's Wedding*?

CB: Yes and no. The characters are different, and it hints at what's taking place: the supernatural elements and the cultural elements. These characters have all these conflicts from the past that are also part of their lives today. It's also about racism.

MW: One thing that strikes me is that you're just as much a part of a community as you are a filmmaker. Many filmmakers that I know make films filled with references to film. Your references are to life.

CB: Earlier I explained some of the problems when I was growing up. I identified with lots of kids that didn't make it. Life cheated them. It was a waste of people, and it continues—even more so now. I arrived at the notion that you owe it to somebody to do something. I also think that's entertaining, because what's entertaining is not car chases and stuff like that, but the subtle things that happen between people.
MW: That's why you're an independent.
CB: There are a lot of independents who have a unique point of view—like Haile Gerima, Victor Nuñez, Julie Dash—who find the fact of being independent allows them to choose their subject matter regardless of the commercial success. For example, Victor Nuñez, who lives in Florida, makes films about Florida. One of the bad things about Hollywood is that you lose your perception of what a story is—whatever that means—and the implications of what a story does and what it's for. There is a notion that the sillier the story is—they don't put it in those terms, they say "entertaining"—the more people will go to see it. They don't have any obligation to the public. I feel that I have one.
MW: What has that cost you, in terms of your own ability to make films?
CB: It hasn't cost me too much. Life is a struggle, and I'm engaged and trying to do something that's very difficult—make sense out of life, explore things, grope about and dig out meaning in these events.
MW: Do you think you're an optimist?
CB: It depends.
MW: A pessimist? Are you a cynic?
CB: I think I'm very pragmatic. I'm a cynic on one hand, because I know that the only way I can make films is to do it myself—cynical in that sense. But I'm optimistic about my own ability. I know the world's a struggle—like the guy in *Killer of Sheep*, the only thing he can do is try and continue to try. That's that metaphor of Sisyphus, pushing his rock up the hill. You can't turn round and swim back now. You're too far gone. . . .

The House of Spirits

Samir Hachem/1989

Published in the *Village Voice*, August 12, 1989.

It's a sweltering July day in South Central Los Angeles. On a quiet block of 20th Street, inside a sprawling, creaky, two-story Craftsman house with lace curtains and a worn-out front lawn, a crew of about fifty people is making a movie. In front of the Panaflex camera, an older man sits on the edge of a double bed, wearing only a burgundy pajama top, his gray pants pulled halfway down his legs. A woman in a floor-length pink nightgown, his wife, rushes in. "Gideon, what's wrong?" she says. "I'm worn out," he says. She finishes pulling down his pants and slips him under the brown and white quilt. "You stay inside," she instructs. Gideon is having a stroke. His wife goes over to the window to pull the shade up. When she turns back to him, she raises her hand up to her mouth and exclaims, "Oh my God, oh!" Gideon is foaming at the mouth. They do the scene a number of times. And each time they do it, a production assistant has to hand actor Paul Butler a Styrofoam cup full of foaming liquid to store up inside his mouth so he can drool it slowly on cue. When the gleaming water bubbles up out of the sleeping actor's lips, some crew members look on intently while others have a hard time holding back their chuckle. At one point, writer-director Charles Burnett says, "Let's do it once without the foam."

The name of the movie is *To Sleep with Anger*. It's about three generations in a middle-class black family wrestling with its own values and those of a new culture that, in the words of one of the producers, Darin Scott, "has become extremely materialistic. . . . It's a dilemma that minorities in particular face as they move into higher social groups than their parents." Tipping his hat to folkloric characters found in black and Native American myths, Burnett introduces to the action the character of Harry, whose unexpected visit to the Gideon household deepens its conflicts, turning brother against brother. Harry brings to the film mystical and superstitious southern tales and customs. When a small boy accidentally touches him with a broom, the indignant Harry turns it upside down and spits on it. "Boy, that is bad luck to touch a fellow with a broom," he yells.

"He's a character that comes to steal your soul, and you have to out-trick him. You can bargain with him. But you have to be more clever than he is," says Burnett, who got Danny Glover to star in this reportedly $1.2 million budget (nonunion) film, totally financed by SVS, a subsidiary of Sony. "I hope people can see another side to black life they can share. It's about a man struggling to save a son and give him a foundation," says the director, whose first feature, the remarkable *Killer of Sheep*, was shot on weekends in 1973 as his thesis film at UCLA for just ten thousand dollars. Burnett's new script has objects, inanimate and live, that draw power out of their sheer simplicity of presence. A half-eaten apple lies next to a sleeping child. An egg falls on the kitchen floor. Someone has a fish bone caught in her throat. In one scene, Glover even gets to hypnotize a chicken.

Much of Burnett's storytelling skills can be attributed to his grandmother, a solid Mississippi woman who taught him his first lessons and tall tales. Unsurprisingly, the script for *To Sleep with Anger*, which contains, the director acknowledges, "collections of people that you hear about," teems with characters who have a knack for grabbing a listener's attention so they can tell a story about a preacher who had committed the worst sin of all, or the story of the man who wanted to try out heaven and hell for himself.

It is Female Slut day on the morning I visit the set. Women on the crew (which is unusually race- and gender-balanced) wear lacy bloomers, tight denim miniskirts and cut-off jeans, fake tattoos, boots and high heels. A feeling of conviviality rules the set. Out on the porch, Danny Glover, bare-chested, his hair in a net, sits with his teenage ninth-grader daughter lounging on his lap. Two children compete in a game of throwing ice cubes and Styrofoam cups into a trash can. ("Those cups don't fly good," says one.) Across the street, an ice cream truck is parked, playing its jingle over and over again. Two women stop by the set selling the Jehovah's Witness magazine.

There are just a few days left to wrap the production, and the pressure is on. "This film," says Harris E. Tulchin, one of its three executive producers (Glover and Ed Pressman are the other two), "would cost 30 or 40 per cent more if it were union." He admits that it was "hard to get an all-black film off the ground." Even the Corporation for Public Broadcasting, which initially financed the script development, backed out because "they didn't like the fantasy elements in it," recalls Burnett. By the time it was picked up and funded, *To Sleep with Anger* had accumulated six producers.

"This is [my] first Hollywood money," says Burnett. "It's an eye-opener." What it has taught him are things "that are not for print!" he says, rolling his eyes. Even with a cinematographer already celebrated for his stylish atmospheres and economy-conscious methods (Walt Lloyd, who shot *sex, lies, and videotape*) and a hard-working crew that's been slaving away on thirteen-hour days, "the emphasis becomes on getting it done, not how," laments the director. The script has more than 190 scenes, and there are only 28 days to shoot them in. "We're averaging six scenes a day," says Burnett, yawning uncontrollably. He admits to having slept very little the night before.

"We're having a problem with the chickens," a P.A. storms in to say. The sound recordist says she can still hear the hammering from the nearby auto body shop. Not to mention the lawn mowers and leaf blowers and barking dogs and the ice cream truck. "There's a BMW blocking somebody's driveway," a message comes over the walkie-talkie. "Is it a van?" Burnett asks. Actress Vonetta McGee's face breaks into a smile as she turns to her director and says, "BMWs don't come in vans, Charles."

The Long-Distance Runner: Charles Burnett's Quiet Revolution

Lynell George/1990

Published in *LA Weekly*, October 12, 1990. Reprinted by permission of the author.

When the American Film Institute's Black Independent Cinema panel convened last spring, attendees with natty dreads and bulging Filofaxes scanned the room, hoping to catch a glimpse of the latest local son done good—Charles Burnett. They had their business cards at the ready, questions carefully rehearsed for Burnett, who had captured the attention of industry types, both here and abroad, with his stately portrayal of a black family in Los Angeles. *To Sleep with Anger*, Burnett's first major feature film (it received a Special Jury Prize at the U.S. Sundance Film Festival in Park City, Utah), offers an exquisite, long-overdue cinematic look at working-class black life. Yet as black filmmakers, including Julie Dash (*Daughters of the Dust*), Keenen Ivory Wayans (*In Living Color, I'm Gonna Git You Sucka*), Wendell B. Harris Jr. (*Chameleon Street*) and Warrington Hudlin (*House Party*), assembled on the dais to share horror stories smoothed by sound advice, an empty seat awaited Burnett.

More than likely, Charles Burnett was taking his "well-received" film around film festivals in search of the distributor. "Have you ever noticed that every time you see Charles he's out of breath?" a friend of his asked. Which is accurate. The three times that Burnett and I meet, he's either running behind schedule or running hard—making up, one senses, for lost time. In the twenty-three years since he began film school, he has directed only five movies: two student projects and three independent features. His first feature, *Killer of Sheep*, won prizes at the Berlin International Film Festival and the U.S. Festival. He's received Guggenheim, NEA, and Rockefeller Foundation grants.

Yet it was the MacArthur Foundation Fellowship in 1988—the "genius" grant that showered him with $275,000, no strings attached—that thrust him uncomfortably into the media spotlight. "I remember that Charles was pleased," says Kenneth Hope, director of the MacArthur Fellows Grant program. "But I don't think he was one of those people who went bouncing off the walls."

Now *To Sleep with Anger* has a distributor and Charles Burnett has achieved recognition, but maybe for all the wrong reasons. It's troubling that so many people find the image of a unified black family unusual. Equally irksome is the media's nervously reverential treatment of a director as gifted as Burnett—who also happens to be black—as a shimmering piece of exotica.

Burnett gracefully deflects the inevitable comparisons with Spike Lee (Lee's work is labeled "issue driven, confrontational"; Burnett's is "subtle, textured, and poetic"). The director prefers the low profile that has allowed him to traverse his neighborhood streets unnoticed. But lately, he finds it harder and harder to keep the business of The Business from distracting him. In the last two months, he's traveled to Cannes, Munich, Toronto, and Spain. But if you "take a meeting" with him on home ground, he'll suggest someplace low-key and convenient for both parties, Sizzler or I-Hop. He arrives—out of breath—casually dressed in a fresh white T-shirt, the factory creases still at sharp points, a warm-up jacket, and crisp blue jeans. Lowering himself into a booth, he politely requests coffee or a single glass of white wine that he'll nurse for three hours. The conversation winds through expansive terrain, from gruesome tales of hangings in German military prisons to the films of Vittorio De Sica to Ray Charles's proclivity for grabbing one's wrist on first acquaintance ("to gauge weight, height, and carriage"). Burnett touches on his extensive research for projects that never saw the light, such as his hours taping ex–Black Panther Elmer "Geronimo" Pratt in San Quentin. "Make sure you have Charles tell you a story," an old school friend of his insists, "*any* story. Charlie tells a great story." That's clear from his new film which, like his conversation, is full of storytelling. Burnett tells stories with his hands, with dark, serious eyes, continually tempering and reshaping them. And the best of his stories always circle back home.

In Charles Burnett's neighborhood no one wanted to be a filmmaker. For his family, he remembers, "It was sort of embarrassing in a way.

That just wasn't one of the things that you considered as an option. It was something that you didn't want to tell anybody. After I'd been in it for a while it sort of dawned on them I was very serious. Then they were very supportive." Burnett had moved with his working-class family from Vicksburg, Mississippi, to Watts when he was three years old. "I lived in a neighborhood where people looked out for one another and for one another's kids. We were very close-knit. It was the fifties, when a lot of the black middle class, among them carpenters and wood masons, still lived in South Central, before civil rights."

Burnett recalls long, dusty afternoons playing on the undeveloped land where Los Angeles Southwest College now stands. "Devil's Dip" offered a place where he and his friends could slide down untamed hills, tear clothing, and break limbs. There was a golf course where they would take BB guns and bows and arrows for long afternoons of exploring. After the rains, Devil's Dip would become a muddy swamp where they'd collect tadpoles, or journey to its farthest extremities on homemade rafts that sometimes sprang leaks. Many of these details appear in *Killer of Sheep*. Sometimes he'd take his trumpet (which turns up in the hands of a small boy in *To Sleep with Anger*) and, if he could find an interested horn or two, assemble an impromptu jam session.

Burnett remembers his childhood as a "sunny period"; yet he refuses to disregard its darker aspects. "I remember pressure from the police. They never let you forget who you were. Also the schools, I suppose there were some conscientious teachers out there, but at that time the school system was a mess. There was no justification for any of that. It was wrong and you have to attack things that are wrong. Later, when I could, I felt obligated to do something about it."

Burnett grew up an eager moviegoer, traveling to neighborhood drive-ins with family and friends to see Tom Mix and Buck Jones shoot-'em-ups, or moody noir films like *Double Indemnity*, or thrillers like *The Red House*. A high school English teacher ran 16mm reels in the classroom, but Burnett didn't look to film as a career: "I would've liked to have taken a photography course," he recalls, "but it wasn't the right environment." He was headed for the "practical route." After graduating from Fremont High School, he enrolled in classes at Los Angeles Community College and was working toward an A.A. degree in electronics—until a writing instructor inspired him by revealing the virtues of subtlety. "There were no set rules. She showed us a gentle way of arriving at what art is."

At the time Burnett enrolled in UCLA's theater department with an emphasis in film, his classmates included directors/writers Penelope Spheeris (*The Decline of Western Civilization, Parts 1 and 2*) and Colin Higgins (*9 to 5* and *Harold and Maude*). "I'd ask myself, 'What if?' What if you weren't in a certain socioeconomic bracket, had different opportunities, how would life be different?" recalls Burnett. "I was trying to view the solutions. What I saw in mainstream films—portrayals of black life—had nothing to do with what I saw day to day. They didn't address realistic concerns."

At UCLA in the late sixties and early seventies, when the Black Muslims and Black Panthers were making their steely presence known on and around campus, Burnett became part of a small, tight group of black filmmakers—Haile Gerima, Ben Caldwell, Larry Clark, Jamaa Fanaka, Julie Dash, and Billy Woodberry. They made films that followed neither the Hollywood "black exploitation" strain, with its pimps in platform shoes, nor the static and airless educational reels that, if the filmmaker were lucky, made the rounds on the high-school circuit. What emerged instead were cinematic vignettes that reflected the spirit of the civil rights movement: from African wind goddesses to working-class women in Watts, these images of strength and resilience celebrated the race.

Burnett's thesis film *The Horse* (1973) was an eighteen-minute study of five young men's emotional reactions to the shooting of a sick horse. "The studios were clamped so tight at the time that the only way to deal with the situation was to look at film as a hobby. You made films because you enjoyed making films. If you didn't make an educational film or a crime film, it was underground cinema," Burnett recalls, "films at midnight. You just didn't get your films shown."

Throughout school and afterward, Burnett juggled odd jobs as a clerk at the downtown library, a teacher's assistant and as a reader for a talent agency. To drum up minority-student interest in film, he also found time to teach a class in ethno-communications. All the while he continued to putter, making gritty films about black life. "A filmmaker must have a background in making independent films outside of the Hollywood product; one gains experience by working and through dialogue. It's like long-distance runners who know how to pace themselves; they don't worry about who's ahead, they know the pace that's right for them."

Burnett and his colleagues forged a strong alliance. They alerted one another to open slots at festivals; when funding was scarce they learned to apply for grants. As Billy Woodberry recalls, "There was a tremendous cohesion among these people. Minority students at the school were a new thing. They were all young and excited and dynamic and getting their hands on this thing for the first time. There were different ideological tendencies: some of them were into Pan-Africanism, some of them were into Marxism. So you had to have a position about culture and film and politics. You had to earn their respect."

Woodberry knew of Burnett, long before he met him. Sometimes he would catch sight of him across campus, but more often heard stories that he haunted the upstairs editing rooms after dark. "He was totally unassuming," says Woodberry. "He looked younger, slightly built. You didn't know that he was in the school or was as far along as he was. It was his manner."

Burnett's films were full of images and details that appeared nowhere else. Woodberry remembers a collection of icons pulled from Burnett's neighborhood that quickly became trademarks: a butcher shop on 103rd Street that sold live chickens or the nearby neighbors who kept a handful of grazing horses that somehow remained oblivious to the urban noise. "He was working in a way that was not exploitative or stereotypical," Woodberry points out. "He had decided early on that those lives were epic in quality. The people who lived in the stories didn't realize it, but it was his job as an artist to give them form and shape."

Beyond the boundaries of their small group, these filmmakers battled with the outside world. Skeptical police would stop and interrogate black film crews shooting on location. On campus, they faced insidious, insulting images dreamt up by white (often times well-meaning) colleagues. Tempers blazed at the screening of Steve (*Fritz the Cat*) Krantz's *Coal Black and the Seven Dwarfs*, which featured wrap-around Cadillacs, black women with more-than-ample backsides swaying to Cab Calloway—(the voice of Coal Black) singing "Hi-De-Ho."

The filmmaker, Caldwell recalls, saw the film as a tribute to black people. "He thought we were being too sensitive. The professor agreed. One sister cried. I was angry and vocal. But afterwards I wasn't sure what difference it made. We were just beginning to realize the power of media, how this new art form could strengthen the movement. We all watched the film *Superfly* change black people's consciousness. We felt that we had to get out there and do something. Charles never really showed anger in a verbal way. He just did his work. He expressed his feelings that way." Burnett's work veered away from sharp political messages. He was influenced instead by the poets and essayists who emerged from the ashes of the Watts rebellion: "It was that celebration of blackness more than anything else," says Burnett.

We are sitting in the Sizzler on Stocker Street, near the Crenshaw-Baldwin Hills shopping center. Dinner is long finished. Burnett glances up occasionally to wave a greeting to friends who wander by. He is talking about the more marginal films at the Sundance Festival that impressed him, *Rodrigo D.* (from Colombia) and *A Little Fish in Love* (from the USSR). What they have in common with his own movies is their love for stories—stories as history, stories as moral lessons.

In the African American tradition, storytellers—be they as formal as the African *griot* (storybearer) or preacher, or simply a chatty great-aunt or mournful bluesman—provided a sense of history when there was nowhere else to go, thus preserving and strengthening the culture. Burnett points to the legacy of early black filmmakers—Oscar Micheaux or Spencer Williams. They too were storytellers who, in the twenties and thirties, were plagued by the same obstacles that Burnett butts up against today: tight budgets, short shooting schedules, and limited distribution. Like them, he has learned to work with what's available. And he's discovered that there has always been something—or someone—to fall back on.

Killer of Sheep (1977), which was shot on weekends on a ten-thousand-dollar shoestring budget with the help of close friends and family, springs from a story Burnett "collected" during a cross-town bus ride. In this film, L.A. appears as a mirage, its palm trees mere silhouettes that shoot up behind the gray haze of smog; it's a smoky backdrop to the somber particulars of life among the black working class. Burnett fleshes out these sketches by setting rich moods with deep shadows and song—pulling from old blues, jazz, gospel, and smoky torch songs. When pained lovers, who can no longer find adequate words to express their confusion and their despair, sway in half-light to Dinah Washington's "This Bitter Earth," "with that music," the director explains, "a voice singing with a band, you see everything that black people were dancing to. You see black culture."

Burnett's camera examines the problems, and the deleterious conditions contributing to them, that with time can either destroy a spirit or make it stronger. There are no neat resolutions; he shuns sentimentality and, without heavy moralizing, celebrates the survival of the black family, even when societal factors threatening to erode it often seem insurmountable. As with *Killer of Sheep*, both *My Brother's Wedding* and *Bless Their Little Hearts* (directed by Billy Woodberry and written and shot by Burnett) are firmly planted in the family. The unit threatens to crumble from within as unemployment rates, a sliding economy and the hard, more immediate anxiety of too many mouths to feed work in concert to chip away at self esteem. With ripe silences and long, probing glances, Burnett allows the atmosphere of this life to leisurely unfold.

A more interior film, *To Sleep with Anger*, tackles the struggle between good and evil within a family. Dabbling in the talismans and charms of southern folklore, Burnett makes the venerable customs of the oral tradition the centerpiece of his movie. As early morning tales are shared over a sunny kitchen table, Harry Mention (Danny Glover), an old acquaintance from "down home" who's paying a visit to his friends in the big city, eases into the role of the classic trickster summoned up from African American folklore. (Zora Neale Hurston collected oral histories about a notorious apparition named "Daddy Mention" who spent time in various Florida jails, prison camps, and road farms, for her book *The Sanctified Church*.) Harry casts an ominous shadow over a splintering family whose father mysteriously falls ill. "It's one of these stories that happens in the mind," explains Burnett. "What becomes the battleground is Gideon's [the father's] body. They're fighting over the house inside, getting Harry out. And what's at stake here is the family. So it's more of an interior thing, with references to the past and future, set in a world that is neither real nor fantasy."

Festivals aside, Burnett's been encouraged by the response from screenings in cities like Atlanta, whose black population, like others around the country, is starved for a film that reflects a familiar experience. "Everyone was saying, 'I'm going to bring my parents . . . because they can relate to it.' [People] want to feel like they're part of this human community and films, quite frankly, have really been disrespectful to black people."

For too long, Hollywood films have defined black Americans in Anglo terms, the "black" product packaged and touted by the media is more often than not conceived in the imagination of white America. Charles Burnett has found himself in the formidable position of recasting the African American experience on film, capturing a full range of black urban life from black class distinctions to the resonant and disparate cadences of black speech. "Charles is very much steeped in our culture," says Carol Munday Lawrence, *To Sleep with Anger*'s post-production supervisor. "Yet he taps into all of mankind. He really is a storyteller and we—black people—need to be allowed to tell human stories. This film is about people, what makes it black are the trappings, the approach, the layers we bring to it. He does such a beautiful job articulating particular black people. Charles recognizes that we are not monoliths."

Though his current projects (a couple of documentaries and a film to be shot in Louisiana that will pair him once again with Billy Woodberry for an *American Playhouse* production, *My Father's House*) will take him well into next year, the battle is far from over. In many ways he's just begun scaling walls, working to demystify and humanize the black image on screen. Overseas he patiently explains to European audiences that African Americans do indeed own washing machines, possess father figures, and have intact families. Unwittingly, he's become a spokesman for the African American experience. "Even in this country, whites in some communities don't see black people," says Burnett. "People don't interact. So they have that European mentality here; all they know is what they get from the media—that blacks are cheating each other or rioting."

Bérénice Reynaud, the New York correspondent for *Cahiers du cinéma*, concurs, pointing out that *Killer of Sheep* was one of the first films in which European audiences saw a sensitive, uncondescending portrayal of a black family. "There is a quality of generosity in the way he looks at his characters. There are two kinds of directors; one who loves his characters, and one who doesn't. Charles is the first kind. He is a great creator of images—a closeup of a face of a black woman goes into the soul of that person. The Renaissance painters like Leonardo inserted a glow—Charles Burnett does this when he looks at faces."

Like the others who gathered on the dais at AFI, Burnett has horror stories of his own to share. After months of looking for a distributor, with plenty of curious nibbles but no takers (until Samuel Goldwyn Company picked the film up early this summer), Burnett is now looking at the whole issue of marketing. Filmmakers and producers throw up their hands over how to mount a campaign to sell a black film that doesn't boast a "slammin'" rap score or a familiar face plucked from pop culture. "*To Sleep with Anger* is a different kind of film. A lot of distributors were interested in it, but one guy came up to me and said, 'Well, Charles, we like the film but there's no sex, no drugs, no violence, no car crashes or any of this, so how do you sell it?' Some of these distributors you talk to ask you, 'What kind of movie are you going to make?' And I'll say, 'I'm going to make one that's going to heal society.' And they say, 'Get this *mess* out of my office.' But if you go in and say I want to make a cheap movie that's going to make $20 billion and it's gonna have rap in it, and we're going to sell the script for $3 million and we're going to have sex scenes from one end to the other—nonstop—and we're going to have five hundred murders and we're going to have this guy rapping over this guy's dead body: 'You wouldn't have died if you hadn't've dissed me.' Then they say, 'Oh my God! Just what we're looking for!' It's that sort of stuff.

"This film is not for everybody," Burnett admits, "and you don't want to compromise yourself to try and attract people. So you make choices. You have to expect that some people are not going to try and analyze things. The people who stand at the door and determine what people should see are very close-minded," he explains. "They don't want diversity. They think that they can tell what reflects the marketplace by looking at either the Nielsens or trying to understand the mind of an eighteen-year-old white male. These people are irresponsible. They're not catering to intelligent people, and it's keeping the masses dumb. You have to have someone with a passion, who is committed to making sure that the people *you're* interested in get a voice. You have to be prepared, because you have to fight each step of the way."

Early in the morning, when the crews were setting up, adjusting lights, clustering in small circles over morning coffee, lining up for the "Andy Gumps," children began to explore the area cordoned off by heavy cable and wire. Local families residing on or around 20th Street near Adams Boulevard wandered over to see what all the trucks, food, and noise were about. The two-story wood-frame bungalow upon which Harry Mention, hat in hand, would descend, became a community gathering place. Whispering residents waited on tiptoe, hoping to catch a glimpse of Danny Glover, Carl Lumbly, or Sheryl Lee Ralph. Some carried scraps of paper to collect autographs, others simply stood at the sidelines watching the machinery at work, still others became extras. "I didn't have a closed set," says Burnett. "We had kids, people walked around and observed. It's like anything else. You're building a house and people look at it. Somebody on the crew looked around and said: 'You oughta have a child-care center with all the kids around.' It was no big deal. No one disrupted anything. They just wanted to see what was going on. They don't often film in these neighborhoods, and when they do, they tell them to get back, saying 'You don't know what you're looking at.' It's the simplest thing, for example, to explain what a lens does. Kids understand it, and you never know, maybe they'll go out to be a filmmaker after that."

The Black Familiar

Lisa Kennedy/1990

Published in the *Village Voice*, October 16, 1990. Reprinted by permission of the author.

Back in 1965, Daniel Patrick Moynihan really screwed things up for us with his essay "The Negro Family." But first there was slavery. The absent father became the progenitor of laziness, apathy, hopelessness, poverty, pathology, ad nauseam. (Forget the male bias that lurks in Moynihan's call for black men to assume their patriarchal rights.) The riches and disasters of family life have rarely made an appearance in film. Source of proper names and long lists of begats, each clan has lost some of its idiosyncratic meaning to that monolith—the "black community."

Even though Charles Burnett's new film, *To Sleep with Anger*, is about family, we're an hour into talking before we brave the sociological.

"The black family has always been in crisis, because it's always been attacked," he offers, sitting in his hotel room. Casual, in jeans, a white pullover, and high-tops, he adds softly, "It's always being 'saved' by someone from outside, some social worker, or social program, not a person of color." As a friend would say, this kind of narrow casting sees its death in *To Sleep with Anger*.

This year has already seen two stabs by black (male) filmmakers at trying to answer the question "Where's Poppa?" That this should be the only item on the agenda creates its own set of problems, of course. Reginald and Warrington Hudlin's *House Party* may have been a raucous cartoon in living color, but its emotional heft came in Kid's relationship to his harsh, hardworking father (played by the late Robin Harris). And then there was the prologue and epilogue of Spike Lee's *Mo' Better Blues*—its father, son, mother triptychs. The match was slightly altered: Bleek (Denzel Washington) does his father one better, a resolution noteworthy not in itself, but for its significance in a community where fathers are portrayed as notoriously absent. (The process of securing the father takes place outside the film too: by using Bill Lee's scores and musical direction, Spike remakes a name for his father.)

Charles Burnett's 1977 award-winning short feature, *Killer of Sheep*, opens onto a crowded frame. Like the prelude of *To Sleep with Anger*, it's powerful and disjointed from the movie, a symbolic tone poem. There's the voice of a father—his back turned to us—and the face of a sullen and very apprehensive son. The father is lecturing him about the importance of family—apparently he's just popped his brother: "If something were to happen to me or your mother, he'd be all you have."

"In many ways my father and I never spoke. I don't think I've said a hundred words to him." Burnett pauses. "Though he and my brother were like twins." Given this, is *To Sleep with Anger*'s sibling rivalry autobiographical? Perhaps. But in it, saving the father, the son, and, finally, the image of the black male, is less an ideological, rancorous, or youthful enterprise than the outcome of a labor of love. The family is not only a repository of genealogy, but also our history as Americans. When Gideon (Paul Butler) asks his son Babe Brother (Richard Brooks), "What do you think we are, slaves?" the wound is poked, the deeper meaning inescapable. At that moment, something akin to a Freudian slip passes, an undercurrent of historical meaning wells up.

Burnett is a master of revealing the black familiar. Both *To Sleep with Anger* and *Killer of Sheep* confirm that our lives are symbolically rich. Other films have touched on this territory. But for a film to be black without trying to explain blackness (to whites) is a subtle, important shift. Photos and portraits are everywhere, on the fridge, on walls, wedged between the wood and the mirror of a chest of drawers, so each is remembered in reflection, and the preener cannot forget her place. High beds; wispy curtains; a bouquet of greens; a greasy box of chicken; a woman observing herself in the lid of a pan, the kind collards would simmer in; a child saying "skreet" for *street*. All these are the subtle tools of a generous chronicler.

In Burnett's work, the quotidian becomes adventurous, though each adventure is shaded by potential disaster. When *Killer of Sheep*'s Stan and a friend go to buy a motor, they enter a sparsely furnished apartment where one man lies, head bandaged. The motor sits in the middle of the room. Taking it down to the pickup, Stan and friend teeter. The camera lingers intently on their feet, on the flimsy stairs, on the awkward motor, making a perfectly normal descent nerve-wracking. Burnett nails the tension in the everyday, isolating every movement for longer than ordinary moments deserve.

This tension exists in *To Sleep with Anger*. The visit Harry (Danny Glover) makes to Gideon's household is not business as usual. In it, the folkloric becomes eerie; the stranger a disruptive force. The home is a parallel universe, with one piece of furniture out of place, a toby (a charm) misplaced. This is storytelling at its finest. The film's brilliant moment comes as both Gideon and his guest sit robe-clad in the living room, Gideon steadily losing strength, Harry claiming the household as his own.

To Sleep with Anger is not artful docudrama, not comedy, but the work of a visual novelist. The company Burnett keeps is not with his would-be peers—Lee or the Hudlins or the Wayans—but with Toni Morrison or playwright August Wilson; being a filmmaker, though, this makes him hard to pigeonhole and harder to market.

In the sixties Burnett took creative writing classes at Los Angeles Community College. He enrolled in UCLA in 1967. "I stayed at UCLA as long as I could," he says, "to keep making films. Back then you couldn't dream of making a film outside of school. The only way to make films was to stay in school." Staying put paid off. He's a skillful filmmaker, able to render the mundane lyrically; the little details move us. The camera on its own—separate from the narrative and the powerful music—is damp with meaning. In *Killer of Sheep* there are haunting shots of Judas goats at the head of a ramp, below them the dumb, sweet faces of future lamb chops now hesitant, now gullible, finally carcasses and parts lining the walls of Solano Meat Company.

On a greed-inspiring stretch of upper Fifth on a perfect October night, Burnett walks off a cocktail party held for his latest project, a documentary on the immigrant experience called *America Becoming* he's doing for the Ford Foundation.

"When I grew up, everyone told jokes and stories. It isn't that way anymore," Burnett sighs. "Having stories when you're a kid, organizing perception in symbolic ways, is so important." That said, Burnett admits he resisted his calling. "I hated the blues." He smiles. His films are buoyed and swayed by them. "I couldn't understand how people liked greens." They're a staple in his movies. "A lot of music my mother played, I couldn't stand—old 78s, they were as hard as stale biscuits. All of a sudden, as a teenager, I had a craving for greens. It was like a fix; I started to learn how to cook greens. I started doing that with a lot of things. You can only stay away from home so long."

Originally, home was Mississippi, but when he was a child, during World War II, his family moved to South Central Los Angeles. "My mother hated the South. My grandmother was always telling stories about it, my mother hated it, she never wanted to go back, never went back. My uncle's the same way. But I have a cousin who's a country preacher and when we go to visit him, you're in church all day. We've always had this love/hate thing in the family about the South. I think there was a kind of denial at work. I remember a time when being called 'country' was the worst thing that could be said about you."

In both his feature films, the L.A. we think we know falls away, becoming a soundstage to a more rural locale. Southern roots are something most black Americans, those who didn't immigrate, share. The roots are a little more exposed in Burnett's film. In *Killer of Sheep*, dusty South Central alleyways evoke the roads of Mississippi, Alabama, Arkansas, which is where most of the neighbors of his youth came from. "Then you knew your neighbor," Burnett says wistfully. "Until the civil rights movement, and the riots, this community held steady," he pauses. "Isn't that strange, that after civil rights it fell apart?"

Burnett tells a story of a friend he used to get a ride to work with during the rough times. "Every day, the battery in his car was dead—he had a generator problem. So every morning he'd steal one." I begin to laugh. "Do you know what it's like to have your battery stolen?" he asks. "You turn the key and there's nothing, nothing." He recalls another incident, this too made it into one of his films, when he walked into someone's house and saw the front end of a car. Burnett asked, "Why do you have the front of your car in your house?" The response: "So it won't get stolen." "All I could think was: 'This is madness.'" He smiles, still a little awestruck. "It's not the way I'd do things." It's not the way he does things. "But I can at least express a life."

Interview with Charles Burnett

Michel Cieutat and Michel Ciment/1990

Published in *Positif*, no. 357 (November 1990): 40–47. Reprinted by permission.

Editor's Note: At Burnett's request, a few passages from the original interview that suffered in translation from English to French have been silently altered to more accurately reflect his intent. (Conversation with Burnett, Los Angeles, March 29, 2010).

The American Black independent filmmaker Charles Burnett, born in 1944, was noticed for the first time by French critics in 1981, on the occasion of the showing in Paris and at the Berlin Film Festival of his first feature film *Killer of Sheep*, a remarkable account of the alienation of a worker from the Black district of Watts in Los Angeles, shot under very difficult conditions in 1977 (cf. *Positif*, no. 243, p. 49). This movie had been preceded by two shorts, *Several Friends* in 1969, a Super 8 graduation film for UCLA, then *The Horse* in 1973. Burnett, to this day, has remained an outsider, both to the greater American film industry, which has opened its doors to certain representatives of the "tough" but nevertheless "exploitable" Black community (from Eddie Murphy to Spike Lee), as well as to the uncompromising independents from various ghettos (his friends Haile Gerima, Billy Woodberry, Julie Dash, Ben Caldwell, or Alile Sharon Larkin). Whether he shoots on a ridiculous budget or the equivalent of *sex, lies, and videotape* ($1,200,000), he never makes the least concession to the label "Black," and he films his own reality, which is that of daily life, at the same time simple and complex, the daily life of people whose behavior is more or less unconsciously inflected not only by the deplorable conditions in their direct environment, but also by various dissonant cultural inheritances. After the commercial failure of *Killer of Sheep*, Charles Burnett survived by taking on various jobs, mainly as a cinematographer. In 1984 he completed his second feature film, this time in color, *My Brother's Wedding*, which also met with a certain amount of indifference. The incontestable quality of his third effort *To Sleep with Anger* in 1990 earned him an invitation to the Directors' Fortnight at the last Cannes Festival, where the movie was, with reason, very favorably (belatedly) welcomed by international critics.

Positif: How did you manage to make this movie with a higher budget than you had for your earlier films?

Charles Burnett: I worked on movies between *My Brother's Wedding* and this one, but *My Brother's Wedding*, which couldn't be distributed in the United States, had driven me to bankruptcy. German television had helped me out by supplying the camera and some film. Since the picture didn't have any chance of finding a distributor, we sent it to Germany, then to Canada where there were some people who wanted to invest in it. In order to finish it we needed to cut about thirty minutes, but we couldn't get the eight thousand dollars necessary to do it in 35mm, and we declared bankruptcy. I went back to work as a cinematographer on an Iranian film, *Guests of Hotel Astoria*, directed by Reza Allamehzadeh, who lives in Amsterdam. I took various jobs to survive and then this movie came along. I wanted to make a movie about a girl who had been killed in my neighborhood because of drugs. She had witnessed the murder of a taxi driver by a gang and she'd testified. One of the gang members murdered her, and since there weren't any other witnesses, he was released. CPB (Corporation for Public Broadcasting) wanted to work with me. I went to see them to ask them for money, but it took them a year and a half to finalize the contract and again I had to work at various jobs. I wrote a script for Billy Woodberry [1] and a project for them. They promised me they would never interfere with the script, because it was based on a true story that I liked a lot, but actually they wanted to change some things. Sometimes I don't care, but from the point of view of the construction, I know when it's possible and when it isn't. So I said to myself, "Why not do something that would be entirely fiction, where it would be okay to make adjustments?" and I began to write the script of *To Sleep with Anger*. But Billy Woodberry wanted his script immediately and CPB's deadline was approaching. I sent them the script, which they hated. They started wanting to make changes again. I gave them a second version, but they wanted me to eliminate everything that was fanciful, they wanted me to stick to reality, to the broad lines of the story, to drop the folklore. However that is precisely what constitutes the essence of the film. It wasn't worth the trouble to continue working together. I sent the screenplay to Cotty Chubb, and he worked with it a lot and presented it in a few places where the door was slammed in his face, since no one understood the script. He finally found money, thanks to Jeff Ringler and Michael Holzman of SVS.

P: How did the script develop?

CB: I realized that textbooks didn't say anything about the Black contribution to American history. You don't find anything in textbooks about Black folklore in the South, for example. If you live in Los Angeles or New York, that's your state of mind. You are a people of nothing, with no support and no roots. Out of this I wanted to draw a story that would incorporate a kind of oral tradition, like the animal tales, the "hairy man," the swindler you encounter in African or Indian stories, and I wanted to insert it in a contemporary situation, like the role played by violence in the family. I also wanted to have strong characters, like in real life, characters people could identify with. What would make it different would be the contribution of this folklore element, which would lead to a moral problem, not only a forced relationship between roles, but a real problem of life and death. The story would be as fundamental as an abstract idea, and then it would all become clear.

P: Then you decided to have this middle-class family . . .

CB: *Killer of Sheep* was about a working class character, but the problem in America is that there are a lot of movies about Blacks and every one of them wants to show everything at once, all aspects of Black life. *Killer of Sheep* has been perceived as being inaccessible to a lot of people who didn't want to watch something about the working class with its problems, but *To Sleep with Anger* was conceived as something more pleasing, more attractive, but at the same time it would have a subplot that would tell a different story.

P: When you write your script, are you already thinking of the precise framing of your scenes?

CB: I employed a cameraman instead of shooting the picture myself as I did for *My Brother's Wedding*. I had set up a storyboard, but I realized that Walt Lloyd and I saw things in the same way. The team included other people I'd already worked with, and I thought it would be good to let them bring their own contributions, to be creative. Sometimes Walt would conceive a shot differently from the way I had, but I didn't oppose him in this. There was a genuine trust between us. We were in a house where it was difficult to do much and we always tried to have a lot of elements in the scene. Simultaneously, there would be actions to follow in the background, in the middle ground and in the foreground. We would prepare a shot according to this alignment, corresponding to the different simultaneous actions of the script, and we ended up with more stories on different levels.

P: Is your script written in its definitive form before shooting, without any room for improvisation?

CB: Oh no! But in this case it was nearly impossible, because we had to anticipate the budget for everything down to the last penny. The movie cost $1,200,000. There were a lot of people, a lot of sets, a lot of scenes. We explained every scene very precisely, every prop was calculated down to the inch, and so there wasn't any room for improvisation. We shot the film over twenty-eight days, to which were added two days with the second unit. If we had come to the set without having everything prepared, we wouldn't have been able to get what we wanted. We had only a few days of rehearsal, but the actors worked hard, and when they arrived on the set it was as if we had had the time to do a lot of takes, whereas we only had a day and half to shoot a scene.

P: How did you come up with this idea of the two brothers, one who is on the father's side and the other one opposed to him?

CB: It's actually about a crisis, a struggle within the family. Shooting the Black community at this moment of their success, when a few of them are leaving their community to live on the outside, where they form a sort of network, that creates this tension between the ones who've succeeded and the others. There's Babe Brother on the one hand, and Junior on the other. It's quite a classic problem. The first to leave are those of the middle class, and they've left a void behind.

P: And the character of Pat?

CB: In the script, Linda, Babe Brother's wife, is supposed to be a light-skinned girl (which would be the typical image of a woman who belongs to the middle class), while Pat is supposed to have dark skin. But during rehearsals, the two actresses were so good that—since I wanted to make a comment on this stereotype of skin colors—I reversed their roles.

P: Is there a relationship between your family and the one in the movie?

CB: I have a brother, with whom I get along well although we're very different. He wasn't lucky enough to be able to go to school, and he was always in trouble. We're always arguing about what's good and what's bad. Our worlds are entirely opposed, but we're still very close.

P: In American movies in recent years, there has been a conspicuous return to the theme of the family, with very sentimental movies like *Dad*. Your film, instead, is about violence within the family.

CB: That's right. There are a lot of studies on the working of families, like those of John Bradshaw, who's written a number of essays and articles on the crisis of the family, and you realize the impact that, for example, an alcoholic father can have: the child sees his reality regularly perverted by the fact that he has to adjust to his father's neurosis, and so he develops his own neurosis and never finds out who he is. On the other hand, in the United States, violence within the family has increased, which has entailed quite a lot of psychological disturbances. The kind of stories that interest me are not romantic tales about a boy who wants to marry a girl.

P: Your film doesn't present a classic construction. It is at the same time a drama and a chronicle. The characters had a life before the movie started and they will have another one after it ends. You seem to show us only a part of their existence.

CB: I like Russian writers like Dostoyevsky a lot, and living in Los Angeles, with the people and the problems I'm confronted with, it seems to me that there's no solution to this endless daily struggle. Two things happened to mark me. In the first place, in this neighborhood, which is very violent, a young guy had been involved in a robbery and a murder. He'd killed the guy who was running after him to try to stop him. I knew the young man because we had grown up together. I argued with his family. He was convicted of murder and was facing the electric chair, and for my part, I thought that Junior—that was his name, Allan Paul—was in the wrong. His cousins and my brother told me, "Junior did what he had to do; he fired in a situation of legitimate self-defense." But I reminded them that it was Junior who had started it. That was the major argument and there was absolutely no way we could agree on this. The second thing was something that happened at a barbershop in Watts. I was arguing with a couple of older men about the student protesters who wanted to change the world, and I brought up Paul Robeson. It was shortly before Paul Robeson's birthday, and I thought everyone was in favor of celebrating that, but I was shocked when these guys said they respected him as a great singer but not as a patriot, because they felt that he should not have talked ill about his country. I said, 'What? This is a guy who was fighting for you, standing up for your rights, protesting segregation, and so forth.' They asked me what I knew about picking cotton, about segregation and all those things. I'd made them angry. Then there's this story that's in the movie. It's a true story about this guy who'd picked cotton in the hills and moved into town. We'd gone to Mississippi, where I met an old preacher who invited me to his place in Greenville. Earlier, he'd lived in Chicago. He told me about his brother. In the beginning of the 1930s, he'd worked for a white man who owed him some money. The white man told him he had problems; the brother had words with him and killed him. Then he went home and told his wife everything and ran away to the hills. They caught him and they tied him behind a car and dragged him from out of the hills back to town. And this guy told me that the world was changing, because you can hardly even call things like this bad. When you're young, you want to experience everything. You want to kill everybody, throw bombs, go out on strike against this or that, like at the time of the strike against UCLA, Cambodia or the anti–Vietnam War movement. There's a sort of irony in this. You become aware of the sincerity of people who've experienced things directly and not by way of the movies. They're humbler, their experience has changed them.

P: The movie contains a lot of humor.

CB: It comes from the folklore, from those southern animal tales. I'm originally from Vicksburg, Mississippi. My parents left for Los Angeles when I was very young, but in our neighborhood there were people who came from Jackson, Mississippi, the cradle of the great storytellers, the great liars, with their very tall tales. So I wanted to superimpose the animal tales, the "hairy men" I mentioned earlier, and all sorts of things like Brer Rabbit. They're stories that start out very normally, like for instance the one about the man who tries to save his soul by being more cunning than the man who's trying to steal it from him. To a certain extent, it's told in a very serious manner, but there is always an element of humor, of satire, like in the story of Brer Rabbit, where the fox grabs the rabbit, and the rabbit begs him not to kill him: "Don't kill me, or go ahead and kill me, but please don't throw me in the briar patch!" There's always this touch of humor all along the course of the narration.

P: This mood of the tall tale, was that something that existed in your family?

CB: We weren't allowed to listen to stories that were off-color, but most people told some funny stories.

P: How did Danny Glover react to his character?

CB: He had a lot of ideas about his character's youth and what had caused him to turn out the way he did. He wouldn't have anything to do with the Method, but he would search for the kind of walk Harry had to have, whether his voice had to be rough, subtle, or disturbing, and so on.

P: What was your very first film?

CB: My very first film was shot at UCLA in standard Super 8, without synchronous sound (the sound was added afterwards), and back then I didn't know anything about filmmaking. At the time—unions were powerful—there were no Black filmmakers. Furthermore, I never told anyone in my neighborhood that I was taking courses to become a director. They would all have died laughing. So I went my way all the while telling people that I wanted to become a cameraman. I had written a script that was about the life of some of the young people in my neighborhood. It was called *Several Friends* and the subject was this sensation you get sometimes when you reach the point where you have the feeling that you're worthless. I also wanted to do something longer about real people placed in very strange situations, but it didn't pan out. Then I moved on to the sound film. The competition was very extreme at UCLA—they only accepted ten students for their graduate program—and a certain originality was demanded of you. You'd be killed if you turned up with conventional ideas.

P: Then you shot *The Horse*, before tackling the feature film with *Killer of Sheep*.

CB: To tell the truth, *Killer of Sheep* and *The Horse* were filmed at the same time. For *The Horse*, which is a strange story, I was influenced to a certain extent by Faulkner. He wrote a story called "The Bear," and I wanted to make a movie of it. It's a kind of metaphor, something he was very gifted at. And I wanted to do something on his personal South, where everything is said and explained in a symbolic way. As for *Killer of Sheep*, it stayed in the can for nearly five years. At the time there wasn't any way to get it distributed. There wasn't a circuit for movies like that. Haile Gerima, who was teaching at Howard University where there was a symposium on communication, saw my movie there, and then Oliver Franklin saw it also. The Philadelphia museum he was with organized a circulating program of Black films and filmmakers. My film was shown in the Walker Art Center in Minneapolis. A lot of people also saw it at the Robert Flaherty Seminar, and then there was the word of mouth phenomenon. But it never amounted to anything. Then a group of people including Ard Hesselink, Catherine Arnaud, Catherine

Ruelle, and Ulrich Gregor arranged a program of movies directed by African Americans, which was presented in Berlin, Amsterdam, and Paris, and attracted the attention of the European press. That was wonderful, because no one talked about it at all at home.

P: Do you have regular contact with other Black filmmakers, like Charles Lane or Spike Lee?

CB: Haile Gerima, Billy Woodberry, Allan Siegel, and myself form a group, and we communicate a lot. I don't see much of Charles Lane. He went through a bad stretch and wasn't very productive, but he has just made a movie. With Haile and Billy Woodberry, especially, I often discuss the aesthetics of film.

P: Does there exist at the moment in the United States a group of Black actors anxious to work with filmmakers like you?

CB: It's complicated. It's very difficult for them to be wholly engaged in this profession, because nothing is ever certain. It's only when financing is assured that they are really interested in our films. At that moment they all say they want to work with us, but it's difficult to get them to support you from the beginning. I think that Black actors, above all the women, should create organizations that would find screenwriters who would work for them.

P: How did you succeed in financing *Killer of Sheep*?

CB: I won a grant for three thousand dollars at UCLA, in a competition with the first script. I wanted to use it to make a movie, but the actor I had chosen was in prison. I kept hearing he was going to be paroled, but it didn't happen. I stayed at the university waiting for him to get out, because he was a very good actor. So in the meantime, I shot *The Horse*. Since the actor still hadn't been released, the university insisted that I make my thesis film, and, after a first refusal on my part, they invoked the rule, because my time was up. So I took another actor, Henry Sanders, and we made the movie.

P: How did the idea for this one come to you?

CB: It's an odd sort of reflection of events that really happened. They seem absurd, like the motor in the house, but it's the kind of thing you see in a very poor neighborhood, among kids who don't have any parents and live among themselves. There was this guy who had the front end of his car in his house, and I didn't understand why. I thought that was really weird, like the guy who kept a series of car batteries in his closet and used them to power his radio. But when I asked him why he had this crazy little car in his house, he told me it was so it wouldn't get stolen, and that made sense. Another guy had a bad generator in his car that kept burning out batteries. At night he would go out and steal a battery from a car somewhere. One day I came to look for him. He had just stolen his neighbor's battery and the neighbor, who suspected him, was watching him over the fence. The battery was in the trunk of his car, the trunk was open, and the neighbor was there, watching him.

P: Were the conditions of the production of your second feature film, *My Brother's Wedding*, closer to those of *Killer of Sheep* or *To Sleep with Anger*?

CB: *To Sleep with Anger*. Financially this wasn't too bad. We lacked money at any given time, but things worked out. The movie was shown on German television and it's been distributed in England.

P: What is your relationship with Black music? In *To Sleep with Anger* you use blues rather than jazz.

CB: I was raised with music, with blues. The first piece you hear in the movie is "Precious Memories" by Sister Rosetta Tharpe, which my mother played all the time when I was a child, but I didn't really appreciate it until a long time afterward, when that melody would haunt me. It was the same thing with blues. My mother had a lot of blues records that she was constantly playing and replaying. At that time, rock 'n' roll was our big thing. In people's minds at the time, the blues were linked to alcohol, but I felt like I was forced to listen. Later on, jazz became fashionable. If you happened to be in the same place as jazz artists, you were considered a progressive. It was a good time for Blacks, because it wasn't violent. You tried to be up to date. The word progressive, lately, seems to have a sense close to aggressiveness, but at the time it was a political term. People "progressed" in the social sense of the term. It was more acceptable, a lot more cool . . .

P: Like Sidney Poitier in *Guess Who's Coming to Dinner*?

CB: Right. Everybody was talking about the jazzmen, everyone was an expert on Miles Davis, on Art Blakey . . . Then it became more serious, more pretentious: Miles started on the trumpet, a clique was formed and it wasn't exciting any more. And all my friends who loved the old blues, the blues of B. B. King, missed that music then. But it was only much later than I could listen to those blues records and discover that I loved the blues without knowing it, that I needed it. And when I made *Killer of Sheep* I wanted to preserve those old records that no one listened to anymore and put them in the movie. In *To Sleep with Anger* there are several pieces that we couldn't get because the rights were too expensive, but all the same the film showcases the music of Bobby Bland, someone people don't usually have the opportunity to hear.

P: Were you familiar with the movies of Black filmmakers of previous generations?

CB: No. I knew the Black stars, because my parents talked about them. And when I came to Los Angeles, at that time in Hollywood there were "race movies," like *Hallelujah!*, *The Green Pastures*, or *Cabin in the Sky*.[2] But I didn't know there were films directed by Blacks until people like Elyseo Taylor and Willie Bell organized a festival at the university.

P: You mentioned Russian literature. One could think in particular of Chekhov, because your way of telling stories is very circuitous, in contrast to Spike Lee, who addresses himself directly to the public. Your own commentary on the society is just as strong, but you express it implicitly.

CB: I prefer to remain allusive, to proceed by metaphor. It gives more meaning and poetry to things you can't explain. I've never met a person who wasn't complicated. There are always several layers of meaning, several intentions in what people say. So it's necessary to be suggestive . . . I am a great admirer of Van Gogh. I love his paintings. I read the complete edition of his letters to his brother, and one of the most interesting things you find there is that according to him, the essence of expression is situated in gestures. It's by gestures that you can express the exact temperature of a bath, the right shoes. That's the case in *The Potato Eaters*, where you can feel the heat escaping from the potatoes through the exaggerated expressions of the characters. It's better to capture the essence than to be limited to photographing reality. I had a professor in creative writing, Isabelle Ziegler—she died two years ago—who had a great influence on me at the time when there was a lot of discussion, especially in France, of the *nouveau roman*. She tried to make us understand what happens in *The Voyeur* by Robbe-Grillet or in Nathalie Sarraute's works. The important thing was not so much a new style as to create something from your character's experience. You can hardly do more than to develop that. And I think that in every case nothing is satisfactory, because you mess things up, then you go on to the next thing and you try again.

P: Was there a period of the history of the cinema that interested you more than others?

CB: The movies I loved the most when I was a kid were *D.O.A.*, *The Red House*, and especially *The Southerner*,[3] which for me precisely recalled the South, especially through the relationships among the characters.[3] And years later, when I was taking those film studies courses, one of my teachers, strangely enough, said that no European was capable of making a movie about America, giving as a prime example *The Southerner*, directed by a Frenchman! I nearly choked. What is important to notice is that as Blacks we were isolated. We needed an audience in order to communicate and we had the feeling that no one was going to like our movies, because everything was different. People appreciated the light shows, the hippie stuff—the reality of the moment was what counted then. I was completely lost until the day I enrolled in a course on the documentary film with Basil Wright, who afterwards brought me to meet Joris Ivens. Ivens, in justifying his way of making films, said something that was important for me, namely, "Respect the topic first; don't ever forget that you are dealing with human beings, don't ever exploit people; you are only there to record their behavior." That's similar to the concern James Agee expressed in *Let Us Now Praise Famous Men*, this constant anxiety that made him wonder, "Am I doing the right thing in speaking to people and revealing the situation they are in?"

(Interview recorded in Cannes, May 18, 1990, and translated into French by Michel Cieutat. Translated from French by Kathie Coblentz.)

Notes

1. *Bless Their Little Hearts* (distributed in France under the title *Bluesy Dreams*), for which Charles Burnett was also the cinematographer.
2. Respectively by King Vidor, William Keighley and Marc Connelly, and Vincente Minnelli.
3. Respectively by Rudolph Maté, Delmer Daves, and Jean Renoir.

An Interview with Charles Burnett

Bérénice Reynaud/1991

Published in *Black American Literature Forum* 25, no. 2 (Summer 1991): 323–34. Reprinted by permission of the author.

Completed in 1984, *My Brother's Wedding*, Charles Burnett's first 35mm feature, was less commercially successful than it deserved to be (perhaps because it dealt with the difficult issue of class differences within the African American community), and the filmmaker was, once again, faced with the nightmare of waiting years before he could find financing for another project. Then, in 1988, he was awarded a prestigious MacArthur Foundation Fellowship and, in 1989, a Rockefeller Foundation production grant. Meanwhile, Burnett had met Caldecot Chubb, a young producer who admired Burnett's *Killer of Sheep* and wanted to help Burnett find financing for the story which was to become *To Sleep with Anger*. When Chubb joined forces with Ed Pressman in 1988, he took the project with him. Pressman, a self-styled "risk taker," gave such filmmakers as Terence Malick, Brian De Palma, Sylvester Stallone, and Oliver Stone their first chances, and produced such "daring" movies as Fassbinder's *Despair*, David Byrne's *True Stories*, Alex Cox's *Walker*, Kathryn Bigelow's *Blue Steel*, and Barbet Schroeder's *Reversal of Fortune*. The making of *To Sleep with Anger* was further aided by Danny Glover's involvement. Asked initially to play a small role in the film, Glover became so enthusiastic about the project—which featured an all-Black cast and afforded him the chance to work with a respected African American director—that he agreed to play the role of Harry, accepted a reduced fee, and invested money in the production. Glover's talent and charismatic presence are among the film's assets.

In addition to the fine performances of Paul Butler, who plays the family patriarch Gideon, and Mary Alice, who plays Gideon's wife Suzie, the film benefits from the presence of Richard Brooks (of *84 Charlie Mopic* fame) as Babe Brother, the "angry young man" whose materialism, frustration, and confusion become easy prey for Harry's pernicious influence. Because Babe's part was developed after the casting, he becomes one of the most interesting characters of the film, at least the most vulnerable, because he somehow embodies all the contradictions of the family, the uneasiness and hidden anger that, before Harry's arrival, had remained unspoken. Babe's character is a sort of inverted mirror of Pierce, the "socially maladjusted bother" in *My Brother's Wedding*. Babe represents the ambitious young professional, married to another Buppie, but the contradictory resentment he feels towards his more traditional brother Junior (Carl Lumbly), "better loved" by their parents, parallels some of Pierce's similar frustrations. And Junior is as fed up at being "the good son" as Babe Brother is at being constantly criticized by his family.

From the outset, *To Sleep with Anger* is a dark comedy—in the best tradition of Chester Himes. The ultimate joke comes towards the end of the film: An incongruous corpse imposes itself on the protagonists, who have to fight back to resume their normal social and family lives. For bureaucratic reasons, the authorities refuse to remove the corpse, which provokes a wisecrack among the onlookers: "If it had been a white man's, they sure wouldn't have left him there!"

As in the original "trickster" stories of the South, Harry is a mythological character, half-sacred/half-sordid, whose arrival disturbs a family's (mis)functioning. As played by Glover, he is fascinating and disquieting because he is so *ordinary*: a braggart, an entertaining storyteller, maybe even a murderer (but there is nothing extraordinary here; if one is to believe the newspapers . . .). Harry exudes a mute, veiled sexuality, flirting only with unattainable women to better indulge in male bonding; a suave parasite, he shows a surprising lack of resilience when Suzie finally sees through him, yet he remains a mask, a cipher, a void in which the members of the family lose themselves.

To express this subtle battle between good and evil, Burnett uses a half-tone palette. With sensitive close-ups, he explores the interplay of feelings, the conceit of human love that always does "too much" or "not enough," the trials of survival, the daily struggles to assert and retain human dignity. For Burnett, the main character of the film is Gideon, whose strange nightmare is enacted in the pre-credit sequence, and who spends most of the film in a semi-coma. What are the dreams, the fears, the hopes of those who go "to sleep with anger," without having made peace with themselves and with others?

The text that follows is an updated version of an interview with Charles Burnett done prior to the 1990 Cannes Film Festival.

Bérénice Reynaud: What does it mean, *concretely*, to be an independent filmmaker?

Charles Burnett: With independent cinema, you have all the time in the world, to some degree. But when you're in production, it's do or die. You have to get it, and if you miss it, there's very little opportunity to go back.

BR: What happened between *My Brother's Wedding* and *To Sleep with Anger*?

CB: I really wanted to direct the story of Dimitria Wallace, a girl that got killed by a gang against which she was going to be a witness in court. So I took it to CPB [the Corporation for Public Broadcasting], and they agreed to develop it. But as soon as I turned in the treatment, they told me how it should go. So I said "No, it's not going to work. Maybe I could give you instead something I am not too close to...." So I gave them *To Sleep with Anger* and again they started to stick their hands in it. I said "No," and they dropped the project. Then Cotty Chubb, who was looking for something to produce, got in touch with me, at the suggestion of a friend. I gave him the script to read, and he said he'd like to do it. He spent almost a year trying to find the money, but eventually closed his production company and joined forces with Ed Pressman. Then things started to roll. We started shooting in the spring of 1989. It took twenty-eight days, plus three days for the second unit.

BR: Could you talk about the credit sequence?

CB: Gideon has a dream, a nightmare, born out of anger and frustration. He's lost his Toby. He sees himself burning in hell for the first time, and then Harry shows up.

BR: You keep Harry as a cipher. We don't really know what he is, what he wants, etc. You use him to reveal what the whole family is about. The characters of the family are very subtly described. Did you write or rewrite the parts with the performers in mind?

CB: For Babe Brother's character, we expanded the role a bit more, added a few more scenes, because the main struggle in the film concerned Gideon and Suzie. But when we were looking for an actor to play Babe Brother, we thought we'd get someone with a name, and so we added more scenes to develop his character. But other than that, it's pretty much the same.

BR: There are some correspondences between the theme of *To Sleep with Anger* and that of *My Brother's Wedding*: divided loyalties towards different parts of the Black community.

CB: I think that most problems exist within the family. It is the base of civilization, and its erosion and breakdown, the destruction of the extended family, are a constant theme for me.

BR: In *My Brother's Wedding*, the parents are a "good," hard-working couple, yet they are alienated from their children, they don't understand them. And you show with great understanding and subtlety the tension within the couple in *Killer of Sheep*.

CB: The main source of the problem is being frustrated and not knowing why. Babe Brother has only a vague idea of what he wants—same thing with the protagonist of *My Brother's Wedding*. He has good intentions, but the wrong ideas—the wrong analysis of life. These characters are definitely based on observations—a collection of things I have seen in people, in my community, in my family.

BR: Your personal visions give a magical aspect to your films, but they also have a very realistic understanding of daily life, of interpersonal relationships in the Black community. What made you decide that making these kinds of movies was going to be your life's work?

CB: One of the things that influenced me, I suppose, is the division I experienced in the community I came from. In Watts, before the civil rights movement, everyone was grouped together; the upper classes and the lower classes had to coexist. So there was a direction, a sense of who you were. After that, it somehow broke down. People moved out because new opportunities were open to them. They left a big vacuum in the community. You grew up seeing a lot of your friends getting into trouble. And, maybe because I have a serious speech impediment, I always felt like an outsider—an observer—who wasn't able to participate because I couldn't speak very well. So this inability to communicate must have led me in a certain direction—to try to find some other means to express myself and my concerns. I really liked a lot of the kids I grew up with. I felt an obligation to write something about them, to explain what went wrong with them. I think that's the reason I started to make these movies.

BR: Are you still in touch with the filmmakers of what Clyde Taylor has termed the "L.A. Rebellion"?

CB: I talk to Haile [Gerima] all the time. Julie [Dash] came to L.A. [to work on the post-production for *Daughters of the Dust*]. But it wasn't a rebellion. Clyde and I argue about his use of the term. When we all went to UCLA, we tried to form groups at different times to facilitate filmmaking. But it wasn't a "school" of Black filmmakers, or a conscious effort. Things just happened. Of course, everybody was more or less rebellious at that time. It was the late sixties, the early seventies. The Viet Nam War was still being fought, and people were disillusioned. What UCLA did was to inspire a certain amount of dissension and critical analysis, a certain desire to be original. And you had to be able to put a group of people together in order to get a film done. This may have given the impression that we were involved in a "movement." But when we look back, we don't see it that way. We were just trying to do films at the time as well as we could, and some of us—especially Haile and Larry Clark—had a particular idea about what they wanted to talk about in terms of social issues, etc. So they were like political groups. We were expected to do something different and to talk about social problems.

When I got to UCLA, there were only a few Black people there—myself, Bob Grant, Don Blackwell, and John Henry—some Latinos, and, as far as I can remember, two Asians. The faculty was not ethnically diversified. A whole cinema was left out [of the curriculum]: the emerging Third World cinema and, notably, African cinema. So Elyseo Taylor wanted to start a program, and, in order to get support, he encouraged a quota system that would allow students from other colleges to register in the film department. He then started a communication program where several of us—myself and a young Latino—taught classes to minority students. The idea was to encourage them to make films about their communities, their particular situation. And I think that such initiatives started a lot of things. I believe Larry Clark came under that program, Montezuma Spalsa, a lot of people who are now in the Chicano Coalition, and most of the future founders/leaders of Visual Communications. We saw a lot of Ousmane Sembène's work, and other Third World movies such as *The Day of the Jackal*, and that gave us a sense of what we could do with cinema. But, even before that, there was the influence of people like Joris Ivens.

When I had arrived at UCLA, there were no feature films you could identify with. But Basil Wright was giving extremely good courses about documentary films, and the way he was discussing this kind of work opened up a possible way of thinking about film. So, before I discovered Third World cinema, Basil Wright's class started a lot of things for me. In the films he discussed, every shot contained a human element and touch. The subjects in front of the camera were treated like *people*, not just props and objects and things to be manipulated. A certain amount of reverence was visible throughout the work, because the person you are and the things you have to say are the same thing.

BR: So, maybe it wasn't a "movement," but there is an obvious stylistic similarity in the films made around UCLA at that time.

CB: There is a big difference between then and now. When we were in film school, we didn't have any of the kind of distribution [for Black or independent films such as that which exists today] or the hope of going to make a Hollywood film. Except there was a filmmaker by the name of Walter Gordon (Jamaa Fanaka), who made *Penitentiary I, II*, and *III*. He was one of the few Black people who was designing films to go directly to Hollywood, to make money. We were convinced that there wasn't any outlet for our work. So we had a chance to indulge a little bit and be creative and say what we wanted. We didn't have to answer to anybody, except to the public.

It was just before blaxploitation started. In the sixties we were all influenced by the idea that either you're part of the problem, or you're part of the solution. And to us it was quite obvious that exploitation films were part of the problem. We had a sense of direction. At that time—this was just after the riots, and before the killing of Martin Luther King—people still believed that they could do something for their country. There was a certain optimism around. Now, students are just going directly into making twenty-minute films designed specifically like a showcase or a portfolio to go into Hollywood and get a three-picture deal. They no longer care about developing their craft, or their vision.

When we were students, UCLA encouraged competition, even among the Blacks, and we tried to be as exact and thorough as possible and say everything that had to be said. I also think that one of the things that the Black filmmakers had to suffer from at that time was that you had to "say everything" in each film, not only because you were never sure if you would be able to make another film or not, but it was somehow *expected* from you. Every time you'd take your film to another screening, a different audience, you could never totally satisfy everybody. If someone was happy, someone else was unhappy, because

"the film didn't reflect his or her reality." You never felt really successful. You might get a standing ovation in one auditorium and, in the next one, a bunch of boos, for talking about poverty in Watts is a far cry from talking about poverty in Detroit or the South Bronx.
BR: What do you think of the current state of Black cinema?
CB: I don't think too much of it. There are still people able to do their work. Haile is doing a film right now. And so are Billy Woodberry and Julie Dash. Charles Lane is a man with a vision. What has to be developed in filmmakers is a sense of who you are, what you want to say, and how you want to say it—a worldview or a perspective that you can express in your own terms.

Black commercial filmmaking does not bother me. I am after one thing, and most of them are after something else. We are working in separate camps, so to speak. One of the things that Spike [Lee] has done is to call attention to the fact that Black films can make money. The down side is that now everyone is looking for a Spike Lee. So if your film does not appear to be a Spike Lee kind of film, you're blown out of the water.

I am trying to do something of my own, without knowing if it's going to be commercial. What I can say about [my producers] Ed Pressman and Cotty Chubb is that, when they have confidence in a director, they say, "Okay, we've agreed to do it; we're going to live and die by it." It's not like doing a studio film. You can argue back and forth with them, and the last decision is yours.
BR: Was *To Sleep with Anger* shot on location?
CB: Entirely. We found the house right away. Interestingly enough, it's in a place that used to be called Sugar Hill. Los Angeles was once entirely inhabited by white people. Then, during the early sixties, a lot of Blacks were able to move into this area called Adams Heights. A few well-known Blacks in the entertainment industry used to live there—like Hattie McDaniel, Sugar Ray Robinson, etc. So it became a rich, middle-class Black area. After that, it went downhill, and poor people moved into those big houses. Now, gentrification is coming back. Anyway, we needed a big house for the camera and all the equipment. We looked around, and this was the best place, exactly what I needed.
BR: How did Gideon manage to get enough money to buy this house?
CB: His wife is a midwife, and he works for the railroad. I once talked to a guy who worked on the railroad as a porter. He got so many tips that

he was able to buy two homes in L.A. Doing a porter's job is different from laying tracks, but even Gideon could make a good salary working on the railroad. And people of his generation who made sacrifices and knew what they wanted were able to accomplish things. This has changed. When I was working on the documentary I just completed, *America Becoming*, I found out that the hope of being able to accomplish something, and self-esteem itself, is totally missing from the Black community now. It is a feature-length, made-for-TV documentary on ethnic diversity in America, financed by the Ford Foundation, and produced by Dai Sil Kim-Gibson. It's about the coexistence of different minorities in America. We will try to show the interaction of different groups. We are focusing on cities within six different states—such as Chicago, Miami, Philadelphia, Houston, Garden City (Kansas), and Monterey Park (California).

BR: So, what do you think has changed for the Black community?

CB: We shot part of the film in North Philadelphia, where the poverty is extensive. When I was in New York in the seventies—I stayed in the Bronx—it was as if someone had dropped a bomb on it. But in Philadelphia today you have a massive, *massive* poverty. It's amazing how this country can let people live like that. How can America have a community completely blinded? There's graffiti everywhere, and people don't even see them, they're so immune to it. Crack and poverty have destroyed a lot of young people, taken away their motivation and their will to compete with the "regular" society. And it seems planned! One of the kids we interviewed said, "We're going the way of the American Indians. They killed our spirit, our self-esteem."

The successes of new immigrants are always compared with the lot of Black Americans. People say, "How come these new people come over here and are very successful, and look at Black Americans—they're still living in poverty." But you have to look further into the problem. Black Americans weren't "invited" over here; they were brought on slave ships, and they continually have had their spirit broken, eroded. The [welfare] programs or lack of programs are disrupting the Black American family. And this society doesn't offer Black people anything else but below-minimal wages. If you don't accept it, they think you are lazy, and the jobs are taken by the new immigrants, who are accepting lower wages. This creates a competition between new immigrants and Blacks on the job market. But established residents cannot work under such conditions, when they are offered no job security, no health benefits, etc. This is what happened between the Cubans and the Blacks when the Cubans arrived in Miami. Now the Cubans are established, and the Nicaraguans are coming and taking the jobs away from them. There's an ongoing cycle.

BR: What do you think a solution might be?

CB: Self-esteem has to be rebuilt. And very few films contain things that could inspire their audiences—such as *real* heroes—everyday people who accomplish something and make sacrifices, real people you can applaud, and not basketball players. Commercial movies are escapist. Not everybody has fantasies about judo-chopping someone to death. We need stories dealing with emotions, with real problems like growing up and coming to grips with who you are; movies that give you a sense of direction, an example.

BR: How do you work with actors?

CB: First, *To Sleep with Anger* was a very low-budget film, and everything had to be the result of a compromise. The actors were really wonderful, because they were all professionals. One of the things you want them to do is to help you help them. Each one operates differently. One may need more direction; one needs a certain kind of dialogue, of relation with the director. But you have to meet their needs. Most of them want to help you get your vision across. And so there shouldn't be any tension in that regard.

BR: How was it to work with Danny Glover?

CB: Danny's great. He's always willing to try different things, and work with you and spend time developing the character.

BR: There is a sense of ensemble playing in the film. Did you rehearse before you started shooting?

CB: We tried to get a weekend of rehearsal with everyone, but that was impossible. We had one reading with everybody. And I rehearsed before each scene. And we tried to get rehearsals at least individually with the actors a couple of days before. We had hoped to have the experience of rehearsing as an ensemble, but the logistics of the financing didn't allow that. We had to hurry and get as much as we could in a short period of time. But Paul Butler and Mary Alice were terrific. They had a lot to offer.

BR: This was the first time you worked with a cinematographer, rather than shooting your own film. How did you like the experience?

CB: I don't really like being behind the camera. If I did it on my previous films, it was just to save money, to have one less person on the crew. Working with a cinematographer was a good experience because it gave me more time to talk with the actors and deal with all the technical aspects of the film.

What happened with Walt Lloyd is that I was looking around, I saw the films he had shot [including *sex, lies, and videotape*], and I thought, "I like that guy's style." We discussed the look we wanted to give the film before the shooting. But what you really have to do is to stand back and be flexible enough to allow the cinematographer to contribute his own ideas.

BR: It's still very much your film, because of the way you handle the close-ups: a combination of the frame, the light, and the direction. You show so many nuances and subtleties on the faces of the performers.

CB: I use close-ups to express the intentions of the story. For example, when Harry and Marsh are facing each other at the table, during the party, the close-ups express the tension between them. There is a sort of subtle revelation between the two of them about what Harry might have done in the past—a sort of confrontation. It automatically suggested the use of close-ups. I usually storyboard before shooting. And often Walt, the DP, would have the same idea on arriving on the set, because once you are on a location, there are always some obvious things to do. When I shot Alile Sharon Larkin's *Your Children Come Back to You*, people told me that her film had the same "look" as *Killer of Sheep*, that it was due to my "style" as a filmmaker. But I don't have a conscious style. I discovered that the reason the two films looked alike is that the locations looked alike. And each one had a similar angle that was the best to shoot from.

BR: Are you still going to do some camera work yourself?

CB: I did it for *America Becoming*. I will also be the DP for Billy Woodberry's new film *In My Father's House*, and I hope he can raise the money for it. It is an attractive project, with a good story, for which you could be very creative visually.

BR: Do you get involved a lot in the editing of your own films?

CB: Yes. I collaborated closely with Nancy Richardson, who is a very good, very creative editor.

BR: What was your shooting ratio?

CB: We shot an average of three takes. I think once we shot about eight takes because we disagreed on how the scene should be played. The biggest problem we had was for a scene which didn't even make the final cut, involving the kid and a chicken. We tried to get the chicken to fly over the fence. We had to reshoot this chicken over and over again. That really added footage. And to try to get the kid to do right was another thing.

BR: You often have children in your films. Is it especially difficult to work with them?

CB: There's a difference between using child actors and getting real kids. The latter are not "acting," they are somehow "reliving their lives," so it's not hard to get the character. The child actor we used was a nice kid, but he'd never used a broom before, he didn't know how to handle it. It's really unusual. You could find a kid in South Central who not only uses the broom but perhaps knows how to change tires, etc. Child actors don't have too much experience in real life, but they're very good at remembering their lines and getting their cues.

BR: I like the way you used the music in the film.

CB: When I write a scene, I usually have a specific piece of music, a record or a melody, in mind. The first piece of music, for example, "Precious Memories," by Sister Rosetta Tharpe, was included in my original conception of the scene. But there was some dance music—by Johnny Taylor, for example—I had written into the script, but that we couldn't use because we didn't have enough money to secure the copyright.

BR: All the secondary parts are wonderfully drawn. Were they inspired by real people?

CB: Yes. For example I have a friend of mine whose husband died, and one of her brothers-in-law proposed to her just after. So that story *is* true. You always have people like that around you—family friends and the like. I know these kinds of characters very well.

BR: How do you make a living now?

CB: I quit [my nine-to-five job] around 1987. Now, my main source of income comes from the MacArthur grant. It came at a very good moment. I'm not really making a living through my films.

BR: How do you perceive your role in American cinema?

CB: I consider my role in American cinema as my contribution to society. It's not enough that your family is able to eat. You have two kids and you want them to have the best—but then you look around and you also want other kids to have the best. A lot of people go to bed hungry. The issue is how to live with that and, if you can, do something about it. You can use film as a tool: It can have a redeeming value by offering insights.

BR: If you weren't a filmmaker, what would you be?

CB: I would be a writer. I even considered medical school at one time.

BR: The MacArthur grant and the release of *To Sleep with Anger* mean definitive recognition in the United States. But you used to be one of the African American artists who were more recognized in Europe than in the United States.

CB: That's a problem for all the people I've talked to that have had the same experience—it's true of musicians as well. But, as someone said, one is often better recognized outside of one's own country. Yet, it's different when a German or a French person goes out and finds recognition abroad. For a Black person, who is already aware of the fact that he or she is an outsider [in his or her own country], it is a doubly frustrating situation.

But recognition in Europe has meant at least one thing. When you're in the midst of doing a film, there're moments when things aren't going very well, and what supports you is the fact that you have made a film, and that it was successful. And success [for me] initially came from the European response. It gave me the sense that the films I had made were *real* films.

BR: What are you doing now?

CB: I am developing a screenplay for Warner Brothers; it's the story of a Black soldier who kills his platoon commander in Viet Nam. But nobody knows it, and when he comes back, he's a war hero, and later works in urban development. If it is accepted, there is a good chance that I'll direct it.

One on One: Charles Burnett and Charles Lane

Charles Burnett and Charles Lane/1991

Published in *American Film*, August 1991, 40–43. © 1991 American Film Institute. Reprinted by permission.

"I saw one of Charles Lane's films, *A Place in Time*, in Paris in 1980. There was a special program of Black American films screened at the FNAC. His film went over big. I met him a year later at the Berlin International Film Festival. He was wearing a trench coat that made him look like Humphrey Bogart. He had become very much the business man, chain-smoking, Scotch on the rocks at 7 a.m, with business cards that looked like something one would give out on Halloween night. He had just obtained a lawyer who was going to help him with a film he had been wanting to do for ages, *Thou Shalt Not Miscegenate* [now in development as *Skins*], which has become quite the theme of several films being made now. The sad part was that it took so long for him to get his next film off the ground. He is a filmmaker who should have been making films right after he did *A Place in Time*. Viewers are in for something special now that Charles is finally on the scene."—Charles Burnett

"I first met Charles Burnett in 1981, at the Berlin International Film Festival. He was presenting his award-winning film *Killer of Sheep*. I found Charles to be quiet, gifted, and confident. The following year I borrowed five hundred dollars from Charles to pay my rent and phone bill. Eight years later, in 1990, I managed to pay him back—because that's the kind of great guy I am. In all sincerity, Charles Burnett is a gem of a friend."—Charles Lane

Lane: Let's start by discussing favorite films. I'll start by asking you . . .

Burnett: What my favorite film is? Well, one comes to mind recently because it was just shown. It's *L'Atalante* by Jean Vigo. It is a film I marvel at. You wonder, how could someone construct a film like that, with that vision? I find it is very difficult just to conceive of something like that. That's one reason why I like it, and secondly, because it works on all levels and it is just very cinematic, just poetry.

Lane: Do you have a favorite type of film?

Burnett: No, not really. Whatever works. I like neorealism a lot, because the subject matter and style of those films are so close to the kind of things that I'm interested in. And because of the fact that they speak about the same kind of situation, of this physical notion of getting at the truth.

Lane: There are three at the top of my list, and they are Hollywood movies. One would be *North by Northwest*, you know, the Hitchcock film. To me that film was perfect in terms of combining the elements that I like—comedy, action, drama, romance, good musical score. *San Francisco* is another Hollywood movie from 1936, from MGM in its heyday. I like that because it has a big, historical . . . Clark Gable and Jeanette MacDonald . . . like a bit of a musical. But it is also about the history of San Francisco in the 1906 earthquake, and it is about religion and it's about opera, and it's, like, a conglomeration of many things. And it all comes out nicely in the end—I find that fascinating. The third is a 1969 movie, *Midnight Cowboy*, which is not a Hollywood movie because no one wanted to make it. It's like *Dances with Wolves*—no one wanted to touch that movie. It was made in spite of everybody, and it kicked big butt. It has a heartfelt sincerity about it, and comedy. The thing about comedy is that I just discovered it. Over the years, it was never the main thing in film that I liked.

Burnett: Really?

Lane: Yeah.

Burnett: It's strange because, after seeing *A Place in Time*, you think of Charlie Chaplin's *Gold Rush* and *Limelight*.

Lane: I started out in film as a dramatist . . .

Burnett: Yeah.

Lane: . . . Serious issues. I did not respect comedy, and I did not respect black-and-white and silent films. I just did [*A Place in Time*] a challenge. Because I respected Hitchcock, I understood the power of visual filmmaking and certainly the power of comedy and satire. And then I grew up. But that wasn't the way I started, which is why I like to mix social issues and comedy these days.

Burnett: Well, it says a lot for typecasting, doesn't it?

Lane: You're not exactly a tragedian. I mean, you have a sense of humor that pervades your stuff as well. I'm thinking about the last scene in [*To Sleep with Anger*]. Basically, you know, there is a dead man on the floor and people go about doing their thing.

Burnett: I think in my situation, I don't separate drama and comedy. My concern is with a theme, a message, and whatever works to get it across. I don't just go out and say, Well, I'm gonna do a comedy because I like the genre or the style or something. It always starts off with me as a story that has a message and takes a certain form. Like in *To Sleep with Anger*, which includes the human condition and tragic humor.

Lane: But you don't start out with, Umm, I'm gonna make a dramatic film—I mean, with the "labels" in your head.

Burnett: I look at irony as a basis for humor. If I wanted to do a story about black filmmaking, which I'm thinking about doing, I look at that as humorous from the very beginning. But there is also an absurdity about it, you know, that takes the shape of humor in the sense that it's not so much a statement about man's condition, but rather, it's a story about the peculiarities of people being frustrated by trying to do something and then being misinterpreted by the public that it is intended for.

If you do a film about a black subject, you know you are going to offend someone. You are going to hear, Why didn't you do a film about doctors? Why did you do a film about the working class? Why did you do a film about the poor? You just can't satisfy everyone. I find there are a lot of things that can be said through humor.

Lane: In the past, I started out with ideas that dictated the genre. I did some bad Super-8 films, and they had stories and all, but I approached them with the genre and style and form I wanted from the inception. The next film I'm going to do is going to be a comedy-satire, *Skins*, an interracial love story.

Burnett: What is *True Identity*? Is that a comedy or satire?

Lane: It's a comedy, an action-thriller.

Burnett: A comedy-action-thriller?

Lane: Yeah, something like that.

Burnett: Was it difficult using other people's material, in terms of having a script that was already there and then having to rework it?

Lane: Yes, because the script, as it was originally written, had some things that I disagreed with in terms, mainly, of the main character and his point of view about being black, let alone the metamorphosis into this white persona. I understood that the character had to be a black man who was prideful and who understood—fuck the title—but who understood his identity. When he put on white makeup to save his life, the audience had to understand clearly that he is doing this because he has no other choice in order to save his life. I also wanted them to see that he is not enjoying being white for a minute. And that wasn't a part of the original piece. The original piece focused on the character getting off on the fact that he had this white makeup on and feeling like it was okay. But I wanted to have a harder edge than the studio did, and I think . . . they were not prepared for it, initially.

Burnett: Was it originally written by a black person or a white person?

Lane: A white person. Andy Breckman had written the original idea for an Eddie Murphy *NBC's Saturday Night Live* sketch called "White Like Me." I don't know if you saw it, but it had Eddie Murphy going underground to see how white people really lived in America. It was a wonderfully funny sketch. But it was a five-minute sketch and, as a feature film, it needed a lot more elements to sustain itself.

Burnett: Was this a case where you ask, Can white people write about black people? Was this a case where it worked, or were there some cases where the person was completely oblivious of some of the . . . perhaps potential stereotypes?

Lane: It was a combination of hits and misses.

Burnett: Were some of the things that the studio executives gave you to consider in terms of the story, were they ludicrous or were there some comments of value?

Lane: Yeah, some of their ideas were from left field.

Burnett: For example? Because I ran into some . . . I'm just curious.

Lane: There was a scene I had written where the main character [Miles Pope] is in his white persona and he goes into a bar in a black neighborhood and he gets ribbed and he gets hassled because his skin is the wrong color and he is in the wrong place at the wrong time. We, the studio and myself, had lots of discussions about this scene because this scene had an edge to it. And the way black people in the scene responded to the character was kind of edgy, like, You're in the wrong fucking place, honky. The double meaning for me was that this guy could take off the makeup to show that he is really a brother. But he also had to take this abuse because it shows how racism, in many ways, can be reversed. The scene is actually double-layered because he's a black man experiencing discrimination from his brothers and sisters and not being able to do anything about it because if he took off the makeup, the response would he, Oh you're black . . . Wait a minute . . . Why do you have this makeup on? . . . Do you want to be white? . . . So he can't take it off. He has to take the abuse. The studio thought that the scene was really not a part of this movie. Their suggestion was to get rid of it. That was unacceptable as far as I was concerned. We now have a variation of the scene and what happens is that this character, in the white makeup, goes through an alley while going to his girlfriend's house . . . and the same kind of thing happens. The scene is rough. It also feels real edgy, and it's hard.

Burnett: Were there any black executives involved in making any comments on how the story should go?

Lane: Good question—no. None of the executives I worked with at Disney were black.

Burnett: So did you find it difficult? I know working with the studio can be extremely difficult. For an artist to be questioned every step of the way, you know, it would be very difficult to write a story because it's no longer that creative process, one's vision. I just did a film [*America Becoming*] with the Ford Foundation, with eighteen people or so involved in it, and each step of the way we had to have it approved. By the time you get excited about an idea, it gets killed because it has to go through this whole process.

Lane: Right, that's one of the things I found most distressing. I have not worked that way in the past. I don't like to work that way. It's not fun, and it takes the joy out of it. It's business and I understand that when you are talking about dollars, thousands of dollars, let alone millions of dollars. But it is not the way that I find joy in working; it's the studio way, it's the reality. What I've found is that it's like directing a film—making a film—by committee. I would like never to work that way again, where every step, every *thing*, becomes a meeting.

You know, I'm an independent filmmaker, you're an independent filmmaker, and there is a spirit there that just soars and wants to go and be unleashed. [The studio process] can be very debilitating. I found it very debilitating.

Burnett: That's why IFP [Independent Feature Project] celebrates the independent spirit. I think just working with [*To Sleep with Anger* executive producer] Edward Pressman is a true delight, you know, because once he decides on a project, that's it. He doesn't come in and screw around. The next day you don't get six notes or something from people who are in reality Harvard business graduates, lawyers who know very little about art, in a sense. They may support it by going to the philharmonic or whatever but in terms of actually being filmmakers . . .

Some people manage by getting a negative pickup, where you don't deal with any of these people until you bring the film in. That's one of the best ways, I think, to deal with it. There is one guy, I won't mention his name, but he is doing that now with a project at Disney.

Lane: And they get a kickback.

Burnett: Yeah.

Lane: Yep. That's still, I think, the best way to go for an independent filmmaker. The thing is, to be absolutely honest and accurate about my experiences with [Disney], ironically, in some of the meetings—although I did not like it and I don't want to work that way again—there has been some good input, to my surprise. I rebelled against it while it was happening and I did not dig it because it was a lot different from what I thought was going to happen, given my understanding coming in. But I must say that there have been times when it was helpful to the project, and when it comes out, when we see it all together, I hope I still feel the same way.

Burnett: Well, I could see where studio executives can act as a devil's advocate, or as a means to make you think more deeply in a certain sense, but I don't think that they can contribute other than to make you question the process. You have people who don't interact with black people or any other person of color. And their reality is limited by their whole situation. And so how could they tell anyone of color who has a particular knowledge, intimacy, or certain sensibilities about the subject, how to think and what's real and what rings true and what doesn't? Do you know what I mean?

Lane: Yeah, absolutely, absolutely.

Burnett: You know, it's like if I was an executive and a Native American Indian came and said, Well, this is a project that I want to do. I'd sit down and say, Well, you know, I don't think you should make the Indian chief look like this, you know?

Lane: Oh, I agree. With executives and studio people, the focus is about bottom lines, box office, cosmetics, and what sells. This Indian chief, from a studio's point of view, we're not talking about an independent film, so from their point of view it's like, let's get a big star to play the Indian chief because that's box office. That's their concern, and it's legitimate. But that's what puts any filmmaker who's independent and working in the studio context in a difficult position. That's what I found because that's the business at their end, that's what they do . . . If you do want to get your vision in there and work within the system, but try to change things, then it's a matter of constantly compromising. And there's a constant split between your vision and the reality of the box office, your vision and the studio . . . what the studio deems intelligent and sees as good business practice. And that always affects the story for better and, definitely, sometimes for the worse.

Burnett: I can understand . . . but my problem is the studios having so much control over images. And, how people perceive Black Americans and the perception that anyone can direct a black story. The producers don't really try to get a black director to do a black theme. I think a black director can lend something to a black theme.

Lane: Right, right.

Burnett: But the studios are not concerned about going below the surface of anything. They think it's a story and anyone can do it, so let's make this, let's package it. It's all about making money and not necessarily about presenting people in the way they should be presented.

Lane: Yeah, I hear that.

Burnett: I think that the studios project this image of being really what they're not, sort of liberal institutions. But, in reality, there aren't a lot of people of color and women involved in the decision-making process and . . . I think a lot of the films do perpetuate racism. The studios are not really interested in depicting life in a realistic way, and that's why I think that this notion that anyone can direct a black movie is acceptable to them, in a certain sense.

Lane: The rationale is, why not cover your bets and get a white director? After all, they are "better," "safer." That's the mentality, and so, you know, it's up to us to shake this shit up.

Burnett: I think films create myths about black people. Most of the films they show are action-packed dramas with drugs and so forth and so on. To a certain point, they have to be held responsible. The only perception these people have of us are basically drugs and mothers who prostitute themselves. I can sell a plot to a studio, I believe, about situations where a girl is on drugs, her brother is on drugs, their mother is on drugs, and their father disappeared and there is this white guy who is going to come and save the young boy, or something like that.

Lane: Yeah . . .

Burnett: And I think what it has done in the past is, it's enlarged their humanity but restricted ours, because it makes it appear that we are constantly being rescued and saved and I think the studios are largely responsible for that public perception.

Lane: I just think that now is a good time, because we do have a lot of black people who are working not only as actors but as filmmakers, and who are getting chances to do their work. I think the numbers are indicative that this can be turned around or, at least, we can make a dent in it. That's my belief. What do you think?

Burnett: Well, I don't know. I think it really depends on the quality of the person. I don't think that just being black is an issue. I mean, it is and it isn't, because you can get people who are politically correct or politically wrong on an issue, but if they don't feel a part of the black struggle, then I think that's a problem.

Anyone who is capable should make a film, but I don't think one can say, Well, we have a black person doing this film and that it is all right. I had dealings with a black studio vice president who was more interested in the packaging of the project than in being true to the story and to the author's intention of the story. So it's not a question of color as much as it is of one's sensibilities, you know?

Lane: Right, I agree. My whole point about my good feelings for the future is a simple mathematical one. Clearly, it is not a color issue per se. But just mathematically, we have more black filmmakers now, who are and will be given a chance to do their work. I don't fear that it's going to get a repeat of the black-exploitation period of the seventies, where we had black faces in these white plots. You know, just a black lead character whose goal is: Let's get Whitey! I think we have talented people, you know. You and I have worked with a lot of them, and I think that this is going to make things change.

Burnett: Once there is a lull in the box office, we no longer will have these opportunities. This notion about Hollywood and who it embraces reminds me that when Spike Lee was one of the few visible black filmmakers out there, the studios were looking for another Spike Lee. They weren't looking for diversity.

Lane: Spike's film was financially successful, so why not pigeonhole it—and possibly have the same success? It's a very limited way of thinking. What do you think about the way black women are depicted in motion pictures today?

Burnett: I think that in films which are action-driven, most of the characters are one-dimensional anyway. If you say you are making a movie about a woman, or a woman's story, that's a no-no. So there's a lot of hostility toward women in this business, it seems.

Lane: I think the people who support these films are modern men and their dates, so that doesn't speak very well about the women's roles that you will see depicted. And when talking about black women, that's a seat behind the back seat in films, and in general.

Burnett: Perhaps getting better writers and having the writers and people involved have a commitment—you know, a social commitment, in a sense. I find it very strange: Say, for example, you are a trumpet player—you treat all the notes the same, all are a part of this composition. If you are a painter, you have all these different colors, and you use them effectively. Whereas in terms of people, it seems like a conscious effort to exclude elements of your art. It seems to me it's your job as a person, as an artist, filmmaker, or writer, to write the best story with characters that are fully evolved.

Lane: But some people by nature aren't artists, and they can only express what their limitations allow them to. I think part of the problem, unfortunately, is that there are not enough women represented in film. You ask the average man, sensitive though he may be, and it's still a limited perspective. He's going to write, you know about this little boy or man or this father, etc., and then there was a girl who lived next door—and that's it. If you had more women filmmakers, it would be a different perspective because they would be writing from their perspective. I don't expect that when women filmmakers come into a plenitude that we are going to have many films from them about the guy next door, but what we will have is somewhat of a better balance than what we have now. I think that's part of the problem, that we don't have equal representation.

Burnett: In general, American films and stories really have to be improved, and that's just one of the symptoms of a general problem.

Lane: Well, I think the fact is that Hollywood has told stories and they've kind of run dry, the well has run dry, so these stories are kind of, for lack of a better word, boring. You know, we've seen them. But it's a new day, and we've got a lot of stories. There are a lot of dimensions to show.

Burnett: I think it's sort of an ironic situation because actually the majority of the people who go to see the movies—a lot of black people will see the movies, but those who really count, in a sense—are the large body of this white teenage audience. And they are still not interested in black stories. I don't think anyone ever gets tired of seeing themselves on the screen. A lot has to do with the distribution and promotion of the film, what an audience likes or doesn't like or knows about. But it is also the fact that America is such a strange culture . . . unless it is exotic to the point of being lewd and exploitive. It's hard; if you go to a studio and say, We have this film about a black family, well, no one wants to see a film about a black family—or a white family.

Lane: But the thing is . . . *A Soldier's Story* . . . I remember when that film came out, and it didn't get the distribution that I was hoping that it would get, but it did make a big noise, and it did get made and it's in the annals. A great story; a very, very good film.

I'm thinking about . . . you said you saw *Dances with Wolves*. I saw it once, and I loved the film. I remember when the film was trying to get made and people rejected it and so on, because it wasn't typical of the Hollywood film. It was also very demanding on one's time, at three hours, and people had to read. I'm saying that there is a signal coming through which redefines things. I hope I'm not being naive, but I am being very hopeful about it. I think *Dances with Wolves* was distributed well but it was a film that should not, by Hollywood standards, have been made, that should not have worked, and I feel the same way about the potential of what we do and our work.

Burnett: The fact is, it makes it difficult for one to confront history when it has to be watered down. Sometimes to make a film gives the impression that everything is fair and that whenever you depict the dominant culture, you have to show it in a good light. It's like a committee imposing on the structure. That's one of the reasons why we haven't made social progress. We just saw Rodney King get beaten to a pulp, and in Boston where this guy killed his wife and blamed it on the black community, the whole nation wanted to hang everybody there. You can't even walk down Little Cicero or even drive through Beverly Hills now without being harassed. We don't use film as a means to confront real issues that over time will create a better society.

Lane: Well, let's take on the challenge through our own work.

The House I Live In:
An Interview with Charles Burnett

Aida A. Hozic/1994

Published in *Callaloo* 17, no. 2 (Spring 1994): 471–87. © 1994 The Johns Hopkins University Press. Reprinted with permission of The Johns Hopkins University Press.

Killer of Sheep, Charles Burnett's first feature film, was made in 1973 as his thesis project at UCLA and shot in its entirety on location in South Central Los Angeles. Beautifully filmed by Burnett himself, the film tenderly recounts a few days in the life of a slaughterhouse worker, Stan, whose existence is as bounded by invisible threads of hopelessness as that of the sheep that he is forced to kill each day. At the time of the film's original, sporadic theatrical release in 1977, the *New York Times* critic Janet Maslin dismissed *Killer of Sheep* as "amateurish" and "boring." Since then, the film has won awards at festivals in Houston and Berlin, acquired honorary protection by the National Film Registry accorded to a select few "masterpieces" such as *Citizen Kane*, and aided its author in winning a prestigious John D. and Catherine T. MacArthur Fellowship, popularly known as the "genius award." Even in this world where justice—if, indeed, there is any—lives elsewhere, things occasionally, as Charles Burnett would say, "balance out with time."

I first saw *Killer of Sheep* just recently, on video, with a group of my high school friends from Sarajevo currently seeking refuge in Los Angeles from the war in Bosnia. We expected to see an award-winning film, possibly a cinematographic masterpiece—but most especially a film about a world that we were neither part of nor could ever join. In spite of all the intellectual comparisons which are currently being made between the war in Sarajevo and the sealed-off war zones in Los Angeles, South Central Los Angeles seemed to us as distant as China's

Forbidden City and as irrelevant as the war in Somalia. We had our own tragedy selfishly to worry about.

And then, just fifteen minutes into the movie, we were all crying.

The children were playing on the minuscule TV screen, throwing rocks onto passing trains, fighting with each other, wrestling in the dust, and doing the "bump." Our entire childhood on the dirty streets of Sarajevo came back in a flash—we too used to throw rocks at busses and climb onto streetcars instead of trains. Also, there was a song in the background that we paid little attention to, although we knew the words by heart and continued to sing it long after it had ended in the film's sequence: "What is America to me? . . . /The grocer and the butcher/The faces that I see . . . /The children in the playground . . . / That is America to me."

A few weeks later, thanks to my friend Orson Watson, who had learned the song in a Russian Pioneer Camp, I learned that its title was "The House I Live In" and that it was sung by Paul Robeson. I realized that it was truly unusual that we Bosnians knew by heart the words of a song that most Americans have never heard, and, in retrospect, that we were crying not only because of the images of the "children in the playground," but also because of this music locked somewhere in the back of our minds: how strange that the memory of one of the greatest African Americans of this century—Paul Robeson—was unconsciously, unintentionally, and paradoxically, retrieved for a moment by a group of refugees from Bosnia who could not even understand its significance!

Memory in and for the Black community, as Charles Burnett says in this interview, "is a strange phenomenon." For the people whose history is continuously being eroded, "memory is like coming on an island, something to catch up on and hold onto." Burnett, enduring resident of South Central L.A. and the Black independent filmmaker whose name is revered by all other like-minded filmmakers for his talent, courage and, above all, for his exceptional human decency, has devoted his entire career—and life—to the safeguarding of such islands.

Charles Burnett was born in Vicksburg, Mississippi, but his family moved to South Central L.A. at the time of the great Black migrations North and West, when "progress" seemed possible and owning a home was "not a dream." Most of the characters in Burnett's films are, much like Burnett himself, first- or second-generation transplants from the South. Uprooted yet again, they are continuously torn between remembering and forgetting, between being who they are—people stripped of everything but their dignity—and what the world expects them to be—docile and servile citizens with no past or future. Their memories, once recovered, do not seem theirs any more. They are, as Stan's wife says in *Killer of Sheep*, already spoiled—"like half-eaten cake, like rabbit skins stretched on the backyard fences."

Charles Burnett has, thus far, made three feature films (*Killer of Sheep*, 1973; *My Brother's Wedding*, 1983; *To Sleep with Anger*, 1990), two shorts (*Several Friends*, 1969; *The Horse*, 1973) and one feature-length documentary with Dai Sil Kim-Gibson (*America Becoming*, 1991). The films were, as one critic noted, "made at a tortoise speed" and scattered between the years of despair and the continuing economic decay of the streets and people that Burnett loves. In a country in which even "community" and "neighborhood," two inherently positive terms, have acquired negative, racial, connotations, Burnett's films are a rare testimony that the Black community can, does, and will continue to exist without explicit references to the white world which surrounds it and constrains it.

This interview was conducted in two parts. We first met on a warm, sunny afternoon, on December 12, 1993, in "The All American Burger" place in West Los Angeles. The second meeting took place on January 26, 1994, on the grounds of Raleigh Studios in Hollywood where Burnett was finishing the work on his latest film, *The Glass Shield*. An unlikely pairing—a Bosnian refugee and the Black filmmaker—we spent several hours talking about films, filmmaking, and, inevitably, about the crumbling house that we all live in.

Hozic: Can we talk about Los Angeles for a moment? Ever since I came here, I've been fascinated—in the negative sense of the word—by this city. "Appalled" may be a better word. It is about the most segregated place that I have ever been to and, having lived in the South, I find that pretty ironic.

Burnett: Yes, that's true. But that's why you have episodes like the riots. They are the result of all this segregation and lack of empowerment. That is why you have crime in certain areas more so than in others. It is a serious problem, a very serious problem which L.A. government officials refuse to address. There've been recommendations after the Watts riots which still have not been implemented. Since 1964 or 1965—I do not remember the exact date any more—there have been two reports done on a national scale about the riots and, then, there has been one done locally. That in itself shows you the lack of interest and concern which certain political structures have for certain people. After the most recent riots, again, there was this immediate wave of people wanting to do something and then the interest vanished. The same thing happened to "Rebuild L.A." The city has truly become the place of "haves" and "have-nots." We have a huge population of homeless people—who *can, want to* work. They are educated people. When I was growing up in L.A., you had to go downtown or go to the mission in order to see a homeless person; there was no begging on the streets on the mass scale you see now. People had the prospect of owning their own homes. It was not a dream, it was possible. All that now seems just impossible, particularly for Blacks. There was this exposé about banks not lending money to Black people who certainly qualify for the loans; these institutions help create these all-white areas, these Black islands, and then they wonder "Why? What's the problem with these people?" Because people in L.A. have this weird illusion that they are isolated and sheltered until there is a disruption such as the riots. But the question of race is always present—by the very absence of interaction. There are all of these underlying ownership and housing laws which prevent interracial contacts. For instance, if you look at deeds on a lot of homes in Los Angeles you will find that they stipulate that the houses cannot be sold to non-whites, and that is what makes the racial situation in this city so volatile and so precarious—the problem is there, but people do not want to confront it, they want to maintain the illusion of the melting pot. It is sicker than denial. It has a lot of repercussions for the school system, on supermarkets, on transportation. The entire quality of life is affected by this de facto segregation.

Hozic: More and more often, we can hear the voices which blame desegregation for the current situation.

Burnett: But it is a mistake to use desegregation as a starting point. If you start from desegregation then the only possible conclusion is that it has changed the community. But the community was segregated before that and, true, segregation created small businesses, separate powers, a sense of community. Imagine what kind of world would have been there without segregation—a much larger, a much healthier community. I do not and I cannot look at desegregation as a negative. Perhaps history will prove that it was the best thing that ever happened, because back then it was really apartheid, much more so than it is now. One could perhaps say the same thing about Soweto—if the walls go down, the community will be dispersed and people may start complaining how they lost their lovely neighborhoods. But is that any reason to keep the apartheid going?

Hozic: You have lived in South Central L.A. all your life. How truly unsafe is South Central these days? "Crime" and "danger" seem to be easily attachable stigmas, helping to divide the "untouchables" from "well-bred" citizens.

Burnett: A lot of people, a lot of families still live in South Central. Gangs make life difficult, but then they are mainly fighting each other. This country is very violent. Los Angeles is very violent. One does not have to be in South Central to be shot down. Anybody who wants to carry a gun can carry one. I do not find it any more dangerous than any other place. Maybe the problem is magnified because of the job situation and housing. But people adjust to it.

Hozic: How did you manage to "get out" of the ghetto?

Burnett: In a strange way, I do not actually perceive myself as "out." I went to UCLA by accident and just recently did a film that people have heard of. I wrote some scripts in the meantime. But, other than that, I've been pretty desperate myself. When I was in high school, no one was expected to go and get any higher education. The teachers were very discouraging. They had the attitude that since you would not amount to anything, why even bother? That was the school and that was the lesson—except for sports, perhaps. We did not even know what else existed apart from carpentry and plumbing. I just happened to enroll in college. I was waiting for the draft when I heard that if I got the student permit I could stay in school and would not be drafted. And then, I discovered film and took off.

Hozic: When you say that you never "got out," it seems to me that you actually did get out, but you never became Spike Lee or Arsenio Hall. Which then makes me wonder—what is the perception of the people in the community of you? Are you considered a success or a failure?

Burnett: Anything is considered a success. Having a job is a success. I think it is a sort of happiness: "Someone made it out." Actually, there are a lot of kids who made it and who are doing well, surprisingly well, in spite of all the obstacles. And then, of course, there are a lot of them who are not doing well. There's a number of kids, even when I was in school, who dropped out. They went off and took menial jobs. They did not feel the need for school. The difference was, at that time, most kids did not believe that they would live longer than twenty-one. Now, they do not believe that they will live longer than sixteen.

Hozic: That's incredible, that's a war mentality.

Burnett: I know.
Hozic: Tell me about your family: you came from the South?
Burnett: Mississippi.
Hozic: Do you ever go back there?
Burnett: On occasion.
Hozic: Most of the characters in your films have this ambivalent relationship towards the South—it is both "back home" and something to be forgotten and left behind.
Burnett: No.
Hozic: No?
Burnett: No. I think that in *To Sleep with Anger* there is this double meaning to "back home." What Harry means by "back home" is not the same thing that Gideon has in mind. For Harry it is corn liquor and chocolate carrots, but there is also a derogatory of his soul called "Hairy Man" [Georgian folk character, A.H.], and whenever he speaks and whatever he tells, it always refers to either death or hell. For Gideon "back home" is much more simple—it is the South which has values and family ties.
Hozic: What about Gideon's sons and the other kids like them who grew up in L.A.?
Burnett: Their relationship with the South has always been problematic. When I was growing up and when we called someone "from the country," it was bad, it was really bad. There has always been a lot of self-hatred, a lot of resentment in the Black community. A lot of kids grew up despising the South, and there are many things to be despised about the South, a lot of hardship related to it. My mother, for instance, hated it. She does not even want to remember it, she wants nothing to do with it. We could not drag her down there, because of her experiences. But, at the same time, the South has always been for some Black people a symbol of a lack of continuity. We have always been disjointed, because there is this part of history that people want to deny. Whenever you talk about slavery, there is a mixed response—some say "Yeah, great, let's discuss it," the others ask "Why do you want to dig up the dirt?" It is a strange phenomenon, memory in the Black community.
Hozic: Can the historical continuity ever be re-established?
Burnett: I think that it is the artist's job to establish links with the past, to give some self-respect to the people, to create the sense of a center. I think that erosion of memory is the design of the establish-

ment. When I was going to school, there was no text on what Blacks have contributed to history. It was all just negative, you just saw them shuffling and moving things around. Even now, it is the same struggle. Hollywood insists on perpetuating these myths about Blacks, dangerous myths, and this is going to destroy Black people. I think that these are their means. Without history you are nothing. Memory is like coming on an island, something to catch up on and hang onto. I think that we have to create the past—no, not to create—to define the past. I was reading Frederick Douglass recently. The collective consciousness of writing was his big theme as well, particularly concerning slavery. He did not want Black people to forget it.

Hozic: But what if you succeed in defining the past and then the message never reaches its intended audience? There is this whole Hollywood machinery which continuously teaches us what Black film actually is, and this machinery controls 97 percent of the market in this country.

Burnett: There are a lot of Black independent filmmakers whose works address the concerns of the Black community—Ben Caldwell, Julie Dash, Haile Gerima, Sharon Larkin—many people who are continuously making films or at least trying to, and who find it very discouraging to get no response to their work. Haile might be an exception. But, I think, the idea is that if you can affect a few people it is still something. The idea is not that something is going to change, but that you should create some form of debate and open up the problems. And even if the film reaches the audience, they are so conditioned by the Hollywood kind of film that, unless they are politically conscious, their idea of going to the movies is to be entertained. It is the question of approach. How do you get people into a movie without being presumptuous about the message, but still maintain the faith that what you are doing stands on the right path and would affect people's consciousness and the way they see themselves? You can only go so far without the compromise affecting you. But then, you also find how a little can go a long way. We filmmakers have a tendency to put everything in one film, to dump it all into the kitchen sink. We become very wordy and pedantic, which does not work. It is just a very fine line that one has to walk all the time.

Hozic: Can Black film exist under such circumstances? Does Black film actually exist?

Burnett: It is hard when you have Hollywood to reckon with. You have to be very strong. Black film is like regional cinema, like Victor Nuñez who makes films about Florida or like Italian cinema. There is more than language that differentiates cinematographies; there is something that we can call a "cultural film." If a film is about cultural issues then it becomes Italian, Black, Japanese. I don't think that the *The Tree of Wooden Clogs* could have been made anywhere else but in Italy. Oscar Micheaux, for instance, touched upon the issues of light and dark skin and of class in the Black community. I am sure that many cultures shared these problems, but it was through the eyes of Black people that they see the world and become aware of them. That's important and that it does make a difference. But if the film is about gangsters and money, if it is about money-making, then it is about nothing. Then it does not have any identity to it.

Hozic: Speaking about cultural identities and their reception, are you aware that there is more written about you in French than in English?

Burnett: Yes, as far as the written word goes, that is probably true. But that has always been the case. I think that when we started, when Black independent film became somewhat of a phenomenon, festivals such as Berlin, Amsterdam, Paris formed the category of the "Black Independent Film" and the art journals in Europe started writing about us. I mean there has always been Black independent film—right after *The Birth of a Nation* there was a response to it, then there was Oscar Micheaux, and in the late 1960s "Blackploitation" films. But, except for the "race movies"—they were called "race movies"—which were truly relevant and which significantly informed the Black independent cinema—there was never a conscious effort to create and recognize "Black cinema." However, even when the Europeans "discovered" the Black independents, nothing comparable happened here. When my film won some recognition in Germany (Berlin International Film Festival Critics Prize in 1981) I read in the American papers about the Berlin Film Festival and there was no mention, not one mention of my film. They mentioned what was on the menu at the gala, but nothing about the film. And in Germany it was the cover story in all newspapers. It's always been like that. It was the same story with jazz. It seems that you have to go across the ocean to be recognized, and then, perhaps, these guys here might eventually catch up.

Hozic: Why do you think Europeans like you?

Burnett: I don't think they like me. [*Laughs.*]

Hozic: Why do you think they pay attention to you?

Burnett: I think it is a strange phenomenon, like Wim Wenders in the United States. I think all indigenous artists do well outside of their own countries. In your own country, they might not like what you are saying. Other countries will accept you because you are talking about somebody else. But I also think that Europe, because of its closeness, is more diverse. Europeans seem more inclined to reach out. In Paris, you can see African art, visibly displayed in shop windows, as you walk down the street. In England, they don't have the same thing as our ghettos. They have working-class neighborhoods, which are basically mixed racially. One group may be culturally dominant, but it is never a total vacuum as it is here. So, you get a different set of attitudes, people travel more. They are not as chauvinistic—oh, I guess they are, one should not romanticize them—but there is certainly a difference.

Hozic: The first reviews of *Killer of Sheep* here were devastating. Did it hurt? Did you care about the reviews?

Burnett: I did. But I was also looking at who was talking about the film, too. I mean, that's the way that people are in the times like these. Critics are like all other humans: they respond to things differently, what moves one person does not have to move another. I mean, you always expect bad reviews, but when it happens it is still painful, because it is so personal; you are taken out and examined. But that is the matter of growing up. I don't know, I thought at the time that that critic saw the wrong movie. I don't mind criticism, but that was a vicious attack, as if the reviewer was really insulted by the movie. So I kept on wondering what I did to offend her. But it all balances out with time.

Hozic: How did you maintain the faith in yourself? It took four years for *Killer of Sheep* to get released, and then another four to get the award at the Berlin Film Festival.

Burnett: Yes, the movie was made in 1973 and released in 1977. At the time we were not making movies with the design to make a living out of it. Film was not a money-making thing. I always had a job so it did not really matter. I was doing all sorts of things. I was working right here, a few blocks up the street, at the agency—reading scripts, writing synopses, etc.

Hozic: You must have been a really peculiar script reader, given that your taste in movies is almost the opposite of what goes down well in Hollywood.

Burnett: It was hard. What was really strange was teaching film writing at UCLA with kids who wanted to sell everything that they wrote immediately. I took a writing class with a wonderful lady, Isabelle Ziegler. It was a great class. We read and wrote everything—short stories and novels and plays. It was at Los Angeles Community College, which was a junior college, a working-class kind of a place. People there had experience. If you go to UCLA where everyone is nineteen years old, has seen the same movies, and has the same background, you cannot learn anything from each other. It is no wonder that the kids can only think of selling movies. Junior college was the best thing in terms of both diversity and experience particularly in the arts but perhaps in everything. Theater was great because they had people who were entertainers, department heads who were old men—I mean not really old but in their fifties—and they were casting these young guys, putting on beards to look older. It was a wonderful experience. But—getting back to reading scripts—I had to adjust. I was just amazed at what kind of things could get done, and I guess I still am—but that's the game. People are not interested in talking about issues. I have been lecturing at colleges and find it very frustrating. The kids just want to earn a certain number of credit units. It is maddening. At UCLA, the students are not interested in experimenting; they want to learn how to write these very slick movies. When I was going to school in the 1960s, one of the great things was that you better not come back with a film that was a cliché or ordinary or something that someone had seen before. There was this demand on being original, on having your own ideas. It was very competitive in this sense: people were afraid of sharing their ideas and they guarded them like babies. And if you worked on something, you did not do it because you needed a job—you just did it because you had a passion for it. But now, God, I was over there and I was so disappointed. I felt raped.

Hozic: But are the filmmakers really to blame?

Burnett: Well, the audience also makes things difficult because they accept movies with no substance. I had to babysit the other night, and I had the kids over. Each one wanted to see something different—one wanted to see *Wayne's World*, the other *Addams Family Values*. So, I took them to a dirt-cheap drive-in where we could see both movies. I think you have to be mad to pay money to see *Wayne's World*. But it was the box-office hit of the weekend. So if you do something serious, people have a tendency to put on a different cap and be more cynical of it than of the things that have no substance to them.

Hozic: Perhaps that's why, when you finally made *To Sleep with Anger* and when Julie Dash made *Daughters of the Dust*, the same critics who once slashed *Killer of Sheep* now wrote that independent film was using "Hollywood tactics" and becoming "mainstream"?

Burnett: I don't think that we ever became "mainstream." When I made *To Sleep with Anger*, it started off as my own idea. Yet I wanted to do it "properly" and get money from the regular sources. I gave the script to the Corporation for Public Broadcasting. They hated it. At about the same time, Michael Tolkin, your friend and an independent filmmaker, contacted Cotty Chubb and told him, "If you ever get in the position of producing a film you should talk to this guy Burnett." So Cotty called me just when I got this awful letter from CPB. The same thing happened to Julie Dash. It started off as a "raise money" kind of independent film but then American Playhouse, where she applied for money, wanted to make changes to the script. To go back to your question, I do not think that the core of our films changed at all; they are still considered non-commercial films. The fact that *To Sleep with Anger* happened at all was the result of the right combination of things. Edward Pressman, the producer of the film, did not make me change anything at all and the distributor just wanted a few minutes less.

Hozic: What did CPB hate about the script?

Burnett: [*Laughs.*] Its "Blackness": the mysticism, the references to the South. They wanted to make it acceptable and accessible. And that meant that the focus of the film should have been on the Black middle-class couple and their problems, forget about the rest. They were probably thinking that middle-American sensibilities would be more inclined to understand what the Black middle class was about as opposed to, I don't know, the complexities I was trying to portray.

Hozic: You had similar problems with the documentary about the immigrants *America Becoming* which aired on PBS in 1991.

Burnett: Yes, it was difficult. When we started filming I thought that we were supposed to be objective about what was going on in this country. When we finished, it turned out that we were supposed to paint a rosy picture of American immigrants. As usual on these kinds of productions, we had a group of scholars that we worked and consulted with. But our visions of reality were not always the same. We had to be very careful in dealing with race—often it was "too heavy" or "too much," or there were "too many Blacks." The language used by the people we interviewed was not always appropriate. When we wanted to have a Native American narrator, it was suggested that we rather use a neutral voice. What saddens me the most, however, is that we could have anticipated all these riots and problems that different ethnic groups are facing in America today—and we did not.

Hozic: What kind of tensions did they want you to eradicate?

Burnett: I do not think that they were interested in eradicating any tensions. Rather, they wanted to explain the positives—the melting pot, that it's working, that immigrants do well, that they bring a lot of resources to this country. They did not want to get into the social dynamics, into the problems which really have nothing to do with immigrants themselves but with the way in which business throughout this country is run to keep the competition going—bringing in cheap labor and lowering wages. That is the principal cause of all these tensions. We went to one of those big companies which brings immigrants from all over the world. They isolate them and put them into little trailer parks. Most immigrants come with this notion that it will be a temporary situation. They end up staying much longer than anticipated. Their kids start going to school, they become Americanized. They don't want to leave. The family has saved enough money to go back home and buy a house there but the wife, or the husband, or the kid does not want to leave. The entire experience simply tears the family apart.

Hozic: *America Becoming* was filmed on locations all across the country—in Kansas, Houston, Philadelphia, Chicago, Monterey Park, and Miami. Which part of the country seemed the worst?

Burnett: They were all very different, with unique and specific problems, but Philadelphia, in many ways, was the worst. Visually, it had this look of a bombed-out city. We were quite appalled by the extent of the poverty. It looked so bad, it was winter, and just imagining life there was terrible. There were a lot of vacant, abandoned homes. A lot of homelessness in areas where the homes were collapsing, where even the foundations were shattered. People literally lived among the rubble. The taxes were going down for political reasons and most of the city services were not functioning. Do you know that even collecting trash is now considered a luxury? The well-to-do parts of the community have their own private services while the rest of the community is going down the hill. Nobody questions it though. It is not like it used to be—people taking pride in their whole city. Now, everyone seems to worry only about his or her own little niche.

Hozic: Was this your first documentary?

Burnett: No, I worked on one with a lady who's now living in France. I have not seen either her or the film in a hundred years.

Hozic: Is it a different process than making a feature film?

Burnett: Yes. Although, basically, it's still the film, it's still a camera and editing and sound. The main differences are perhaps in one's intentions and the script. Documentaries are more unpredictable, there is less control over what is taking place in front of the camera. In theatrical, fictional films people can be ordered around to do things exactly as they are scripted. It is impossible to do that in a documentary. The director and cameraman have to be on alert all the time. Some aspects are much easier. There is still responsibility towards the subject, but it is reflected in the relationship between "you" and the "subject" as opposed to "them" and the "subject."

Hozic: Which part of the filmmaking process do you enjoy the most?

Burnett: None of it, actually. I was just thinking about it last night. How did I ever get in this business? [*Laughs.*] Or perhaps I like it all. One of the bad things about doing films on a larger scale is that you begin to specialize. The work becomes strenuous and stressful. There is this big steamroller behind you. It is not a "mom and pop" kind of organization any more—you, alone with the camera, a sound person and a few friends as actors. The film is budgeted up to the very last second of the day. If you work for twelve hours, you have to cut, otherwise it's overtime. Then, there are all the unions and their regulations. It is good; they protect the actors and the crew and whoever else—but most people lose sight of what filmmaking is all about. For most it is a paycheck, a job, money more than anything else. So, production starts with all these ideals and declarations of solidarity. The director gives a little speech, "Let's make this great movie," but the bottom line soon becomes what it has always been—money. Obviously, people have to eat, and money struggles are normal. I just wish there was some balance. Actually, I do not like pre-production; it is stressful. The essence of pre-production is the budgeting of the departments and the shifting of the resources, or the lack thereof, from one department to another. So, everyone is upset from the very beginning. But it is crucial—if you get the house in order in pre-production, then you will have a well-prepared production and you are set. It is strange. As you make bigger and bigger movies, you get further and further removed from production in a sense. All these bubbles pop up around you. The director is supposed to concentrate just on arts: the cast, the cinematographer, the art director. Other people are selecting people underneath. Often, you don't even know who they did hire to work for you until it's too late. And if someone ruins fifteen minutes of the day it is a shot that could have been taken, maybe a very important shot. That can cost a lot of money. So you want an efficient crew, and you do not want to spend most of your time telling them what they should be doing. Otherwise you are in trouble. But you have people who hire people who want to hire people with whom they had worked before—although it's you who have to work with them now.

Hozic: Do you at least like screenwriting, which is such a solitary process?

Burnett: I would if I were able to do only one thing at the time. But when you are working and trying to stay alive, you work on a number of things at the same time, six or seven projects in different stages, hoping that one of them would connect. So you do not have the time to sit down and just work on one script. But I like discovering good ideas.

Hozic: Do you usually visualize the film before you start shooting?

Burnett: Yes, I have to. In order to function on the set, I must have a very good sense of what each scene is supposed to look like. It helps in explaining the scene to the cameraman who wants to know what the scene is supposed to look like. It gives him a vision. It helps tremendously in terms of directing actors. A clear visual sense of where the actors can go and what you are looking for is essential, because very often, actors will come and say, "Hey, I want to show you something." And you have to be able to say, "Yes, great, but let's try another direction." The visual image gives you something to start on. It is a building block. Unfortunately, a lot of times you do all of these preparations and ultimately cannot use them because of logistics or money problems. Everything is a money problem in this business.

Hozic: So would you rather go back to "no money" films?

Burnett: I wish I could be in some way supported or self-supported. One of the positive things about proper productions is that you have health benefits, and when you have kids, that's important. If truly independent films had that, it would be great. But making films independently is definitely the only way to make films that you really want to make.

Hozic: I feel slightly uncomfortable posing the question, since you are still working on it, but aren't you about to finish a new film? What is it about?

Burnett: *The Glass Shield*, the new film, is based on a true story. It's about this guy Johnny Johnson who joins the Signal Hill police department right after a young football player has been killed. Johnson learns what had happened, he is the only Black person in the department, and he gets disenchanted with both the police and all the institutionalized racism. He finally has to leave. So the film is based on his experiences in the Signal Hill police department. But it is also a story about police departments across the country, about their policies, about the court system, about justice.

Hozic: Is this the first time that you are directly tackling the issue of racism?

Burnett: In an overt way, yes.

Hozic: What sorts of difficulties did this present?

Burnett: It was difficult in getting the film off the ground. We could not get the financing for the film in the States, so we had to go abroad for the money. But that happened very quickly. We had the script for about a year or so, and it took us about two years to get the financing. So actually it was not so bad. We just could not get a nibble on it here. Films that have a social message are very difficult to make in the United States—the studios avoid them and a lot of little, independent distributors and producers also do not want to touch them. The message means trouble in this business.

Hozic: This is the second time that you went abroad for the money. *My Brother's Wedding*, your second film, was produced by the German Television ZDF. *The Glass Shield* is produced by the French company CiBy 2000. Does that affect your work in any way?

Burnett: Dealing with foreign backers is a lot of work in itself. They are not interested in making this film into a commercial success, but they are interested in getting prestige and their money back. There is more of a looseness about the way that film work is structured in Europe. It is not as bureaucratic as it is here. But that creates other problems. The Europeans are equally loose about the rules and regulations in this country, which are very strict. This looseness costs time and money; things get delayed, and you have to wait. If you get the money here, you can get it quickly, but then there are a lot of strings attached to it.

Hozic: Do you already have the distributor for the US?
Burnett: No.
Hozic: When and how do you plan to release *The Glass Shield*?
Burnett: The gentleman who runs CiBy 2000 was hoping that the film could open in France in June or July. Here, the distributors have these ideas about a summer film, a fall film, a Christmas film. So it depends on when they see it and which season do they decide that our film could be.
Hozic: Do you intend to send the film to the festivals?
Burnett: I am not so sure. The good thing about the festivals is that they can generate a lot of hopefully positive publicity and save on marketing and advertising. But then, on the other hand, they can work against the film. For, if the film becomes "a festival film," the distributors would not want to touch it.
Hozic: Did you do a lot of research for this film?
Burnett: I did enough not to create a confusion. I first wrote the story, and then I did the research in the police department. Sometimes it is dangerous to have too much information. It may sound like a contradiction, but a lot of times you cannot cover all the bases although you feel obligated to do so. You want to be fair and give all the characters more than just one dimension. In that sense, seeing what the policemen had to go through before I wrote the story could have affected me and my choices and then ultimately the theme. The theme is the main thing, and you have to be constantly reminded of what it is that you are trying to say. In trying to be fair across the board and politically correct, you can run into serious problems. I do not know if this makes any sense. For example, I am doing this thing on Frederick Douglass and the more I learn about Frederick Douglass, the more affected the story line is. It is not about one man, because if you are doing something about Frederick Douglass you are doing the history of America. From the time that he escaped to the time when he became an abolitionist and the time of his death—the scope of his life covers all the major events in America. Then his psychology is very important. Usually, talking or writing about historical figures, you get this notion that they react to something in a positive way, that they knew from the very beginning how they would act. But what is really important is to get into all conflicting and different ideas that went on under the surface of this man—because that is what motivated him to do certain things and not the others. Times affected his outlook, culture affected his outlook, the

notion of what an American man at the time was affected him. It all goes into the story, but it also dictates your choices.

Hozic: You had mentioned that you were trying to raise money for a project. Is Frederick Douglass the project that you are trying to raise the money for?

Burnett: No, no—I am trying to do something altogether different. When you have a fine idea—and it is difficult to find one—then the best way to explain it is to write it down, because that is the only way that it can be done the way you want it. If you try to sell an abstract idea, with no script, then the studio or producer start adding to it, they see someone in the film that you do not, they start making demands. So I would like to be in a position to do a film about Frederick Douglass the way I want it. This is something that I am really interested in. If I could just do the film I want and not worry about how well it's going to do in the market! Limitations are both good and bad. Everybody needs limitations; an artist needs restrictions, criticism, balance—but limitations of the right kind. That's why you always need at least one project that is not affected by bureaucrats.

Hozic: As we talk, at moments, you sound tremendously disillusioned, as though once, in those glorious 1960s and the early 1970s you, and everyone around you, had hoped that the world would become a different place. And now you are realizing not only that it did not change, but that it has changed in the wrong direction. Are you really disillusioned?

Burnett: I think that, as I was growing up, disillusionment was inevitable. Growing up was nothing but battling dreams, hopes, expectations of what life would be. Responsibilities, also, had a lot to do with it, and the time allotted to us to do things played a part in it. I do not think that disillusionment is a bad thing. I think that you have to be able to get on your feet and make a choice—either you agree with the current trend or you don't. You see, illusions are one thing and convictions are something else. Sometimes convictions and illusions get confused, sometimes they inform each other. Illusions and dreams may be lost, but convictions remain. I think that my convictions have been intact. Everyone I know still has those same strong convictions. Perhaps the methods have changed. I sound very pessimistic and negative. I guess it is because of "race." I think that I have finally realized the scope of the battle. It is not just having dreams and fighting for them. It is as if you are doing a surgery and you open the body and you realize that the whole body is cancerous. However, what was that proverb? "As long as there is life, there is hope." I talk to Julie [Dash] and Billy [Woodberry]. They've been struggling to get films off the ground for such a long time. Even co-workers, other filmmakers, can help to create this disillusionment. I think that we all need some sense of camaraderie. Talking it out, sharing thoughts and ideas is important. I talk to Haile [Gerima] a lot. He is way off in Washington, DC, teaching at Howard University. But he manages to survive. There is this relationship between him and his students which sustains him. What saddens me is that there was once this group which had these similar ideas, things that used to stimulate us all along, and as the time goes by we are separating more and more. I guess I will have to learn how to work in isolation.

Hozic: When you got out of UCLA, the group—you, Julie Dash, Billy Woodberry, Sharon Larkin—functioned almost like a family factory for the movies. You wrote the script for Billy Woodberry's *Bless Their Little Hearts*, and worked as a cameraman for him and for Sharon Larkin. Julie considered you her best teacher. What happened in the meantime?

Burnett: I don't know. We are still connecting but not as much as I would like it. Perhaps we are all trying to be practical, trying to survive, doing other things, working. We do not get together as much any more. If there was some institution or just a house where we could all get together and make movies—perhaps it would be different. Perhaps. That's what I would like the most. We talked about joining our resources and buying equipment together, starting our own production company. That's how disillusionment can help you—it helps create other avenues. As you get disenchanted with one route, you find another, better one. The other thing that happened—I was talking to Haile recently—is that as you start making bigger movies, you get caught up in a certain way of doing things and removed from the independent friends that you had earlier. You forget how much you could do with how little and have to be reminded of how much can be done without this whole steamroller and budgeting behind you. And realizing it you start looking around and finding other avenues.

Hozic: You have a tremendous sense of mission which is very rare, especially in this city and in this business. Where does it come from?

Burnett: Arrogance. [*He laughs.*] No, seriously, partly it is my arrogance. For whatever reason I always believed in what I was doing. All artists do, and they love to think that people do not understand their work. But, in my case, because of race and because of color, it always had a much deeper meaning. It reaffirmed my convictions. And, as I said earlier, a large part of it was the early training, the sixties and the sense of indebtedness that somehow became the part of everything I did. Kids who came later with this "me" generation have a completely different attitude. They are more capable of being successful in this business. There have always been hustlers in this business, but I do not think that they were as socially acceptable as they are now. "Make money without any contribution" or without any substance is the order of the day. I do not think that everybody is a hustler, or perhaps it is not hustling at all, but I somehow always associate this "me, me, me" attitude with it. Maybe I should not be so negative, but some of these guys have hundreds of millions of dollars and they seem to be so comfortable with it. Whereas I think that you cannot have that kind of money without being corrupt or getting corrupt. It just puzzles me, I guess—and angers me. A lot of it has to do with anger. Anger is always there. There are all of these guys in this business who are constantly testing, trying to see how far they can push you. I sometimes think that that's all they gain, that's what they are here for—for the superior, God-like attitude and power. On the other hand, there are these two words—"boy" and "slave." Millions of little things remind me of them every day. Maybe I am just oversensitive. But so many people fought against this and the words still resonate, so perhaps that's where my convictions come from.

Hozic: The indebtedness—who or what do you feel indebted to?

Burnett: I just look around and see so many people who are much, much worse off than I am. Plus, in the Black community, I believe that we owe a lot to previous generations, really a lot—for if it was not for their endurance, if they had given up, we would not be here. There are wonderful examples throughout history of people who spoke up not only for the Black community—but for all. They tried to make this country whole and right for everyone, like Frederick Douglass, who fought for the democratic Constitution of this country and everyone's inalienable rights, who fought against the view that the "Negro has no rights that white men should respect." People have accomplished so much even under those conditions and we should not forget it.

Hozic: How long do you think that you will endure?

Burnett: Battles shape you in a certain way. They make you more articulate. You learn how to discern crap right away—and much of this business is about that. You become less tolerant. The promise of my own production company, my own camera and editing equipment, keeps me going. You see, I do not think that it is a bad thing to be disillusioned. You become very realistic. You learn what the odds are. It is just like picking a fight. And you need it both ways—the ideas because they give you a sense of direction and an initial purpose and a reality check. Sometimes, it is good to come to terms with the reality.

An Explorer of the Black Mind Looks Back, but Not in Anger

Michael Sragow/1995

From the *New York Times*, January 1, 1995. © 1995 The New York Times. All rights reserved. Used by permission and protected by the Copyright Laws of the United States. The printing, copying, redistribution, or retransmission of the Material without express written permission is prohibited.

"Faulkner put race on the table," Charles Burnett says, "and he was aware of the black psychology. The right to exist, how to exist, the power to endure were always part of his theme."

Mr. Burnett, a forty-nine-year-old movie maker who grew up in the Watts section of Los Angeles, has Mississippi roots and an expansive cultural perspective. As Carl Lumbly, who co-starred in Mr. Burnett's best-known feature, the 1990 film *To Sleep with Anger*, puts it: "Too often a director's reference points are films or television: 'Give me Ralph Kramden.' Charles can take you to a particular moment in *For Whom the Bell Tolls*."

The American Museum of the Moving Image in Queens will hold a retrospective of Mr. Burnett's first three films and a preview of his fourth, *The Glass Shield*, on Saturday and next Sunday. Because Mr. Burnett has made so few pictures, each new one is definitely an occasion for supporters of black independent film. Miramax will release *The Glass Shield* later this year

The movie stars Michael Boatman as a black rookie and Lori Petty as a Jewish deputy who run up against racism and anti-Semitism as they expose police wrongdoing in Los Angeles. Like all of Mr. Burnett's movies, *The Glass Shield* was done on the cheap; nevertheless, it tries to blend realism and splashy stylization. It marks a transition for the director. After two decades of making art films, Mr. Burnett is trying to appeal to a wider audience.

The Glass Shield follows a trail of corruption to government ranks while exploring the idea that blacks lead double lives. Mr. Burnett was drawn to the plight of the black police officer because he—like Frederick Douglass (a possible future film subject) and Joe Christmas in Faulkner's *Light in August*—exists "in a white world and a black world at the same time." Faulkner, says Mr. Burnett, understood how people with a foot in each world are forced to adjust, "how it affects their speech when they're in one or the other."

What bothers Mr. Burnett is that black film directors have not been able to further the esthetic frontiers that were pioneered by black writers in the twenties and thirties. "We're sixty years behind the Harlem Renaissance," he says. "We're not even dealing with those issues of the language and psychology of a black person, man or woman." Mr. Burnett notes that while the members of the Harlem Renaissance were reacting against the tradition of "having to write from a white perspective about black people for a white audience," black filmmakers today are still hemmed in by the dictates of a white industry.

"Why do blacks make so many violent films?" he asks. "Because that's the kind that sells. You can't talk about integrating black folklore and oral traditions and jazz when you're in a pitch meeting."

Mr. Burnett has found a certain freedom outside the mainstream. He has no desire to grandstand. He does not want to be Spike Lee, or even the anti-Spike. "I want to be able to walk down the street and observe people without people observing me," he says. In three films made with the frayed end of a shoestring, Mr. Burnett has explored untapped areas of black life. *Killer of Sheep* (completed in 1974) is a poetic evocation of working-class life in and around the Watts area of South Central Los Angeles. In 1990, Mr. Burnett's no-budget film became one of the first fifty movies listed by the Library of Congress in the National Film Registry.

Working again with amateur or fledgling actors, he wrote and directed *My Brother's Wedding* (1983), a comedy-drama about a young man torn between the self-destructive street life and the sometimes-phony upward mobility within black communities in Los Angeles. Mr. Burnett won a MacArthur Foundation Fellowship in 1988, giving him $275,000 over five years.

Even with the prestige of a "genius" grant, it wasn't easy for Mr.

Burnett to launch *To Sleep with Anger*, a blend of southern black folklore and contemporary family drama set on the fringes of South Central Los Angeles. Vincent Canby, writing in the *New York Times*, praised the movie as a "very entertaining, complex film, a comedy of unusual substance." Despite an acclaimed performance by Danny Glover and rapturous responses at festivals, the film didn't win theatrical crowds. But a Burnett cult still grew.

Compact and with a tenor voice, Charles Burnett has a southern politeness and reserve even when speaking amid the distractions of his editing rooms at the Raleigh Studios in Los Angeles. Some of his fiercest emotions surface with a rueful laugh or an exasperated shake of the head. Mr. Burnett was born in Vicksburg, Mississippi; his family moved to California when he was three. He sees the Watts of the fifties as a semirural extension of Dixie: "We would ride our bikes out to the swamps, places like Devil's Dip, nothing but hilly areas, or where oil wells used to be." Asked about favorite movies from his childhood television-watching days, Mr. Burnett mentions two black-and-white films from the forties: Jean Renoir's Texas farming saga *The Southerner* (Faulkner advised Renoir on the script) and Delmer Daves's rural Gothic *The Red House*. They both had "solid, adult storytelling," he says. They were also pastoral tales with a moral core.

Mr. Burnett's memories of his early life in Watts are warm but complicated. His mother and his serviceman father split up. "My grandmother raised my brother and me; my mother was working," he says. "But we had a community. Anyone who was from the South had this community that was southern, just displaced." He describes his old neighborhood as stable, with bookkeepers and bricklayers, doctors, and carpenters.

"It was the kids of my generation who had problems as they grew up—not all the kids, but the ones who dropped out or got into gangs," says Mr. Burnett. He broke with them when he realized they lived by a skewed moral standard. No matter what the context, they could justify shooting or even killing as long as they felt physically threatened. Choices he made early on—not to skip school, not to spend day and night in a pool hall—determined his course in life. "There's a little voice inside your head that tells you, 'Nope, that doesn't work.' Somehow you find your way."

After high school he went to Los Angeles Community College, where he learned about student draft deferments and majored in electronics. There he took the most important course in his life, creative writing. He discovered Camus and, yes, Faulkner, and began to work at the main branch of the public library. He also frequented the movies, where he went for resounding moral dramas like *Becket* and *A Man for All Seasons*.

"I didn't know what to do with this passion," he said. "I didn't know what to call it. I didn't know what cinematography was. But I thought: 'Cinematography. That's a nice word.'" So he applied to the University of California, Los Angeles, and eventually received both a Bachelor's degree and a Master of Fine Arts. The reigning mode on campus in the late sixties and early seventies was creative anarchy, with arguments in the screening rooms and the classrooms.

"Slick Hollywood was suspect," he says. "The whole thing was experimentation, personal vision." And ferocious competition. At student screenings, the atmosphere was volatile. "The kids were vicious. Teachers, faculty, everybody else would jump on you, too."

Killer of Sheep, his M.F.A. thesis project, zeros in on a hero who works in a slaughterhouse. He can't count sheep to fall asleep; that would remind him of his misery. He dreams that he's getting somewhere, though his family life teeters on the brink of failure.

Mr. Burnett says *Killer of Sheep* emerged from running debates he had with fellow film students. "Their movies would present an abstract worker against management. And they had this sort of A-B-C-D quality—that if you do A and B, then C would follow from that and things would resolve themselves." In reaction he made a story about a man who toils in frightful conditions. "But where his real problems lie is within the family," he says, "trying to make that work and be a human being. You don't necessarily win battles; you survive."

He filmed *Killer of Sheep* on his own stomping grounds; he was living in Watts when he went to college. The film's absurdist moments had a factual base. One of his friends had an electrical short in his car that would kill the battery every day; rather than get it fixed, he stole a replacement battery every night. "It was so easy to do the wrong thing," Mr. Burnett recalls.

In a darkly humorous scene in the film, the hero buys a used car engine that has been resting in the middle of a weird household's front room. That was based on "this guy who had the front end of his car inside his house." When asked why he kept the car there, Mr. Burnett says the man replied, "Because someone would steal it if I had it outside." Mr. Burnett concludes: "You have to look at someone else's logic. You just can't impose your values."

Mr. Burnett had lean years before the MacArthur award, struggling to make his own films while seeking grants and mowing lawns, doing cinematography and screen writing for friends and messenger work and script reading for a talent agency. He now lives in View Park, a middle-class black neighborhood not that far from Watts. He is married to Gaye Shannon-Burnett, who acted in and helped produce *My Brother's Wedding* and handled the costumes for *To Sleep with Anger* and *The Glass Shield*. The couple has two sons, Steven, eleven, and Jonathan, six. Mr. Burnett showed his new film out of competition at the Cannes International Film Festival last year. Todd McCarthy, a *Variety* critic, wrote: "Although writer/director Charles Burnett throws more weighty social and political issues on the table than he can possibly dramatize coherently in less than two hours, *The Glass Shield* emerges as a powerful moral drama . . . At moments one can see the seed of a modern *Chinatown* here." In *The Glass Shield* Mr. Burnett has created a character who initially accepts the police officers' us-against-them ethics and lies to back up a white deputy's arrest of a young black man, played by Ice Cube.

The director has some firsthand knowledge of law enforcement in Los Angeles. In 1970, when he was in college, he was mistakenly arrested and held in jail for a weekend, because he'd been in a car that was later used in a robbery. In order to experience the world of cops and cons from the other side, he went on a ride-along with police in South Central. "You drive down the street, your adrenaline is high, and it never goes down because it's just one thing after another," he says.

The trip helped him understand the police mind-set. "You can't condone it," says this quiet man. "But you can understand how a Rodney King thing happens."

Burnett Looks Back

Amy Taubin/1995

Published in the *Village Voice*, January 10, 1995. Reprinted by permission of the author.

In 1990, Charles Burnett officially became a national treasure when his first feature, *Killer of Sheep* (1977), was designated by the National Film Registry of the Library of Congress as "culturally, historically, or aesthetically significant and worthy of preservation." In its six years, the film registry has selected 150 films: *Killer of Sheep* is within its purview, but so too is *The Birth of a Nation*.

Honors aside, Burnett is one of the two greatest African American directors, the other being Spike Lee. Unlike Lee, whose politics impel him into the Hollywood arena, Burnett, although based in Los Angeles, has made all of his films within the independent sector. The ultra-low-budget, gritty but lyrical *Killer of Sheep*, which examines the daily life of a slaughterhouse worker, was filmed in South Central L.A. on weekends with money he saved from his regular job. (*Killer of Sheep* might easily have inspired Gus Van Sant's *Mala Noche*, which has a similarly jagged and claustrophobic sense of place.)

My Brother's Wedding (1983), financed largely by European TV, played in New Directors/New Films but never received commercial distribution. One of the few films to examine economic and class relations within African American society, it focuses on an inner-city man whose brother moves up in the world by marrying into a rich family. *To Sleep with Anger* (1990), Burnett's most powerful and accomplished film, was produced by Ed Pressman after it had been turned down by PBS and other public funders. With a great ensemble cast led by Danny Glover, a contrapuntal, Chekhovian screenplay, and a mise-en-scène that blends slice-of-life with magical realism, *To Sleep with Anger* weaves the points of view of three generations of an extended African American family with roots in both the rural South and urban California. The film won considerable critical attention but was ineptly distributed by Samuel Goldwyn and never reached the audience it deserved. Still, it attracted the attention of CiBy 2000, the French production company with a penchant for serious art film directors. CiBy 2000 financed Burnett's most recent film, *The Glass Shield*, an introspective *policier* that has been making the festival circuit and probably will be released by Miramax, although no one is sure exactly when. Miramax originally scheduled an October 1994 opening, but now they're saying sometime in the spring of 1995.

No less a hybrid than *To Sleep with Anger*, *The Glass Shield* is about a naïve black rookie cop who desperately wants to win the approval of his undisguisedly racist fellow officers in the LAPD. Only when he becomes complicit in framing a murder suspect (Ice Cube in yet another memorable performance), and is forced to confront the corruption around him, does he begin to come to terms with his own identity. *The Glass Shield* opens with a title sequence that telescopes the entire narrative into a series of comic-book-styled drawings. The garish color and pulp quality of comic-book imagery carries over into the film proper, where it's offset by the intensely subjective point of view of the narrative. The mix of genres throws the viewer off balance and challenges the conventional expectation that films dealing with race will be couched in documentary-style realism. On January 7 and 8, the American Museum of the Moving Image will present "Inner-City Blues: The Films of Charles Burnett." In addition to the three earlier features, Burnett hopes to show at least a few scenes from *The Glass Shield* in the context of a discussion of his work moderated by *Voice* critic Greg Tate.

When asked why *The Glass Shield* still has no release date, Burnett, who is among the most tactful and reserved of filmmakers (one can't imagine a conversation between him and the Weinsteins), acknowledged that he and Miramax had had some differences about the film but that he hoped they were close to resolving them. According to the festival rumor mill, Miramax wanted a more conventional conclusion, with the bad cops punished and the good cop rewarded. When I saw *The Glass Shield* at the Vancouver Film Festival, the audience clearly was put off by the last scene, not because it's narratively false, but because the acting was unconvincing. What I hoped was that Miramax would finance a reshoot of the ending without changing its meaning. Says Burnett: "The film is based on a true story and I want it to reflect what actually happened. He [the black cop] was the only one who suffered for it. Everyone else involved got to keep their jobs and go on with their lives. He was transferred and drummed out. At the end, he's no longer this dreamy, naïve person. The film is about him coming full circle to find out who he is."

In Burnett's refusal to adopt Hollywood's genres and codes of realism in toto, one senses an alienation from an entire history of film that ruled people of color out of the picture. "One of the things that got me into this business was trying to make realistic movies but going beyond and behind. What appears isn't what's there in a certain sense. Trying to reach beyond and behind, that's where you go off center, somehow."

Violence Sells: So They're Telling Charles Burnett

Wolf Schneider/1995

Published in *LA Weekly*, June 2, 1995. Reprinted by permission of the author.

Is it the public that's not interested in African American movies unless they are violent and action-laden, or is it the film industry that's stuck on pressing black filmmakers into the urban-ghetto-guerrilla mold of *Do the Right Thing, Menace II Society,* and *Boyz n the Hood?*

To see the trailer for Charles Burnett's current film, *The Glass Shield*, is to be bombarded with a fast-moving hip-hop cacophony of arrest and interrogation. But the movie itself uses a jazz score and complex drama to examine corruption's insidious spread and the pitfalls of racial and gender stereotyping.

Burnett's last film, 1990's *To Sleep with Anger*, was distributed by the Samuel Goldwyn Company. Marketed to the art-house crowd, it drew fine reviews but a disappointing $1.2 million in box-office grosses. This is probably another reason why Miramax Films is emphasizing the action for *The Glass Shield* so heavily.

"All of the action is in the trailer—basically, it's all the action out of the movie," says the film's producer Carolyn Schroeder. "The trailer makes it look boom-boom-boom, but it's not." Says Burnett, "They try to get the high points and appeal to the visceral."

Such commercially skewed targeting to the black male audience aged fourteen to twenty-four may be limiting, but it's better than being ignored, which is what happened to Burnett with *To Sleep with Anger*. Since its theatrical distribution rights went one way (Goldwyn) and video another (Sony SVS), the film received a paltry theatrical release of roughly thirty prints. "Anything is a step up from Goldwyn," Burnett says. Then worries, "They're probably going to kill me."

Despite being one of the most highly lauded filmmakers in artistic circles—he's the recipient of a MacArthur Foundation "genius" grant, and his first feature, *Killer of Sheep*, has been singled out by the Library of Congress for preservation (although good luck trying to find it on video)—Burnett is still on shaky ground in the filmmaking business.

Seated at the dining-room table of a tony Cheviot Hills residence replete with sweeping staircase and five bedrooms, Burnett is self-contained and soft-spoken. He never removes his black leather jacket. The house is not his; it's headquarters for Carolyn Schroeder and Gwen Field's Picture Perfect development company. It was Schroeder who raised the funds for *The Glass Shield* from CiBy 2000, which financed the under-$5 million picture and then sold domestic theatrical and video distribution rights to Miramax.

This mansion is worlds from the streets of the 77th precinct in South Central L.A., where *The Glass Shield* is set. The movie is based on the experiences of John Eddie Johnson, a cop who found he had to sell out his own integrity in order to buy into the system.

Miramax will release *The Glass Shield* on 330 prints in 24 cities, and is promoting it with 4,000 trailers and two 30-second and three 15-second TV ads. At Burnett's request, KJM3 Entertainment Group, an "African diaspora" marketing organization that worked on Julie Dash's *Daughters of the Dust*, has been enlisted for six weeks and a budget of about $150,000. The company will spread the word to churches, black cop groups like the Guardians, black employee unions, and the National Association of Black Social Workers.

Test marketing for *The Glass Shield* was as highly targeted as the ad campaign: the film was screened in the South Bronx, where a low-income, fifteen-to-twenty-five-year-old audience screamed in protest at the hero's emotionalism in the original downbeat ending. "The group that was there were more or less rap-oriented kinds of kids who lived with people getting beat up and wanting the good guys to get justice," reasons Burnett. Given the option of a reshoot funded by Miramax, he reluctantly availed himself, opting for a more commercial ending. No dialogue was altered, but now the acting suggests a more positive, redemptive resolution. "It's more obviously upbeat, rather than sort of ambiguous. More of a closure."

According to Burnett, more major compromises had actually occurred earlier, with CiBy 2000 scrutinizing casting and chopping scenes. "In post-production it was a nightmare," he says. "It had to do with personalities, you know, irrational beings making irrational judgments." Specifies Schroeder, "What they wanted out was everything that makes a Charles Burnett film—the texture, the flavor."

Burnett and Schroeder are not privy to Miramax's prints-and-advertising budget, but they expect *The Glass Shield* will go into profit should its box-office grosses exceed $9 million—roughly three times its budget.

Money isn't everything. At the same time, what does it mean that at the age of fifty-one Burnett should sound old-fashioned when he talks of rising through the filmmaking ranks with Dash in the seventies? "We came up in a period where film was to serve, more than to entertain. You know," says Burnett, "it's supposed to have some sort of social effect."

Above It All: Charles Burnett Puts Black Power in Subtle Films

Gary Dauphin/1997

Published in the *Village Voice*, February 4, 1997. Reprinted by permission of the author.

Charles Burnett has a good laugh when he's asked if there are things he wishes he'd done differently. The fifty-three-year-old director of crucially important black independents from *To Sleep with Anger* to *My Brother's Wedding* is to have a retrospective at Lincoln Center, and his reaction to all his work being screened in one place reflects the bottom-line sensibility that a career outside of Hollywood instills. "Every time I see a film of mine I think of things I could have or should have done differently," Burnett explains. "There are certainly things I would have handled differently in *The Glass Shield* [his 1995 LAPD drama]. It's a matter of money and budgets, overall. If you have more money, you do things differently."

The films and videos on view in the retro (aptly titled "Witnessing for Everyday Heroes") almost always open on the deceptively compact stage of Los Angeles's contemporary black workaday, understatement and daily repetition creating African American characters unlike any in the movies. The great line about Burnett belongs to critic Armond White, who once wrote that his films not only depict black life but sustain it. Whether it's the revelatory ache of his signature neorealism in the 1977 *Killer of Sheep* or the icy-hot salve of *To Sleep with Anger*, the light Burnett sheds on black life is at once uncompromising and gentle, able to move between firm critique and familial affection without contradiction.

The retrospectives centerpiece, *Nightjohn*, seems a bit of a departure for Burnett, but that's only at first glance. Produced for the Disney

Channel (where it was broadcast last year), this story of a onetime freeman (Carl Lumbly as Nightjohn) who travels to various plantations teaching slaves to read puts Burnett not only in the unfamiliar territory of the antebellum South but also in the role of director-for-hire. "I came on board just as [Disney and the producers] were interviewing for directors," remembers Burnett. "The script was complete and many of the other parts of the production were already in place. [*Laughs.*] I was just lucky to get the job!"

Burnett found working in television "completely different" from working in feature films. "First of all, in TV production everything is set in stone. The scheduling is tighter, and the layers of organization [studios and producers] are arranged differently. Then there are sides of the business I hadn't encountered before, like standards and practices departments. Some of their decisions seemed a bit . . . weird." Disney's S&P objected to a scene where one slave holds another down for a whipping, but then didn't utter a peep about another slave's finger being cut off by the plantation's owner. Says Burnett: "It was hard to understand their thinking at times."

The odd ways of the denizens of cable television notwithstanding, Burnett's vision comes through quite clearly in *Nightjohn*—a children's film about literate slaves and banally evil owners. The director's trademark evenness in *Nightjohn* allows its characters to rise (and not rise) to occasions according to their own internal barometers. For Burnett it's simply a matter of "an ordinary event that turned ordinary people into extraordinary ones. Learning how to read was a dangerous, secretive thing for slaves; it required quite a bit of courage. You can see that courage echoing in the later lives of great leaders and orators like Frederick Douglass, but also in the commitment to education that still exists in large numbers of people."

On the question of the project's particular timeliness, Burnett is a bit more circumspect, observing that the script was written long before Ebonics became front-page news. "It's certainly timely, but education is always a timely issue—or should be at least. I think if anything the controversy around Ebonics is an opportunity to focus attention on other aspects of education, from funding to the fact that, very fundamentally, parents need to take an interest in their children's education." *Nightjohn*'s themes relate to that, but paying attention to education, in Burnett's view, is "an ongoing process," something that continues after the lights go up in theaters.

Up next are directing duties on a multipart PBS doc about Reconstruction (he's one of four directors doing segments), to be followed in April by the start of production for his next feature, *The Annihilation of Fish*. "It's basically the story of a middle-aged couple who are going through various conflicts. They come from different places in a number of ways—first being that one's from New York and one's from San Francisco—and they have to learn that they . . . need one another." It's a brief description of a film that's going to be eagerly awaited, and like much of Charles Burnett's work, God (or at least love) will be in the details.

Talking with Charles Burnett

Sojin Kim and R. Mark Livengood/1998

Published in *Journal of American Folklore* 111 (Winter 1998): 69–73. Reprinted by permission of the American Folklore Society, www.afsnet.org.

Charles Burnett, a 1988 MacArthur Fellow, has written or directed nine features for television and cinema, often carving his stories of contemporary African American life against the grains of the neighborhoods of Los Angeles, his home. Burnett received his M.F.A. from the UCLA School of Film and Television, and his thesis project *Killer of Sheep* (1977) was chosen by the Library of Congress for the National Film Registry. His more recent and widely distributed feature films include *To Sleep with Anger* (1990), starring Danny Glover, and *The Glass Shield* (1995), which was based on actual events and dramatizes the experiences of a rookie sheriff in a corrupt police department.[1] For Charles Burnett, films can create values and, in his words, "change how people see one another and how society operates." Yet despite the acclaim of film critics, his projects have not been widely popular. He attributes this response in part to his films being perceived as "too ethnic," thus captivating only specific audiences.

We met with Burnett in a café in late March 1996, to talk about his work. Speaking at UCLA a year earlier, he had used the words storytelling, folkways, and community when discussing his films. Straining our ears against the hissing espresso machine and city buses growling along drizzle-slick Sunset Boulevard, the three of us discussed these notions, as well as those of tricksters and tradition, and how these themes thread through Burnett's art. We specifically addressed *To Sleep with Anger* and *Killer of Sheep*, exploring how they are formed by Burnett's experiences of growing up in the Los Angeles neighborhood of Watts and how they both reflect on family and community social dynamics that he associates with a particular way of life.

Our interview with Burnett affords the opportunity to explore how a filmmaker who specializes in creating fictional, as opposed to strictly documentary, worlds thinks about folkloric concepts.[2] Rather than limiting ourselves merely to identifying and speculating about the functions of the numerous examples of folklore within Burnett's films, in this essay we splice together our thinking and excerpts from our interview to address how Burnett himself relates ideas important to folklorists. We consider as well the qualities in his films that we find significant due to their evocation of the expressiveness and cadence of everyday life.

To Sleep with Anger unfolds around sexagenarian Harry, who has dropped by unexpectedly to visit Suzie and Gideon, old friends he has not seen in the thirty years since they moved to Los Angeles from somewhere in the South, "back home." In an early scene, Harry plays cards with the youngest of Suzie and Gideon's two adult sons, Babe Brother. They sit at the kitchen table. In the background, a row of glass pickle jars filled with sprouting plants lines the window; Babe Brother's wife, Linda, and their son, Sonny, watch and listen. Harry pulls a large knife from his pocket, and the rabbit's foot hanging from it attracts Sonny's attention.

> Linda: You're not like the rest of Gideon's friends. Most of them believe if you're not hard at work then you're hard at sin.
> Harry: I'm more modern in my ways. I don't believe in sin, though there is good and evil. And evil is something that you work at. [To Sonny] You mustn't touch. Your mother may not like you handling knives.
> Linda: I think he just wanted to see your rabbit's foot.
> Harry: I let this rabbit's foot take the place of my toby which I lost years ago.
> Linda: What's a toby?
> Harry: A charm that old people teach you how to make. You don't want to be at a crossroads without one. I had one for a long time that used to belong to my grandmother who had it since she was a child. In my travels I misplaced it. And I've been looking over my shoulder ever since.

Harry's remarks suggest his ambiguous character and the fundamental role that he plays in the film. *To Sleep with Anger* revolves around the ways in which Harry, graciously invited by Gideon to "stay as long as you like," affects the lives and relationships of his old friends and the members of their extended family. According to Burnett, his screenplay resonates with a tale:

CB: There's a Georgian folktale called "Hairy Man."[3] And he, you know, will steal your soul. But it's something you bargained with. If a person is looking for something, and manages to run up against these kinds of people, you're always lacking something, some kind of deficiency.

SK: You mean he finds your shortcomings?

CB: Yeah. Or you go out looking for something and are very vulnerable for whatever reason. And you run into this character and you unwittingly make this deal. The only way to get out of it is to out-trick this trickster, you know. So, it's basically that kind of character he plays . . . Harry is someone like in between a real person and possibly this character of a Hairy Man. He appears to tell the truth and this and that. And people come along with judgments and perceptions of him. He can be just an ordinary guy or he could be what they really said he is or what they really think he is. And so I left it vague and had the audience figure it out.

Harry is a trickster, his name borrowed from the character in the story Burnett heard during his youth and based on individuals Burnett encountered when he was growing up—those whom "older people always thought were evil." Appearing out of nowhere, Harry upsets the lives of his hosts, their children, and in-laws. By gaining their confidence and cleverly exploiting their weaknesses, doubts, and internal conflicts, Harry opens the family members to crisis. He casts his spell especially over Babe Brother, the most volatile family member, whose irritation with and distance from his parents and older, more responsible brother, Junior, slowly coagulate as the film progresses. As a trickster, Harry is an enabler who exposes the frailty of the bonds that hold this family together, bringing it to the brink of dissolution when brotherly tension manifests itself as fisticuffs in the kitchen. Yet exactly because he has bared these tenuous alliances, Harry creates strength and facilitates growth in the family, thus assuring that it reassembles more solidly than before he arrived. Neither good nor evil, he creates the possibility for renewal and forgiveness by provoking suffering and rage. As Harry tells an old nemesis who confronts him about his role in a killing that almost incited a race riot, "Strange as it may seem, it might have cleared the water. Sometimes the right action comes from the wrong reason."

However, reworking the tale of "Hairy Man" was not Burnett's primary objective in making *To Sleep with Anger*. Rather, his sense that a distinctive way of life was dying, along with an older population that exemplified it, was a catalyst for writing the script:

SK: What was the reason you began writing that story?

CB: Well, basically it is something you grew up with, you know. You look around and you see it disappear. It's gone. And you wonder why kids today now are without a foundation and such and such. And it just hit me at a time when I thought it was really important to talk about it. One of the things I used to—the guy died just recently—I used to go get my hair cut for the very longest time by a guy in Watts [Los Angeles] at 108th and Central. No, not Central, Compton Avenue. But these old guys used to come in there all the time . . . There's always some degree of storytelling or reciting or recalling the past. And . . . but it's just, you know, there were all these older people who came in there, not too many young people. You realize that there is this missing link and lack of continuity. So it was an attempt to bridge all that stuff, you know. That's why I wrote it.

Burnett's motivation for making *To Sleep with Anger* recalls those researchers who are animated by the desire to document what they perceive to be threatened ways of life. The people who had moved to Southern California from the South had a considerable impact on Burnett when he was growing up in Watts during the 1950s. *To Sleep with Anger* is set in a nonspecific Los Angeles neighborhood, described by Burnett as a place that anyone comes to when they migrate from the South. It's the idea of this place where this generation of people came and had kids, their kids had kids, and they lost any interest in the past, the stories about relatives.

Accordingly, the film investigates the ways in which people and places evolve as each new generation comes of age.

RML: It sounds like when you talk about continuity between generations that you are talking about tradition. How do you interpret that term? Tradition?

CB: It's strange because tradition, information, you know, survival, all of these things are tied in. The wisdom, all that . . . The problem is as you get older, you realize that you should have been wise enough to learn or respect, shape ideas from other people, an older generation. Because again, you realize that when you make mistakes you should have listened and these patterns are set. And it's strange, because if you listen to the blues you'll find a lot of information passed on in very specific ways but with the same thing, expressing values and feelings and things like that—experiences that we can all learn from. It's that sort of thing, something where you can pick up the ball or the torch or whatever it is and hand it off to someone else.

Indeed, the blues are a frequent aural presence in Burnett's films. He also cites the Bible as a "complex, fascinating source of information" for values and experiences, and *To Sleep with Anger* contains explicit biblical references in the plot, in the dialogue between characters, and in small visual cues, such as the image of Adam and Eve printed on Harry's playing cards.

To Sleep with Anger brims with examples of traditional expressive behavior that folklorists will readily recognize.

RML: We wanted to ask you about another word you used almost a year ago when you talked at UCLA . . . We're interested in how you think about folkways and how you incorporate that into the projects you're working on.

CB: A lot of things you forget or want to discard and [you want to] develop new ways of conducting yourself. And there's ways of acting and conducting yourself that certain people do and have a pattern for. It's just a way of living that's come from a place in time. And you know you want to celebrate that, so to speak. I mean, it is something that relates to humanity, seems to me.

Many visual and verbal portrayals in *To Sleep with Anger* illustrate the "pattern" of life of which Burnett speaks and emphasize the values of the members of the community he has created. Although they live in the city, Gideon and Suzie tend a garden and raise chickens. One evening they host a fish fry, for which people dress in their Sunday best and play blues and gospel. More casual and common social calls and activities occur in their kitchen, conveying how the use of domestic spaces can reflect and affect the organization of social interactions (see Glassie 1995:327–424; Pocius 1979, 1991). In describing his father-in-law's home, Burnett stated, "No one goes in the dining room. It's spotless. I mean the furniture is nice. But you go right into the kitchen, and that is where everything takes place. No one ever goes into the front room or the dining room." Significantly, the most important actions and encounters in *To Sleep with Anger* occur in Suzie and Gideon's kitchen: Harry's first interaction with Babe Brother, the fracas between the two brothers, and Harry's death at its threshold.

In addition, Burnett has laced the conversations of his characters with examples of proverbial speech such as "Medicine that works leaves a bitter taste," "Why close the barn door when the horse is gone," "You ain't worth the salt you put in greens," and "An empty wagon make a lot of noise."[4] He has also incorporated examples of traditional beliefs and healing practices into the film.

These examples underscore a central theme of the film, namely the at-times uneasy, although not mutually exclusive, relationship between the unofficial and the official, the traditional and the modern. In one poignant scene, a pastor visiting the bedridden Gideon chides Suzie, saying, "I would think that you would depend on prayer rather than these old-fashioned remedies." Likewise, the healing powers of prayer may be similarly dismissed as uncritical and unsophisticated by others such as Babe Brother and Linda. Burnett therefore explores the tensions and misunderstandings that may arise when the trajectories of differing, often generationally specific, ways of knowing and behaving cross and collide. He also demonstrates how the systems of beliefs people develop in their own lives may accommodate seemingly contradictory ideas. For instance, Harry declares that his ways are "more modern" than Gideon's, but when his foot is brushed by a broom wielded by Sonny, he performs a series of actions to forestall the bad luck associated with the gesture: he puts a dash of salt in the palm of his hand, spits on it, and throws it over his shoulder.

Burnett's earlier film, *Killer of Sheep*, also reflects on the past. A riveting examination of Stan, an insomniac slaughterhouse worker, and his family, the film starkly counterposes the parallel worlds of children and adults. Scenes of Stan's daily struggles are intercut with long, real-time master shots of youths playing that suggest their carefree lives while also conveying the potential cruelty and danger of their games. Echoing cinema verité, Burnett often allows the action to unfold in front of the camera, capturing the results on grainy black and white 16-millimeter film; at times the film lumbers along, at other times it slides out to the edge of dissonance.

Similar to *To Sleep with Anger, Killer of Sheep* is set in a Los Angeles neighborhood, and Burnett's depiction of it reveals his attachment to the area that fired his imagination. In addition to haunting visuals, he has deftly woven the street sounds of this neighborhood into the film—a tinkling version of "Yankee Doodle" from the ice cream van, barking dogs, screaming hook and ladder trucks, a choking car engine—thus conveying a sonorous sense of place. And he has populated this world, as he did in *To Sleep with Anger*, with characters negotiating the ebb and flow of daily life—the struggle to relate to lovers and children, the joy and frustration of payday and the fading satisfaction of money in the pocket, and the varying abilities of people to create and maintain lives within social networks. Burnett's pacing and masterful rendering of place, evocative details, and types and situations of characters produce a realism that tacitly tugs at the seams between features and documentaries.

According to Burnett, *Killer of Sheep* addresses the questions of what it is to be a man, what success is, and how one copes with problems in the community. And as in *To Sleep with Anger*, he depicts the theme of a person's place within a physically defined social network.

SK: How about the idea of community or neighborhood? Do those mean something to you and do you feel like they come out in your films?

CB: Well, I think that the fact of the matter is, again, I moved out. I moved into an apartment, and I never said "hi" or whatever to my neighbors. I never even had a conversation with them. I didn't know that my neighbors downstairs wrote children's books until I was moving. It's so sad because I would be very interested in that now. But you know when I grew up, everyone knew their neighbors, and kids, and so forth, so there wasn't the anonymity. I mean people knew who you were so you couldn't just jump into someone's backyard and steal something. I mean we used to raid peach trees and things like that, and apricot trees and all sort of things, but, you know, you didn't break into someone's house. The doors were open. And so you had to be, and I think you felt that you were observed, so you had to be on your best, good behavior. But now, no one knows anyone anymore too much. Except the older generation, the people who lived in the community a little while . . . A lot of it has to do with not owning houses and things like that.

In one scene of *Killer of Sheep*, two young men awkwardly try to steal a television. They are witnessed, however, by an old man watering his yard and by Stan's young son, who shouts the warning, "He's going to call the police."

In Burnett's films, community, like tradition, is not immune to slow decay and eventual dissolution, forces which result in part because subsequent generations fail to learn the stories, the folkways. Although he is obviously concerned with such a progression, Burnett is not a wistful romantic; he does not celebrate a place and time from the past as an Eden. Rather, in these films, his juxtapositions of different generations and systems of belief and morality express loss and longing, continuity and reinvention, and the complicated texture of people creating order and meaning.

CB: You know, when you're a kid, one of the things, too, I think, that happens is when you're younger and grow up in another generation, you kind of reject everything, question everything. And I did that a lot, like most kids who grew up. That's some old wives' tale; that's an old something, you know. And you know, as you get older you find, well, maybe there is something to it. There's some pattern to life. And then you try to not totally accept it, but respect it in a certain way, you know.

In this fashion, both *To Sleep with Anger* and *Killer of Sheep* are inquiries into evolving cultural processes as much as they are meditations on collective and individual pasts.

Notes

1. *To Sleep with Anger* and *The Glass Shield* are available at most video rental stores. *Killer of Sheep*, which won the Critics Prize at the Berlin International Film Festival and first prize at the U.S. Film Festival in Park City, Utah in 1988, periodically screens on public television. Many thanks to Alan Gevinson, director of the Ethnic-American Feature Film Project of the American Film Institute, for locating a copy of *Killer of Sheep* for us. Other films that Burnett has directed and written include *Several Friends* (1969) and *My Brother's Wedding* (1984). In 1996, he directed *Nightjohn*, a television feature for Sarabande Productions/Disney.

2. For a relevant essay about folklore in literature, see Owen 1965.

3. Donnell Van de Voort collected a version of "Wiley and the Hairy Man" in Alabama as part of the Federal Writer's Project of the Works Progress Administration. This tale was subsequently published and categorized as a "Nursery Tale" in Botkin 1944:682–87 and was reprinted in Courlander 1976:482–86. More recently, a version of "Wiley and

the Hairy Man" has appeared in Richard Young and Judy Dockrey Young 1991:64–68. A probable motif of these tales is G303.3.1.21: The devil as a great hairy man.

4. Respectively, these are versions of: "Bitter pills may have blessed effects" (Smith 1948:47); "It is late shutting the door when the mare is stolen" (Taylor and Whiting 1958:109); "Not worth his salt" (Taylor and Whiting 1958:316); and "Empty vessels make the greatest sound" (Smith 1948:171).

References Cited

Botkin, B. A. 1944. *A Treasury of American Folklore*. New York: Crown.

Courlander, Harold. 1976. *A Treasury of Afro-American Folklore*. New York: Crown.

Glassie, Henry. 1995. *Passing the Time in Ballymenone: Culture and History of an Ulster Community*. Bloomington: Indiana University Press.

Owen, Guy. 1965. "Using Folklore in Fiction." *North Carolina Folklore* 13:147–55.

Pocius, Gerald L. 1979. "Hooked Rugs in Newfoundland: The Representation of Social Structure in Design." *Journal of American Folklore* 92:273–84.

Pocius, Gerald L. 1991. *A Place to Belong: Community Order and Everyday Space in Calvert, Newfoundland*. Athens: University of Georgia Press.

Smith, William George. 1948. *The Oxford Dictionary of English Proverbs*. Oxford, England: Clarendon Press.

Taylor, Archer, and Bartlett Jere Whiting. 1958. *A Dictionary of American Proverbs and Proverbial Phrases*. Cambridge, Mass.: Harvard University Press.

Young, Richard, and Judy Dockrey Young. 1991. *Favorite Scary Stories of American Children*. Little Rock, Ark.: August House.

Invisible Man

Terrence Rafferty/2001

Copyright © 2001 Condé Nast Publications. All rights reserved. Originally published in *GQ*, March 2001, 239–44. Reprinted by permission.

When the filmmaker Charles Burnett was growing up in Los Angeles, he used to play the trumpet, and sometimes, he says, "I'd blow all day, just to hurt people." This is rather a shocking statement, coming from this gentle, soft-spoken fifty-six-year-old man, whose movies rarely raise their voices and always seem more interested in healing than in hurting. But, as the amiable narrator of Burnett's superb short comedy *When It Rains* (1995) observes, "We live with contradictions," and perhaps one of the reasons this major American filmmaker is almost completely unknown to the general public is that his art, at its best, embraces contradiction so enthusiastically: He searches for—and often finds—the messy truth that's tough to reduce to an advertising slogan or a marketing strategy, which means that even the so-called independent-film companies (who pride themselves, loudly, on their adventurousness) won't take a chance on Burnett's most personal projects. "Now, even with the independents, you have to get name actors and things like that," he says. "You have producers like Miramax who are called independent, but they're under a company like Disney and they have some of the same requirements. Whenever people put money into a film, they're going to try to influence the content. It's only a matter of degree."

I don't detect any rancor in his voice when he says this, even though I'm working hard to coax some quotable anger out of him. When I ask Burnett about one of his made-for-television films, which looked to me as if it had been interfered with, he quietly responds, "I'd have to go off the record on that," and he recounts battles with other producers and distributors in a serene, matter-of-fact tone. His equanimity is a little mysterious, but it's consistent with the sensibility of his films, which, like those of Jean Renoir and Satyajit Ray (and depressingly few others), are remarkable for their refusal to be surprised by the idiocies and even the cruelties of human behavior.

To tell the truth, I was hoping for a bit more outrage from Burnett, who, more than most American filmmakers, has ample reason to feel frustrated by the current state of our national cinema. His first feature, *Killer of Sheep* (1977), is one of the most striking debuts in movie history and an acknowledged landmark in African American film: It was among the first fifty movies selected for the Library of Congress's National Film Registry (which places it under a sort of historic preservation). But in spite of the acclaim—which also included major awards at the Sundance and Berlin film festivals—*Killer of Sheep* did not find a theatrical distributor and has never been released on home video. He didn't complete his second feature, *My Brother's Wedding*, until 1983, and that, too, failed to attract a distributor. It was seven years until Burnett's next picture, *To Sleep with Anger*; that film had the distinction of actually appearing in a few of the nation's movie theaters, but despite rapturous reviews it did very little business, and Charles Burnett remained the best-kept secret in American movies.

Of course, none of these pictures were designed to be commercial blockbusters. *Killer of Sheep* was Burnett's thesis film for the UCLA film school; he shot it in black and white with the school's equipment. He filmed it in 1972, but, he says, "It stayed in the can because I didn't want to graduate. There was no place to go to find equipment as cheap." Burnett had enrolled in the film school in the late sixties, after getting a degree in electronics from Los Angeles Community College and deciding that was not his true métier: "The guys in the electronics industry, whom I'd get to know when they came back for refresher courses, were sort of strange to me. They just wanted to be at a certain place in their lives in, like, twenty years—to have security, a twenty-year pin, three weeks' vacation. That was all they were dreaming of. And their jokes weren't very funny." UCLA's film program was, he says, "anti-industry, very anti-Hollywood"; his main reason for choosing it, however, was that it was "dirt cheap" compared with USC's.

Whatever his motivation may have been, UCLA was clearly the right place for Burnett. His favorite movie as a teenager was, after all, Renoir's *The Southerner* (1945), an episodic, low-key narrative of a struggling white farm family—an extremely unusual preference, not just for a black kid from L.A. but for any adolescent, anywhere. "What impressed me," Burnett says, "was the way the film treated its characters—this calm, sort of slow revealing of humanity." This is not a quality, I think it's fair to say, that's generally associated with the worldview of youth: It's the kind of thing people appreciate (if they ever do) only when they get older and less impatient. Burnett, that is, must have been kind of a weird kid, and in UCLA he found a school that would actually nurture his stubborn individuality. The twenty-year pin was not a concept.

"It was all about film as an art form," Burnett says. "We didn't think about working in Hollywood but about making our own personal films. So we just stayed at UCLA and exploited the department as long as we could; we used the equipment until they told us to leave." *Killer of Sheep* must have been exactly what Burnett's teachers—who included the pioneering British documentary filmmaker Basil Wright—had in mind when they talked about "personal films." The movie is a series of not particularly momentous episodes in the life of a black slaughterhouse worker; the plot is, if anything, even less eventful than that of the filmmaker's beloved *The Southerner*, and Burnett makes no concessions to the audience's expectations of action or suspense, or any other narrative convention of commercial movies. The picture is unmistakably personal, and not simply because it's set in South Central Los Angeles, where Burnett had lived for a while in his boyhood, after his family moved from Vicksburg, Mississippi; what's distinctive about *Killer of Sheep* isn't so much its setting as its sensibility, which accommodates a much wider range of experience and emotion than working-class drama ordinarily does.

The protagonist's day-to-day existence is pretty grim. After a shift at the abattoir, he's in no mood to play with his kids or make love to his wife, and he often looks as if even the effort required to crack a smile were just too much for him. But the movie is neither depressing nor monotonous—because, despite the powerful undercurrent of fatigue and despair, there's an odd buoyancy to Burnett's depiction of the South Central community. Although the people are poor, they haven't, most of them, altogether stopped *living*: The grown-ups get by somehow or other, and the kids find ways to play. (Here, as in many of his later films, Burnett takes time out to savor the enchanted self-absorption of children.) There's more than enough humor and beauty in *Killer of Sheep* to keep it from becoming a drab, grinding chronicle of misery, and enough, too, to make us understand the devastating totality of the hero's physical and spiritual exhaustion: He's so beaten down that he's missing some real possibilities for pleasure, which exist even in South Central. We know they exist because Burnett has shown them to us.

Killer of Sheep was a far more complex vision of African American life than moviegoers were used to at that time. Its style, Burnett says, was influenced by the "poetic, lyrical storytelling" of the documentaries he saw in Basil Wright's class, as well as by one aspect, at least, of Hollywood's studio-era manner: "One of the things I noticed about American movies of the thirties and forties was that there was always an ensemble, a mix of all these different characters; I was impressed by the sense of community that it created." The fact that Burnett could combine two such disparate influences, while at the same time scrupulously ignoring every prevailing notion of what a "black" film was supposed to be, gave evidence of a formidably hardheaded artistic personality—the intractable idiosyncrasy of a true independent. The money people in the movie business have a nose for that sort of thing, and they don't like it one bit; they don't trust a filmmaker who isn't auditioning for them.

So Charles Burnett failed to benefit from the filmmaker-friendly climate of Hollywood in the seventies, which enabled Scorsese, Altman, Coppola and De Palma, among others, to indulge their sensibilities with respectable budgets and relatively few aesthetic constraints. The powers that be recognized that although these guys were artists, they also wanted to be *players* in Hollywood. There's nothing scarier to the studios than a filmmaker who doesn't ask for their approval, and Burnett rather obviously fell into that category. "I think a lot of us who came out of film school in those days were very passionate and obsessive about things, and that shows in our work and also in our confrontations with producers," he says. "We're not willing to compromise as much. For us that's not a winning situation, because you don't get the jobs. They'd rather have someone who'll agree to do whatever they want to do. One executive told me that I wasn't a 'shooter'—that's a term they use now—that I wasn't someone who can just go out and shoot the film and forget about all that artistic stuff."

Again, when Burnett recounts such indignities, he manages to sound neither bitter nor self-congratulatory—just kind of bemused. More anger might even have helped his career: The enraged black man is a stereotype entertainment executives understand (i.e., know how to exploit). Burnett's knowledge of racism is too deep to be expressed in political slogans or rap bravado or the pop catharsis of a movie shootout, which may explain why the late eighties–early nineties Hollywood vogue for black filmmakers (Spike Lee, John Singleton, et al.) somehow failed to include him. After *My Brother's Wedding*, which Burnett showed at festivals but never submitted to distributors—he considered it "unfinished" and still does—he had perhaps his best chance for commercial success in *To Sleep with Anger*, which had a major star (Danny Glover) and a reputable independent distributor (the Samuel Goldwyn Company). The picture, besides, came out at a time when the movie audience's interest in black subjects was peaking. And it's a terrific movie. But no one went to see it.

According to Burnett, Goldwyn had no idea how to market *To Sleep with Anger*. "The Goldwyn people never really exploited the good reviews. We couldn't get them to put money into prints and ads. Nobody knew about the movie. They put it in theaters where it was difficult for the black community to go see it, and we couldn't even get them to advertise in church magazines, which would have been very inexpensive. But it was impossible to tell them anything, because they knew what they were doing, supposedly." (Goldwyn has since gone out of business.) *To Sleep with Anger*, like Burnett's two previous features, is essentially a study of family and community but with a heavier emphasis on the southern roots of black Angelenos. In the South Central of his youth, Burnett says, "there were so many people from Mississippi and Texas that it was practically a southern environment." The movie's main characters, a sixtyish husband and wife named Gideon (Paul Butler) and Suzie (Mary Alice), live in a modest, respectable L.A. house but retain a few striking vestiges of down-home rural culture: They keep chickens in their backyard. When an old friend from Mississippi, Harry (Glover), turns up and moves into their house, he evokes in them— quite deliberately—an overpowering nostalgia for the old ways. He's bent on reminding people who they were back when, and his effect on the community is hugely unsettling, almost destabilizing: While everyone's enjoying the fish fries and the corn liquor and the tall tales, some of the older folks uneasily confront aspects of their past they'd rather forget, and some of the younger people—notably Gideon and Suzie's insecure younger son—are dangerously attracted to Harry's air of self-confidence, without understanding that this southern man's slyness and roguish irresponsibility are the aberrant products of oppression and low expectations. The film is an elegant, richly populated comedy of manners, in which ordinary people dance with mischievous ghosts and come perilously close to getting swept off their feet.

After *To Sleep with Anger* flopped, Burnett continued working as he always had, without recognition, his financial fortunes eased somewhat by a 1988 MacArthur "genius" grant. "When the MacArthur Foundation called," he says, "I'd been swamped with bills and people calling to collect money, so I was suspicious at first. When I realized it wasn't a joke, my wife said, 'Let's go look for a house,' and that's what we did. You know, go out and spend the money before they discovered they had the wrong person." Cushioned by the MacArthur money (and the medical benefits the foundation provided), Burnett directed a PBS documentary on interracial communities, *America Becoming* (1991), and began to develop *The Glass Shield* (1994), a fact-based drama about a young black cop in a corrupt L.A. county sheriff's station. For that project, he had the backing of Miramax (pre-Disney) and the French company CiBy 2000, and despite some problems with one of the French producers, he managed to make more or less the movie he wanted: a thoughtful, lucid moral drama with a deeply conflicted hero and no gunplay whatsoever. Miramax's fabled marketing department tried to sell it as a hood movie, dumping it in a few urban theaters with the support of minuscule ads whose most prominent feature was the glowering face of Ice Cube (who has a small role in the picture). "I knew that was a mistake," Burnett says. "Kids went in there expecting rap music, and they were disappointed."

At this point, Burnett might have been more than a little disappointed himself, but in the aftermath of *The Glass Shield* he roused himself to turn out a couple of movies that do not look like the work of a discouraged man. He describes *When It Rains* (1995), a thirteen-minute comedy, as "just a little movie about blues and jazz I made with some friends of mine; we got a camera, put all the equipment in a Volkswagen, and shot here and there and took advantage of everything we saw." The film is a loose, speedy minipicaresque that follows a middle-aged musician in a dashiki around his neighborhood as he tries to raise the rent money for a distraught single mother and her daughter. Some people are broke, some people are mean, some people gladly give him a few bucks, one guy collects a debt from him, and another guy makes him a sinister offer that, even in the circumstances, he *can* refuse. Near the end of the day, an old buddy playing trumpet on the street hands him, in lieu of cash, a rare jazz LP by John Handy, which, to everyone's surprise, the landlord accepts as adequate payment: "I'm hip to John Handy," he says with a big smile on his face. The hero muses, "If I'd looked for common ground to begin with, this nightmare would have never happened. Do I need to say more, except Damn! I'm glad I didn't have a rap album in my hand," The tossed-off quality of *When It Rains* is deceptive: The movie feels improvised but, as in a great jazz solo, every note counts and the shape of the whole is irreducible, inevitable. It's a song about survival—that's the blues component—and you can't get the melody out of your head.

Burnett's next film, *Nightjohn* (1996), based on a children's book by Gary Paulsen, was made for the Disney Channel: Its heroine, a slave on a southern plantation, is a twelve-year-old girl (played by a remarkable young actress named Allison Jones), but the movie's treatment of its subject is startlingly adult. The story revolves around this bright, spirited girl's clandestine attempts to learn how to read—an activity strictly forbidden by slaveholders, who were determined to keep their bound labor force as ignorant and "childlike" as possible. The girl is tutored by the title character (Carl Lumbly), a slave who had once been free. Her frightened elders disapprove, but she's too fired up to worry about consequences: Once a kid's imagination has been engaged, it's a runaway train. Burnett's work has always shown a natural affinity for obstinate, imaginative, even slightly flaky children, and he does full justice here to the inspirational quality of this brave girl's education. But he also incorporates in *Nightjohn* an extraordinarily nuanced analysis of the economic and psychological deformities imposed by the slaveholding culture of the Old South. The movie clears your eyes and then fills them with tears of rage.

Nightjohn was the first film Burnett made from material he hadn't written himself. (The screenplay is by Bill Cain, a Jesuit priest.) Since then he has worked exclusively as a director, with scripts of variable quality. For ABC he directed the Oprah Winfrey–presented miniseries *The Wedding* (1998) and the Wonderful World of Disney production *Selma, Lord, Selma* (1999), about the civil rights struggle in Alabama. Last year he did a Showtime movie, *Finding Buck McHenry*, about a white Little Leaguer's obsession with a vanished star of the Negro Leagues. And coming soon to (a few) theaters will be *The Annihilation of Fish*, a quirky romantic comedy in which a couple of lonely, mentally disturbed senior citizens, played by James Earl Jones and Lynn Redgrave, discover, through mutual pleasure and affection, a contentment that more or less resembles sanity. These pictures have their virtues—in fact they're all better than they have any right to be, because Burnett's restless curiosity about human behavior always manages to turn up something real. But you miss in them the full power of his unique vision of race and family and community, the opening up of new perspectives that the viewer experiences in *Killer of Sheep* and *To Sleep with Anger* and *When It Rains* and *Nightjohn*.

"I'd love to do my own films," Burnett says, "but it takes so long. It just takes an extraordinary effort to keep going when everybody's saying to you, 'No one wants to see that kind of movie' or 'There's no black audience.' You have to pay the rent." He has had no success attracting backers for *The Crazy Kill*, his adaptation of one of Chester Himes's pungent, brutally funny crime novels about the Harlem cops Coffin Ed Johnson and Grave Digger Jones. This sounds like a wonderful Charles Burnett movie to me, and the fact that there's no imminent prospect of seeing it makes me angry. Angry enough, actually, to have made me misrepresent Burnett a wee bit in this piece: He really isn't a complainer. I hope he'll forgive me for venting my outrage, on his behalf, at the people with the power in the movie business. Sure, it's childish of me, but, as Burnett knows, sometimes you just feel the need to *hurt* people.

Set This House On Fire: Nat Turner's Second Coming

Gerald Peary /2001

Published in the *Village Voice*, September 4, 2001. © 2001 by Gerald Peary. Reprinted by permission of the author.

"I was the great-grandson of a slave owner, and he was the great-grandson of slaves," says *Sophie's Choice* novelist William Styron, seventy-six, recalling his friendship with the late James Baldwin. "Jimmy dared write from a white point of view, and I thought that was admirable. It was at his prodding that I decided to jump into the soul of a black man. I never regretted it, though Jimmy predicted I would catch it, and I did."

The fiction that Baldwin inspired was *The Confessions of Nat Turner*, which reconstructs the infamous 1831 slave rebellion in Southampton, Virginia. The 1967 Pulitzer Prize–winning novel (which Baldwin adored) is now among the narratives being used for an omnibus movie in the making that's part documentary, part fictional re-creation: *Nat Turner: A Troublesome Property*. Directed and co-written by Charles Burnett, it focuses on the insurrection that led to the violent deaths of perhaps sixty whites from slave-owner families and of most of the sixty to eighty slaves who participated. The slaves not killed immediately were put on trial (before all-Caucasian juries), and most were hanged, Turner among them.

A 1968 adaptation of *Confessions* to star James Earl Jones was halted in part by the efforts of African American protesters, who felt that a white author had stolen their hero and distorted his character. In the fiery 1968 anthology *William Styron's Nat Turner: Ten Black Writers Respond*, the essayists accused Styron of insinuating that Turner's slave revolt was prompted by his raging desires for a Caucasian girl. Charles

V. Hamilton wrote, "We will not . . . leave unchallenged an image of Nat Turner . . . who dreams of going to bed with white women, who holds nothing but contempt for his fellow blacks."

Styron admits he has felt the sting of his critics, but remains unrepentant. "I find almost all the complaints invalid, irrational, and hysterical, based on bigotry and prejudice," he says today. "I don't want to seem self-assured, but I wouldn't change much."

On the occasion in late June when we speak, on an outdoor movie set at a working plantation in Louisiana County, Virginia, the writer feels especially vindicated. He's been invited here to observe the shooting of key scenes from his novel, more than three decades after the studio filming was stopped dead. "It's high time, after thirty-three years," he says.

The trio of collaborators on *A Troublesome Property*—director Burnett, producer Frank Christopher, and co-screenwriter Kenneth S. Greenberg—debated for several years how to frame their dramatized history. Finally they rejected a Ken Burns–style omniscient voice-over for a postmodern approach. Their movie would not present one definitive "Nat Turner" but shifting, contradictory ones—re-creating episodes from Turner's life from six chosen texts, in which six different actors would play him. One features a sub-literate, primitive Nat, the way he's portrayed in Harriet Beecher Stowe's abolitionist novel *Dred* (1856); in another, he's the eloquent, articulate leader put forth in Randolph Edmonds's 1935 agitprop play *Nat Turner*.

"We take the stories we're given as almost etched in stone," Burnett explains on the set. "Stowe's Nat is a simple, angelic innocent, so we show him with a skunk and a mountain lion. In another story, there's the murderous Nat, so this violent person emerges with a sword."

Styron's Freudian creation is one of the competing Nats. "Nat Turner has conformed to all those who consider him, and been rewritten in the image of people writing about him," says Styron, who approves of the film's *Rashomon* aesthetic. "Even his actual confession is suspect, taken down when he was imprisoned by a lawyer, Thomas R. Gray, who had every reason to twist the words."

Courtly and approachable, Styron plants himself in a director's chair, trying to get by in the ninety-seven-degree Virginia heat. Today he will watch the shooting of the horrific scene that climaxes his novel—the only occasion that Nat Turner murdered someone. Turner (today, Virginia stage actor James Opher) chases, stabs, and bludgeons to death

Margaret Whitehead (high schooler Megan Gallacher), the daughter of a slave owner.

The novelist got into the deepest trouble from his detractors in fabricating the steamy encounters pairing Margaret and Nat. "In the novel, she teases him mercilessly, practically does a striptease in front of him," Styron says. "In his confession, Nat admitted this murder, so it had to be incredibly significant that he chose this particular person."

Styron looks on as the camera rolls: Poor Margaret flees down a country path and trips at a log fence. Coming up behind her, Nat draws his weapon, and stabs.

"Very good! Very powerful!" Burnett announces after three quite chilling takes.

"I never thought I'd see this scene I dreamed up," Styron says, stirred.

Producer David Wolper originally purchased the rights to *Confessions* for six hundred thousand dollars more than thirty years ago. "They wanted to change the story, which bothered me a great deal," Styron says. "They wanted to give Nat a wife and turn it into a bourgeois family. Norman Jewison was going to direct, then Sidney Lumet. I myself got a black screenwriter, Louis Peterson. But it didn't help that it was always a white director.

"Later, Spike Lee took an option, but his company decided not to [proceed]. *Beloved* and *Amistad* seemed to indicate that historic movies about blacks are poison at the box office."

A UCLA film school graduate and probably the most revered African American cineast among critics and scholars, Burnett is best known for *To Sleep with Anger* (1990), a subtle, complex tale starring Danny Glover set in a contemporary middle-class black family, and the TV movie *Nightjohn* (1996), about the private lives of slaves on a harsh southern plantation. His first feature was *Killer of Sheep* (1977), selected for preservation by the National Film Registry of the Library of Congress.

It's after 10 p.m. and thirteen hours of shooting when Burnett finally sits down for a formal interview. He's weary, he hasn't eaten dinner, and he loathes doing publicity. He's also doubtful about the prospect of theatrical distribution for *A Troublesome Property*. "It's a small film, and it's a major proposition, a theatrical release. My films are not just for entertainment's sake."

Postmodernist relativism notwithstanding, who is Charles Burnett's Nat Turner? "When I visited Southampton County," he replies in a roundabout way, "I met white people still fighting the Civil War, who say of Nat, 'He's a murderer!' They can't reconcile that his men killed women and children who were sleeping. They identify with the dead whites but not with the rest of humanity. They don't think about this institution of slavery that didn't care about human life."

For his part, Burnett, a famously gentle man, offers an unequivocal endorsement of Turner. "He's every man who'd fight for the liberation of others, who realized the evils of slavery and wanted his people to live in a normal way. Everyone has inalienable rights, and he, in a sense, was interpreting the Constitution. Nat Turner was more American than those whites who denied him."

Warming by the Devil's Fire: Director Interview

Charles Burnett/2003

From PBS, *The Blues*, www.pbs.org/theblues/aboutfilms/burnettinterview.html. © 2003 Vulcan Productions, Inc. All rights reserved. Reprinted by permission.

Historically, there's a complex, even antagonistic, relationship between the blues—the devil's music, Satan's music—and the church in the black community. A lot of blues players, many of them women, left the church to pursue a career in the blues, and ended up going back at the end of their days. In *Warming by the Devil's Fire*, we mentioned how Son House, who was a preacher at one time, went to jail for murder in self-defense, came out, tried to be a preacher again, then went back to playing the blues. "Georgia Tom" (whose real name was Thomas A. Dorsey) wrote sexually graphic songs for Bessie Smith and others, then he went and wrote some wonderful, lyrical religious compositions later on. Sister Rosetta Tharpe and Reverend Gary Davis did the same thing.

This relationship between the sacred and the profane is the theme of *Warming by the Devil's Fire*. It tells the story of a young kid going back to Mississippi before he's twelve to get baptized. To get saved. But then he's kidnapped by his uncle Buddy—a blues person—who takes him around to experience what he's gonna be saved from. At the end, his other uncle, a preacher named Flem, finds him and puts him on the road to the mourner's bench. And years later, Uncle Buddy also ends up becoming a preacher.

When we started this project, I screened a lot of footage on the blues; if I hadn't, I probably would have made a relatively conventional documentary. But after seeing so many others, I began to think what could I add? How is this going to be different? I also had to consider how to frame the film—because there's so much to the blues, what do you include, who do you exclude? It took quite a while for me to sort these questions out, which must have frustrated Marty Scorsese.

The story I chose for *Warming by the Devil's Fire* isn't strictly autobiographical, but everything in the film happened to a certain extent, and I used these experiences as guideposts to come up with a story that everyone could identify with. I had an uncle who was very much like Buddy. Like the trickster figure in folklore, Buddy awakens things in his nephew and gives him experiences that will help him become a complete person. At the same time, I wanted to tell a story about the blues that echoed the form. There's play within the material; it tries to be loose. And the character played by Tommy Hicks—Uncle Buddy—personifies the feeling of the blues and embodies all of its contradictions.

The story's told from the perspective of the narrator, the young kid who returns to Mississippi and becomes aware of the blues as an art form. It's through his eyes that we, the audience, meet the blues. It's through his ears that we listen to the blues and come to appreciate them. The film includes a wide range of music, from raw gutbucket blues to the more sophisticated R&B, and is representative of both male and female singers.

I wanted to put the music in context, too. The blues came out of the South, and the South has its history of struggles, and it seemed to me you can't really separate the blues from their historical context: how people lived, the hardships they experienced, the texture of their daily lives—it was all related. I was looking for things that spoke to that period, that conveyed the harshness, the humor, and the contradictions. For example, we use a lot of footage of the horrible flood that devastated that part of Mississippi. Lives were lost. The whole economy was damaged. We showed the levee camps that sprang up as a result—another tragic period in the history of black labor. We used chain-gang images. For a black person in the South at the time, it didn't take very much to go to jail. You didn't have to do a serious crime—just look the wrong way. Out of those experiences came the elements for the blues.

The blues encompasses every emotion; people listen to the blues because the blues allows one to come to terms with basic instincts. And it speaks to the circumstances for blacks of an earlier time. When you look at the atmosphere surrounding the blues—racism, hard work and little to show for it; exploitation, humiliation, and the explosive life at the juke joint, where shootings and knife fights were not uncommon—

you get a picture of survival and the will to live and self-destruct at the same time.

I also wanted to include images that were in themselves moving, visual, cinematic. I really admire a work by James Agee called *Let Us Now Praise Famous Men*. He and Walker Evans went across the South and documented workers—black and white—during the Depression. What made that book remarkable was that it provided this sense of history told from a certain perspective. Yet Agee was also concerned about exploiting the subject; he wanted to be as objective as possible. The result was a document that gives a feeling of the period that would have been lost otherwise. That's one of the things I was trying to achieve—to go beyond information and convey a feeling for how these people lived and how they felt.

I grew up playing the trumpet, so W. C. Handy's music was the beginning; his were the first blues I learned how to play. Handy wasn't your typical vagabond blues player, like Robert Johnson and Blind Lemon Jefferson, traveling with a guitar on his back to find work on the street corners. Handy came from a middle-class family, which was unusual. His father wanted him to go to college and didn't think music was any way to make a living. But Handy had a lot of things going for him—he was one of the first African Americans to write and publish his own material. He followed his own dreams, went against his parents' wishes, and ended up being successful.

Handy went blind, then his sight came back, and finally he went permanently blind. I've always been interested in people who have to overcome a handicap like blindness, like Blind Lemon Jefferson, who managed to survive, hopping trains and singing in levee camps, the worst and most dangerous places to work, where there wasn't any law. That he was able to be imaginative and creative and have a sense of poetry under those circumstances is remarkable. His music and lyrics are incredibly moving, but the things he sings about are things you only want to experience vicariously.

During one scene in the film, Buddy plays a record by Lucille Bogan, a singer whose lyrics were very graphic sexually. Her records should be double X-rated; in fact, her first release was too raw to be released. When she sings about "nipples on my titties as big as the end of your thumb" and on and on, you get a clear sense of why the church was so opposed to the blues. On the other hand, Lucille Bogan can be seen as an important figure in that she was unabashed about her sexual desire at a time long before the so-called "sexual revolution." Bogan, Mamie Smith, Ma Rainey, Bessie Smith—these were women at the top of their game creatively who dealt openly with women's themes and issues.

Choosing the music was the hardest part—because there was so much great material to choose from. Every time I came back to the film, I'd wind up choosing another piece of music. To really get a sense of the blues, you'd need to do the impossible, by putting everything in. I chose a Sonny Boy Williamson song, for example, because he's a great singer/harmonica player, of course—but also because he was a character himself, someone with a great screen presence. When you do a film, you always have to consider casting. There were some wonderful musicians we could have used who, unfortunately, weren't as cinematically engaging. A lot of people who were essential to this era probably should have been included for historical reasons, but for dramatic reasons I wound up leaving them out. Movies don't allow for any lulls. So you go for the personality, what works well on the screen.

I wanted to have more of Bessie Smith and Billie Holiday in the film, in fact more of everyone. Especially the women, who came from vaudeville, which meant they had more professional training, as opposed to someone like Robert Johnson, who migrated and picked up things as he went. The early women singers had a big impact on the blues, particularly because of their record sales. They had huge audiences and helped spread the blues. The women had a unique role.

—Charles Burnett

Charles Burnett

Doug Cummings/2003

From *Film Journey* (filmjourney.org), November 13, 2003. Doug Cummings is a writer on film who lives in Los Angeles. Reprinted by permission.

Tuesday night, filmmaker Charles Burnett was invited to screen his new documentary, *Nat Turner: A Troublesome Property*, for a class here at Caltech and facilitate a Q&A afterward. A graduate of UCLA, Burnett is one of the most highly esteemed filmmakers currently working in the U.S. and he continues to be active in independent and black filmmaking circles. Although he has taken a less mainstream—and more ideologically nuanced—approach to his career than popular names like Spike Lee or Larry Clark, Burnett's films (including 1977's *Killer of Sheep*, 1990's *To Sleep with Anger*, and 1996's *Nightjohn*) are visually strong works with vivid characters and complex undertones. As Nelson Kim writes in *Senses of Cinema*:

> Charles Burnett is the epitome of a cult hero—almost famous for not being famous. On the rare occasion his work attracts any notice in the mainstream press, the article will be sure to mention how little attention his work receives in the mainstream press. Despite the public acclaim of critics and fellow filmmakers, the festival awards and retrospectives, the MacArthur Foundation "genius" grant, the Library of Congress' selection of *Killer of Sheep* for its National Film Registry—despite his legendary status among a small cohort of cinephiles, Burnett goes unrecognized by the larger culture, the pop marketplace. His films are known to few. But among those few they're loved by many.

Nat Turner (1800–1831) was a notorious plantation slave in Virginia who organized the only "successful" revolt in American slavery, forming a loose band of marauders who killed fifty-nine people in plantation homes before they were captured and executed. A physician named Thomas Gray interviewed Turner in jail and subsequently published *The Confessions of Nat Turner*, but historians now question its accuracy. In 1967, novelist William Styron fictionalized the events of the rebellion—as well as Turner's private life—and won a Pulitzer Prize for his efforts. While Styron's novel was widely praised in white literary and popular circles, it was criticized in the black community for framing Turner's actions in the context of a disturbed sexuality and his illicit love for a white plantation woman. Instead of viewing Turner as a folk hero who retaliated against his oppressors, Styron's novel suggested Turner was a psychologically disturbed murderer.

Burnett's documentary intercuts talking heads (historians, activists, and commentators) with beautifully filmed reenactments of the various images of Nat Turner through the years, from such sources as Gray's interview to Harriet Beecher Stowe's *Dred* (1856), Randolph Edmonds' 1935 theatrical production, and Styron's novel. The resulting *Rashomon*-like narrative structure presents various images and points of view allowing the viewer to come to his or her own conclusions. It's a provocative mosaic which moves from drama to reflection to exposition and back again with remarkable fluidity.

After the screening, the soft-spoken Burnett talked about his own conflicting thoughts regarding the film. In a refreshing way, he seemed as critical toward his film as any other viewer and commented on how difficult it was to find the funding for the project (a five-year process) and how the final product was a compromise in length (initially conceived at two hours, the film now runs a PBS-friendly fifty-eight minutes) and emphasis (instead of focusing on Turner's position as a folk hero, Styron and his novel are prominently featured). Burnett claims he could never obtain the financing to do the film he would really like to make, a feature about Turner's courage in the face of oppression and his heroic efforts to strike back. This conception of Turner would be impossible to promote, Burnett suggested, in a white-dominated culture that perpetually emphasizes the deaths of the plantation families rather than the horrifying realities of slavery.

It was at this point that several members of the audience—mostly young, white college students—began to openly question Burnett's perspective. "How can you call him a 'hero' if he killed so many people?" they asked. "We're talking about *oppressed people*," Burnett explained. "Sure, Turner's group killed about sixty people, but what is that compared to the five million people who were killed on the boats from Africa?" "Maybe what you're trying to say," one student offered Burnett, "is that you admire Turner's 'spirit' but not his actions?" No, Burnett assured the student, "Turner was a warrior fighting a system that was killing him and those around him on a daily basis—he certainly didn't establish or perpetuate the system of slavery." "Why don't they just keep talking about Harriet Tubman and Frederick Douglass?" one student asked.

As for myself, I was immediately reminded of two films I had seen in the last couple years. The first was Claude Lanzmann's 2001 follow-up to his landmark Holocaust documentary *Shoah* (1985), entitled *Sobibor, October 14, 1943, 2 P.M.*, which recounts the only successful armed revolt on record at a Nazi extermination camp. The surviving inmates conspired together and executed each one of their German guards using hatchets. Lanzmann's film is tough to sit through—it's told in unflinching detail by one of the revolt's participants, who describes the logistics and the brutal efficiency of his fellow conspirators. While their solution is unquestionably violent and shocking, no one in the theatre seemed to judge the Jews harshly for their act of desperation; at the end of the film, Lanzmann lists the numbers and dates of the people exterminated within Sobibor for years, and as each day ticks off additional thousands, the gruesomeness and unfathomable horror of oppression and suffering is simply overwhelming. Rather than a detached moral judgment of the ethics of resistance, one is left simply with a profound sense of sadness and empathy for the sufferers.

The other film I watched recently was *Sankofa* (1993), a powerful film about a fictional slave revolt that its director, Burnett's colleague Haile Gerima, described as his attempt to present a story about slaves taking fate into their own hands. "The plantation school of thought believed [resistance and rebellion] was always provoked by outsiders," Gerima said, "that Africans were not capable of having that human need [themselves]." *Sankofa* is one of the most successful independent films in history—because U.S. distributors and video chains like Blockbuster Video refused to carry it, Gerima and his staff have hand-carried the film across the U.S. and scheduled community screenings promoted solely through word-of-mouth. When Burnett suggests he could never obtain the financing for a film about a slave revolt, Gerima's film is a perfect example.

It struck me that there seemed to be a profound disconnect between many of the students in the room and the realities of the slave trade and plantation life in general. While most educated people would quickly denounce the institution of slavery, the resonant empathy we find in other oppressive situations—like the Holocaust—seemed to be utterly absent. Is it that our culture is simply more inundated with Holocaust imagery? Or is Burnett on to something when he suggests racial and class backgrounds continue to inform one's perceptions of these struggles? After experiencing the dynamics of the discussion on Tuesday, I'm inclined to agree with him.

Independent Lens: Charles Burnett

Scott Foundas/2006

Published in *LA Weekly*, April 20, 2006. Copyright © 2006 by *LA Weekly*. Reprinted with permission of Village Voice Media.

Charles Burnett's first feature film, *Killer of Sheep* (1977), remains to this day a near-mythic object, one of the first fifty films inducted into the Library of Congress's National Film Registry, yet rarely screened and never issued on video owing to unresolved copyright issues. Meanwhile, Burnett's second feature, *My Brother's Wedding* (1983), has suffered such a clandestine existence as to make *Killer of Sheep* seem like *Titanic* by comparison—when I spoke with Burnett during the course of writing this story, he told me that even he doesn't have a copy of it. And Burnett's work of the subsequent two decades has proved scarcely more available. Simply put, there may be no better contemporary American filmmaker whose films are more difficult to come by—or who has more richly evoked the infinite varieties and textures of life, black or otherwise, in our city.

He wasn't born here—who was?—but Burnett moved to Los Angeles from his native Mississippi as a child and took an engineering degree from LACC before, in the early 1970s, making his way to the film program at UCLA. There, in the company of classmates Billy Woodberry (*Bless Their Little Hearts*) and Haile Gerima (*Bush Mama*), he emerged as one of the leading lights in a movement of young African American filmmakers keen to show their people, and the city they inhabited, in ways rarely glimpsed in mainstream movies. Reflecting on their work in his 2003 essay film *Los Angeles Plays Itself,* Thom Andersen singled out Burnett as the herald of a "Los Angeles neo-realism" that ran in blinding contrast to cinematic depictions of L.A. as an oasis of beachside cottages, hilltop palaces and the upwardly mobile upper middle class—a city that ceased to exist south of the 10 freeway or east of the 110.

So the geography mapped by *Killer of Sheep* wasn't merely physical, but sociological—a South Central inhabited not just by pimps, hookers, and OGs, but by poverty-line families eking out meager existences while hoping against hope for change to come. Told as a series of episodes from the life of a Watts slaughterhouse worker struggling to hold his family together, even as his identification with the beasts he slays begins to weigh heavy on him, the film juxtaposes impressionistic fragments from the lives of the working poor against Paul Robeson singing "What Is America to Me?" And yet, what makes *Killer of Sheep* so unforgettable, so Renoir-like in its humanism, are the scatterings of joy Burnett finds amid the gray gloom: fleeting moments—a junk-strewn lot transformed into a playground by the power of a child's imagination, a husband and wife holding each other in a long-forgotten embrace—that are like mirages in a desert.

To see that film again today—on those rare occasions when one can see it—is to be reminded of just how much American movies in general, and African American movies in particular, have suffered for not having Burnett as a regular voice at the table. (Instead, we get well-heeled minstrel shows like *Crash* and *Hustle & Flow*.) Indeed, in the years following *Killer*, Burnett's own life ran nearly as lean as those of the characters he depicted. *My Brother's Wedding*, which told of a Watts dry cleaner marooned somewhere between the professional aspirations of his family and the thug lives of his friends, was plagued by production problems (including the quitting of the lead actor—twice) and never properly released. And by the time of a 1997 *New York Times* profile tellingly headlined "A Director Who Collects Honors, Not Millions," Burnett was candid about the fact that were it not for the MacArthur Foundation "genius grant" he received in 1988, he might have had to abandon his filmmaking career altogether.

Luckily he didn't, and the result was *To Sleep with Anger* (1990), one of the great movies of the nineties and a magnificent dark comedy about how the arrival of a meddlesome stranger (brilliantly played by Danny Glover) sparks a collision of tradition and modernity, religion and superstition, for an extended middle-class family. Another story of Watts, it is a soulful evocation of a place spilling over with black history and folklore, where backyards teem with hen houses and chicken coops, where God works in mysterious ways and where Old Scratch himself may show up on your doorstep with a couple of tattered suitcases and his hat in his hand. It was also the first of Burnett's films to achieve something close to wide distribution, and he followed it in 1994 with an honest-to-goodness Miramax movie, *The Glass Shield*, a bristling fact-based story of racism and other wrongdoing in the Los Angeles County Sheriff's office.

Burnett's characters are forever wrestling with demons—literally in the case of the eponymous protagonist of the underrated farce *The Annihilation of Fish* (1999); figuratively for *The Glass Shield*'s idealistic black deputy navigating his way through an all-white precinct, or for the rebel slave Nat Turner, the subject of an excellent 2003 Burnett documentary. Burnett himself is no stranger to demon wrestling. For all his triumphs, he has too rarely been able to make films on his own terms, and so he has turned increasingly to television, where the material hasn't always been deserving of his gifts (an exception being the lyrical and touching Disney Channel feature *Nightjohn*, about a freed slave who returns to plantation life in order to teach other slaves how to read). There are hopeful signs: As this article goes to press, Burnett is in the final editing stages on what may be his most ambitious project to date—a biopic of Sam Nujoma, the first president of Namibia—and the folks at the invaluable Milestone Film & Video confirm that their long-standing project to issue both *Killer of Sheep* and *My Brother's Wedding* on DVD should reach fruition by year's end. Not that Burnett seems likely to ever rest on his laurels. Such, to borrow the title of his recent film on the history of blues music, would be to risk warming by the devil's fire.

Charles Burnett, in a photo taken in Los Angeles around the time *Killer of Sheep* was in production, in the mid-1970s. Courtesy of Charles Burnett and Milestone Film and Video.

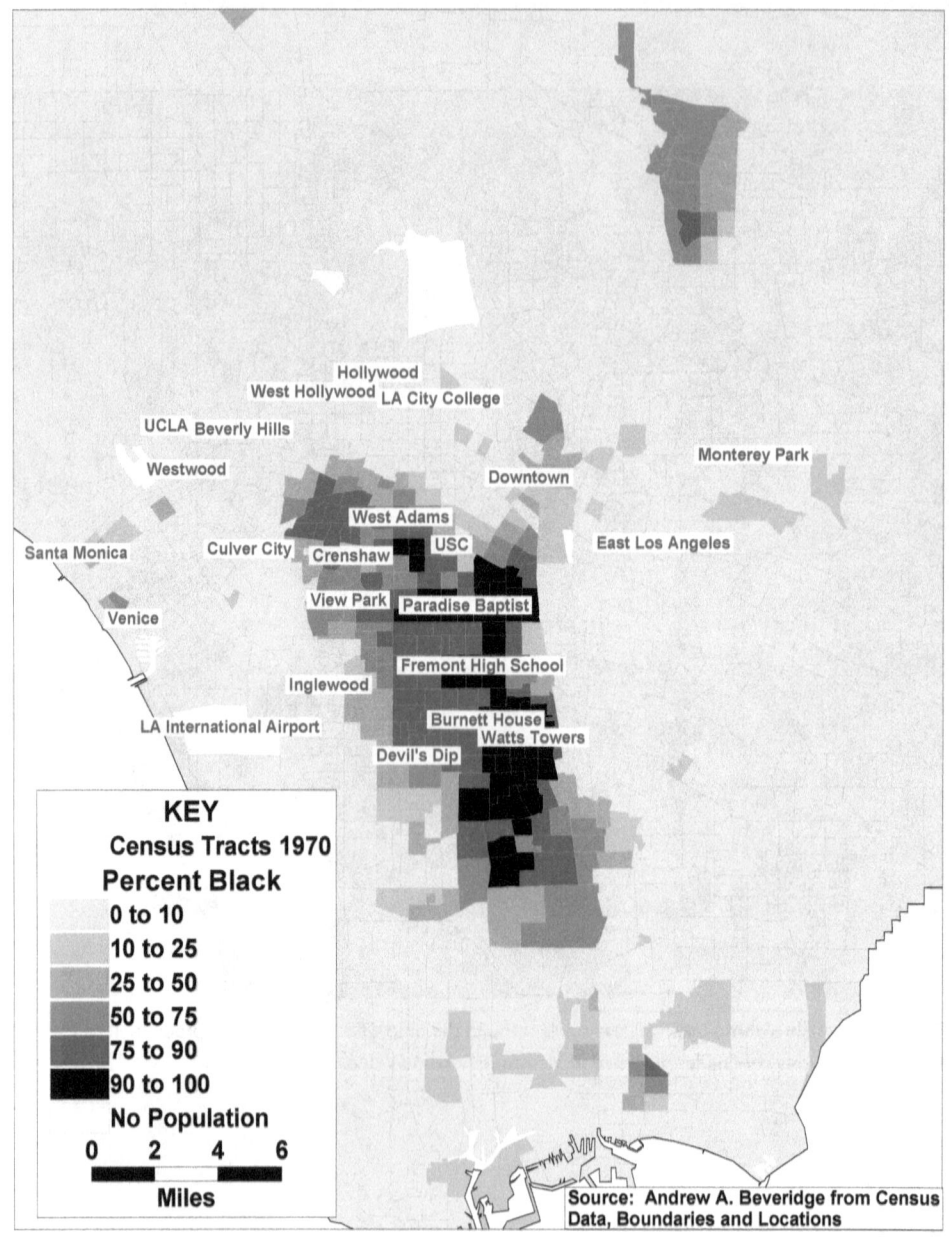

Charles Burnett's Los Angeles, Circa 1970: His Neighborhood

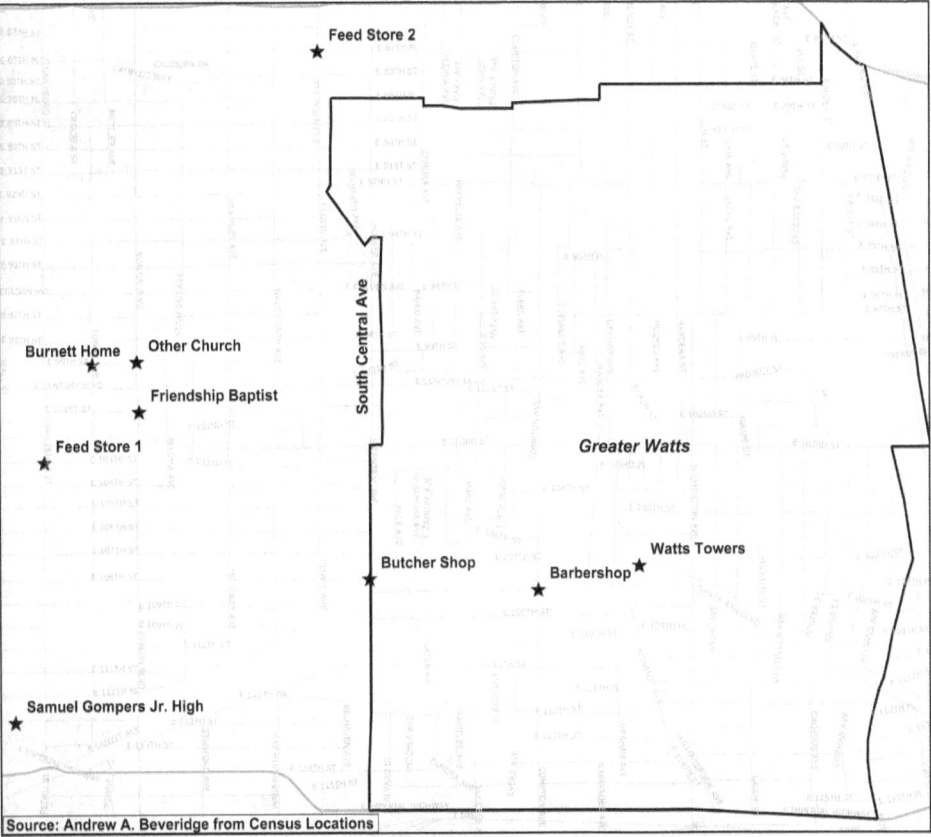

Source: Andrew A. Beveridge from Census Locations

Burnett Home: Burnett and his family lived at 99th and Towne (one mile west of Watts). The scene about the stolen TV from *Killer of Sheep* was shot in the backyard.
Churches: Local churches Burnett attended as a child. The Paradise Baptist Church he used to go to with his grandmother was until 1961 located near East Los Angeles, not far from where the Burnett family lived before moving to South Central in the early 1950s.
Butcher shop: Used as the butcher shop setting in *Killer of Sheep*.
Feed stores: These establishments sold chickens and all sorts of animals you could raise, contributing to the southern rural feel of South Central so effectively captured in Burnett's films, especially *Killer of Sheep* and *To Sleep with Anger*.
Barbershop: Located in Watts, this barbershop is the setting for the anecdote Burnett tells about Paul Robeson's reputation among the barbershop regulars.
Central Avenue: The western boundary of Watts. In the 1940s, according to Burnett, "If you were black, you had to live east of Central Avenue." When Burnett's parents moved from Mississippi to Los Angeles in the late 1940s, they first settled several miles east of Central before moving in the early fifties to their residence one mile west of the avenue.
Devil's Dip: The makeshift playground of Burnett's youth; inspiration for scenes of children playing in *Killer of Sheep*.
Samuel Gompers Junior High School and **Fremont High School** are schools that Burnett attended.
Watts Towers: A Los Angeles landmark and one of the great works of folk art.
West Adams: The once affluent middle-class black area where *To Sleep with Anger* was filmed.

Childhood scenes, Watts, as depicted in *Killer of Sheep* (1977), released by Milestone Film and Video, 2007. Courtesy of Milestone Film and Video.

A husband and wife experience a fleeting moment of joy, *Killer of Sheep* (1977). Courtesy of Milestone Film and Video.

A still from *My Brother's Wedding* (1983), released by Milestone Film and Video, 2007. Courtesy of Milestone Film and Video.

Burnett on the set of *To Sleep with Anger*. © 1990 SVS, Inc. All Rights Reserved. Courtesy of Sony Pictures Entertainment and the Academy of Motion Picture Arts and Sciences.

Danny Glover as "Harry" casts his spell, *To Sleep with Anger*. © 1990 SVS, Inc. All Rights Reserved. Courtesy of Sony Pictures Entertainment and the Academy of Motion Picture Arts and Sciences.

Carl Lumbly and Allison Jones in *Nightjohn*, 1996. Courtesy of RHI Entertainment and the Walker Art Center.

James Earl Jones as "Fish" and Lynn Redgrave as "Poinsettia" in *The Annihilation of Fish*, 1999. Courtesy of American Sterling and the Academy of Motion Picture Arts and Sciences.

Danny Glover's character celebrates the liberation of Namibia, *Namibia: The Struggle for Liberation* (2007). Courtesy of Cinema Libre Studio.

Turner Classic Movies Celebrates Martin Luther King Jr. Day with Charles Burnett Primetime Retrospective, January 21, 2008. Courtesy of the Academy of Motion Picture Arts and Sciences.

The poster and press kit cover of Burnett's most acclaimed film. Courtesy of Milestone Film and Video and the Academy of Motion Picture Arts and Sciences.

Burnett, June 6, 1997, at the Walker Art Center in Minneapolis at a screening of *Nightjohn* (1996). Courtesy of Charles Burnett and the Walker Art Center.

Shadow of Watts, in the Light

Dave Kehr/2007

From the *New York Times*, March 25, 2007. © 2007 The New York Times. All rights reserved. Used by permission and protected by the Copyright Laws of the United States. The printing, copying, redistribution, or retransmission of the Material without express written permission is prohibited.

With the click of a mouse, Kathy Thomson brings a face out of the darkness—the face of a young African American woman, looking with sadness and concern out of a small screened window in a white frame house. The face belongs to the actress Kaycee Moore, a star of Charles Burnett's 1977 debut feature *Killer of Sheep*, and it has been hidden in shadows for almost thirty years.

Burnett, who directed, wrote, produced, edited, and shot *Killer of Sheep*, hasn't seen Moore's face in quite this way since he first photographed it. Back then, he was a student filmmaker shooting on the run with no money to spend on equipment and even less time to set it up, and he wasn't able to light Moore so that she would stand out against the dim interior. But now that *Killer of Sheep* itself is coming out of the shadows, there is a little bit of time and money to go back and make the fixes that were impossible three decades ago.

Thomson is a colorist for Modern Videofilm, the company here that is transferring *Killer of Sheep* to video for its first DVD release, one of many steps in the complicated process of resurrecting a film many consider a lost masterpiece. It is Thomson's job to go through a film, frame by frame, and make the adjustments in color and contrast that make an image pop on the screen.

Looking over her shoulder Burnett was impressed by her magic. "That's nice," he said softly, as one by one the images of *Killer of Sheep* took on a density and detail that had been dormant for years.

Burnett, then a thirty-three-year-old graduate student at the University of California, Los Angeles, made *Killer of Sheep* as his thesis film. Working on weekends when he could gather his largely nonprofessional cast together, he used equipment checked out of the university—"Easy access to those cameras and editing machines was the reason I put off graduating as long as I could," he said—and much of the black-and-white film stock was salvaged from production houses, which would often give the young student filmmakers their "short ends," partially used reels of negative that still contained a few minutes of shooting time.

Burnett never dreamed that his film would get a commercial release. But today *Killer of Sheep* is widely acknowledged as one of the most insightful and authentic dramas about African American life on film, as well as one of the earliest examples of the politically aware black independent cinema that was taking shape in the 1970s.

And in the years since, even as it has become almost impossible to see, *Killer of Sheep* has gathered a reputation as one of the finest American films, period. In 1988 Burnett received a MacArthur Foundation "genius" grant on the basis of *Killer of Sheep* and made his second feature, *My Brother's Wedding*; in 1990 *Killer of Sheep* was named to the National Film Registry of the Library of Congress.

Where has *Killer of Sheep* been? "It was never meant to be shown in public," Burnett said, explaining why he had never obtained permission to use the musical passages—marvelously apposite choices of blues, pop, and jazz—that accompany and accentuate his images. Even though the fragile 16-millimeter film itself had been restored and transferred to 35 millimeters by the UCLA film preservationist Ross Lipman in 2000, no distributor was willing to take on a title with such conspicuous legal problems. The cost of tracking down the owners of the music rights and compensating them seemed to far outweigh any potential profit.

Enter Dennis Doros, who, with his wife, Amy Heller, runs Milestone Film & Video, a boutique distributor with an unconventional catalogue—silent films, travel documentaries, philosophical Asian dramas—that reflects the taste of its founders. Doros heard about the restoration from his friend Lipman, and after meeting with Burnett, decided to take the plunge.

"We thought it would take about six months to get the music clearances," Doros said. "That was six years ago."

The rights ended up costing $150,000, far more than the small company could afford. The director Steven Soderbergh providentially stepped forward with a gift of $75,000, and the project was saved. Milestone plans to open it in theaters around the country this spring, beginning Friday at the IFC Center in Manhattan. A DVD release will follow in the fall.

There is nothing else in American movies quite like *Killer of Sheep*. Thematically the film is a reaction against the "blaxploitation" films that were filling downtown theaters in the early seventies. There are no supercops or superpimps in Burnett's Watts, the neighborhood he has lived in (or near) since his family moved to Los Angeles from Vicksburg, Miss., when he was a child.

This is a community of working-class strivers doing what they can to keep their families together, glimpsed in a series of impressionistic images and fragmented scenes, its rhythms those of chance happenings rather than a four-square, three-act plot. Burnett has directed seventeen movies of varying length since graduate school, including *To Sleep with Anger* (1990) and the television film *The Wedding* (1998), but *Killer of Sheep* remains his most free-spirited creation, the work of a naturally gifted artist who has not yet learned what rules he is breaking.

The hero of *Killer of Sheep* is an earnest young man named Stan (Henry Gayle Sanders). In the perpetual grip of an indefinable sadness, Stan struggles to support his wife (Moore), his son (Jack Drummond) and his small daughter (Angela Burnett, a niece of the filmmaker), by working in a slaughterhouse. He is a killer of sheep, processing the animals that pass through the killing floor, but he is also a counter of sheep, a man who can't sleep, eaten away by unnamed anxieties.

Stan is both an executioner and a victim, forced to acquiesce to a brutal system if he is to preserve what is most tender and fine in his life. But the film frequently wanders away from its main character, following Stan's son as he goes off to play games of war in an empty lot (in scenes that strikingly anticipate David Gordon Green's 2000 film, *George Washington*) or observing Stan's wife as she carefully applies her makeup, hoping to rekindle Stan's romantic interest.

Burnett remembers meeting Sanders, his leading man, when they shared an elevator in a Wilshire Boulevard building, where Burnett, then working as an assistant in a management company to put himself through college, was dropping off a script.

"I thought Henry was the saddest-looking man I'd ever seen, like he had the whole weight of the world on his shoulders," said Burnett, "so I asked him if he'd ever done any acting."

As it turned out, Sanders, a Vietnam veteran who had moved to Los Angeles hoping to turn his autobiographical novel into a play, had already appeared in a handful of films, including one directed by Bobby Roth, a UCLA classmate of Burnett's.

"You'd better be careful who you get in an elevator with," said Sanders, now sixty-four and still a working actor and playwright. "You might end up in a motion picture."

When *Killer of Sheep* finally opens, it will be the same strange, beautiful, despairing, and hopeful film that Charles Burnett made in 1977, though with one small change. At the end the film returns to the abattoir where Stan works, and as we watch him angrily, almost brutally, driving the sheep from their pen to the slaughterhouse floor, we hear Dinah Washington's smoky, romantic recording of "Unforgettable."

Because the owner of the publishing rights to "Unforgettable" ultimately declined to lease them to Doros, that song has been replaced by Washington's searing interpretation of "This Bitter Earth." A more pointed choice, perhaps, but in the context of the film a no less complex one: it's the same song that Stan and his wife dance to earlier in the film, alone together in their sparely furnished living room on a sunlit afternoon, the movie's most deeply felt moment of peace and trust.

A Vision of Watts Still Frozen in Time

Mary McNamara/2007

Published in *Los Angeles Times*, April 1, 2007. Reprinted by permission.

Most student films, mercifully, do not get theatrical distribution. Certainly not thirty years after they were shot or with the combined efforts of crack film preservationists and a most persistent specialty film distributor. But *Killer of Sheep*, which will open Friday at the Nuart, is not an ordinary film.

The UCLA film-school thesis project of Charles Burnett (*To Sleep with Anger, The Glass Shield*) is instead a cinematic tone poem, an elegy, perhaps, or an ode to a certain time and place. Set in Watts during the mid-seventies, *Killer of Sheep* refers to Stan, the main character, a husband and father trapped by his job in a slaughterhouse. There is a loosely constructed plot, but the film focuses on the quiet beauty of the mundane: a group of kids throwing rocks in a train yard, a young woman announcing her pregnancy, a couple dancing in their living room. The message that emerges—life is difficult but lovely just the same—is as understated as it is heroic, and in a sense, applies to the man who made the film.

Shot on 16mm film, using mostly non-actors—friends and neighbors and kids—*Killer of Sheep* was Burnett's response to the era's blaxploitation films, his attempt to show life as it really was for many black families.

"Hollywood, I don't think, tries to portray things realistically," he says. "When they make movies about the community, you only see drug movies or violence. That perception of black people," he adds, "still exists."

He went into Watts and used regular people rather than actors, he says, because he wanted to demystify filmmaking for members of his neighborhood. "When I was growing up," he says, "the idea of becoming a cinematographer was like going to the moon. Kids came up to us, they didn't even know what the camera was. Spike [Lee] has done a great job since then. He's pretty much a household name."

Burnett, however, is not, unless your household includes one or more dedicated cinephiles. Then his name evokes reverence; bring up *Killer of Sheep* and reverence turns to awe.

Earning high marks

With its almost palpable tenderness and artistic imagery, the film became a film-school favorite, used in classes as an example of an exemplary student film and making the festival rounds until it won an award in Berlin four years after it was made. The Library of Congress chose it as one of the first fifty films on the National Film Registry, and the National Society of Film Critics selected it as one of the "100 Essential Films" of all time.

Meanwhile, the world changed, not only in Watts but in the film industry, where film school became too often a mere steppingstone to the studios and independent film took on a brand. But Burnett remained as he was—devoted to telling stories from real life. To *Sleep with Anger* (1990) considered the impact a sweet-talking con man has on a family, *The Glass Shield* (1994), often cited as a precursor to the more over-the-top *Training Day*, takes on fear and racism in the Los Angeles Police Department.

Burnett, a soft-spoken man who looks years younger than his age (sixty), is best known in the film community as a man of reserve and integrity. "Charles is often called the best black American director," says Ross Lipman, a film preservationist at UCLA. "I think he is simply one of the best American directors, and *Killer of Sheep* is one of the best American films ever."

Lipman is the man behind the film's theatrical release. Seven years ago, he was part of a team that received a Sundance grant to restore eight films, including *Killer of Sheep*. Although the film reels were deteriorating, Lipman and his colleagues were able to painstakingly pull out the quality of the original and blow it up to 35mm.

Lipman was so impressed with the finished product that he called Dennis Doros at Milestone Films. But quality is not the only reason student films are not distributed theatrically—Burnett had used a lot of music in his film, and none of it had been through the licensing channels. It took Doros six years of nagging and persuasion and $142,000 worth of check-writing to get the necessary permission. "I just couldn't give up on this film," says Doros.

"Charles is one of the most humane directors in cinema," Doros says.

For Burnett, the process has evoked, understandably, a good deal of nostalgia. "Seeing it now," he says, "it's more emotional. It's a community that doesn't exist, a place that doesn't exist. Now there is so much violence, so many drive-by shootings."

But if being seen as an underappreciated artist bothers Burnett, it doesn't show. He is working on *Nujoma: Where Others Wavered*, a feature film funded by the recently formed Namibian Film Commission about the life of that country's first president. After that, who knows?

"I've had chances to make commercial films," he says, "but I have an attitude problem."

It's not that he's arrogant or belligerent, he says, he just doesn't want to do films that exploit people. "One time they wanted me to do a film but concentrate on the drugs and violence [in the African American community]. I said, 'People have already seen that, and it doesn't reflect necessarily the whole picture.' That," he adds with a rueful smile, "doesn't go over well."

After thirty years in the business, he says, he still doesn't understand why people talk the way they do in meetings. "You have to really sell your projects, and I'm not good at that. It's like they're speaking a different language. Sometimes," he says with a laugh, "I don't even have to say anything to get in trouble. They can tell by the look on my face."

He remembers a time, he says, when people made films to make films, not to make money. "Not that there aren't people doing that today," he says. He cites the Pan African Film & Arts Festival as a refuge for filmmakers telling real stories. And every year a few righteous movies go mainstream. "I think it's good that independent films are being recognized," he says. "*Brokeback Mountain, Little Miss Sunshine*. All films that deal with social issues are good, they just take a different angle."

Over coffee at the corner of Motor and Venice, Burnett radiates a calmness that borders on serenity. He is, as they say, very real. He lives with his wife and two sons in Viewpark. He answers his own phone, sets up his own interviews. There will be no industry air-kisses here.

Danny Glover remembers the imperturbability of Burnett from years ago, when he starred in *To Sleep with Anger*. "Everything would be crazy on the shoot, just crazy," says Glover. "And there would be Charles, perfectly calm, like the eye of the storm."

Whether he's speaking about the idiosyncrasies of filmmaking or the drug problem in present-day Watts, Burnett's tone is matter-of-fact. In conversation, as in his films, the ugly truths of life are just that—ugly, true, and part of life.

He tells a story to illustrate what he sees as the continuing arrogance, and racism, of the industry: A film crew had set up in his neighborhood and Burnett, riding by on his bike, asked what was going on. "This grip looks at me and says, 'It's too difficult to explain,'" Burnett says with a smile that is truly amused. "Too difficult to explain. To me."

So yes, he and Spike Lee have done a good job of demystifying filmmaking in the black community, but filmmakers remain fairly mystified about the black community, which, Burnett says, is continually portrayed in a stereotypical way.

"They said this year's Oscars was so diverse. Why? Because two black people won? Two? Because there were a few Spanish people nominated?" He raises his eyebrows skeptically. "That's diverse? Come on," he adds. "The entertainment-type movies they make are all a distortion."

Not that he denies that drugs and violence are a problem in Los Angeles. "I don't know if you believe the conspiracy theories about Iran-Contra," he says, "how [the CIA] came into the community with guns and the drugs and destroyed it. But I do know that overnight there were AK-47s on the street and these kids, none of whom were scientists, suddenly knew how to make crack. I think that would be a good movie, if you could figure out how to tell it."

Wounded by injustice

Unlike other filmmakers who he says exploit the violence in neighborhoods like South Central, Burnett would like to make a film that addresses the issues without blaming the victims.

"You go to the schools today and they look like prisons," he says. "The blacks and the Hispanics are fighting over crumbs. Where else can a child be shot in the head—something that occurs on a regular basis—and it goes in the back of the paper and no one cares? We might as well be living in Iraq. If this had been in a white community, there would have been an emerging plan."

He speaks and there is passion in his voice, passion and indignation, but not necessarily anger, at least not how anger normally plays, though he says he has been harassed by police officers and has had to teach his sons that cops don't need a reason to pull a tall young black driver over or give him a hard time. He may not be happy at the state of the city or the state of the industry, but he also knows that his life has turned out better than many of those around him.

"A lot of the people I was at school with don't make movies anymore. So by that light, I am very, very successful," he says. Sure, he'd like to make a big film that would make a lot of money so he could take even better care of his family, but he still does what he does for the reason he began.

"I like to do good movies. A good movie has such a positive impact. It can humanize people, explain conflicts that are significant in a way people can understand."

This Bitter Earth

James Ponsoldt/2007

Published in *Filmmaker*, Spring 2007. Reprinted by permission.

"When I stumbled across a 16mm print of *Killer of Sheep* at film school in North Carolina, it was like finding gold. I had never seen an American film quite like it . . . raw, honest simplicity that left me sitting there in an excited silence. It echoed throughout *George Washington*, the first film that David Gordon Green and I made together."
—Tim Orr, cinematographer (*All the Real Girls, Raising Victor Vargas*)

What sort of anxiety exists in the influence of a visionary masterpiece that is virtually unknown by a majority of the mainstream audience?

According to music apocrypha, Brian Eno said, "Only about a thousand people ever bought a Velvet Underground album, but every one of them formed a rock 'n' roll band."

Now consider Charles Burnett's *Killer of Sheep*, shot for less than ten thousand dollars in the Watts community of southern Los Angeles during the seventies and considered a seminal film in the canon of independent cinema.

Have you seen it?

If the answer is no, there's a good reason.

While radically divergent in content, *Killer of Sheep* is a kindred spirit to Todd Haynes's first film, *Superstar: The Karen Carpenter Story*, and *Cocksucker Blues* (photographer Robert Frank's anarchic, drug-fueled 1972 Rolling Stones tour documentary) in that it's been legally prevented for decades from having a commercial release. But unlike those two mythically "unseen" films, *Killer of Sheep* has finally overcome its legal hurdles—a stellar soundtrack by luminaries like Paul Robeson, Dinah Washington, Louis Armstrong, Scott Joplin, and Earth, Wind &

Fire, among others, was largely uncleared—and is now, on its thirtieth anniversary, in theatrical release from Milestone Films with a restored 35mm print by the UCLA Film and Television Archive.

Killer of Sheep, Charles Burnett's thesis film for UCLA, which he wrote, directed, shot, edited, and produced, won prizes at the Berlin Film Festival and Sundance (then called the U.S. Film Festival) in the early eighties, was labeled one of the "100 Essential Films" by the National Society of Film Critics in 2002 and declared a "national treasure" by the Library of Congress. Often referred to as an American *Bicycle Thief*, Burnett's film may have more in common with the stories of James Joyce, who was famously obsessed with allowing his characters to experience "epiphanies," which the author defined in *Stephen Hero* as "a sudden spiritual manifestation, whether in the vulgarity of speech or of gesture or in a memorable phase of the mind itself."

In the opening scene of *Killer of Sheep*, a man lectures his son for not defending his brother in a fight. The father, only inches from the boy's face, says, "You are not a child anymore. You soon will be a goddamn man."

The boy's mother, busy consoling the beaten-up and crying brother, his head in her lap, walks across the room with a serene expression on her face and, without saying a word, smacks her son across the cheek.

The boy takes it like a man.

Like a man.

This notion is at the core of *Killer of Sheep*: what it means to be an adult, and how children learn and internalize grown-up behavior and responsibilities through lectures, through tears, but mostly by silently observing, peeking around corners, usually unbeknownst to their parents. The children of *Killer of Sheep* are witnesses, sponges—loved and shielded, but not ignorant.

What do these children see?

Men like Stan (Henry Gayle Sanders)—a husband, father, and worker in a slaughterhouse, where he hustles sheep to the killing floor, then cleans up the resulting mess. Stan arrives home exhausted, stressed, and unable to please his wife (Kaycee Moore). When he buys a car for "fifteen dollars—and a shirt for collateral" with his friend Eugene (Eugene Cherry), believing that a new ride will prove his worth as a man and a provider, the extended vérité scene that follows, involving a steep hill, an open pickup truck, and poor planning, ends hilariously. Yet the expression on Stan's face as the motor—and with it his mechanized dreams—crashes to the concrete is one of unspeakable devastation.

Still, every morning, Stan goes to work.

While people in the neighborhood steal television sets and disrespect their elders, and thugs plot murders, Stan returns to the slaughterhouse. While the children in the neighborhood play in empty lots, throw rocks and dirt, leap from rooftop to rooftop, learn to imitate the bathroom beauty rituals of their mothers, joyous and fearless and unaware of their own poverty, Stan mops up animal blood. What the children don't know about their parents' jobs can't hurt them, and their play fights bring only crocodile tears.

But the tension created when a young daughter innocently, perhaps naïvely watches her tired father reject his wife's sexual advances, or when children on skateboards zip into the street, unconcerned about oncoming traffic, instills a feeling of minor dread that the youth in *Killer of Sheep* are on the verge of discovering adulthood, with all its burdens and violence. As an audience member, you want the bliss of youth to be pure and perpetual, but of course that's impossible. The kids must learn to be adults at some point. And like the sheep in the factory watching their kin bleed from the ceiling, unaware that they're next, the wait can be heartbreaking.

In a scene midway through the film, an adult character lies on the floor, having just been jumped, and he's told that he always feels sorry for himself, to which he replies, "If I don't, nobody else will."

Killer of Sheep doesn't ask the viewer to feel sorry for the characters in the film, but simply to respect them, to listen to them, to recognize that they aren't giving up, and that they deserve a dignity most films would deny them. It is a film so perfect that it seems impervious to time, as though it's always existed, yet it is so humane, so poetically rendered, that one can't help but utter, with astonishment and gratitude, the supreme compliment: In *Killer of Sheep*, the characters feel alive!

Many critics' Best of 2006 lists were topped by a French film, *Army of Shadows*, by Jean-Pierre Melville, completed thirty-seven years earlier yet never theatrically released in the U.S. until last year. Although many distributors won't release this year's contenders until the fall, it would be shocking if a finer film than *Killer of Sheep*—American or otherwise—is released in 2007. The film is currently out in limited release by Milestone Films.

JP: So you've been in the studio dealing with some music issues on *Killer of Sheep*?

CB: I made it as a student film, and it wasn't meant to be screened theatrically. I made the film and just put all the music in. There wasn't an issue [then] with the rights for the music, but little did I know that today it would become an issue. Dennis Doros at Milestone had a Sisyphean situation. The people that had the rights to the song "Unforgettable" refused to grant him the rights, so that was a big delay. Finally, we decided to repeat one of the earlier Dinah Washington songs [in its place]. There's another song—"Poet and Peasant Overture"—that we're also going to have to replace.

JP: Is this the first time you've tinkered with *Killer of Sheep* since initially completing it?

CB: Yeah. It's the first time I've spent so much time watching it in years. It's hard to take. It's nostalgic, certainly. You see the community in which it was made, and it really was a community. Over the years it's been devastated in many ways. Since we made the film, it's become dispersed, people have moved out, crack cocaine became an issue, gang violence—in the eighties it was very bad. It's mellowed out a bit now, but it's still not the same. Looking back over what you might call "an age of innocence" is tough to watch.

JP: Rewatching *Killer of Sheep*, do you think your craft has changed? Would you do the same things now?

CB: I don't think so. That was an experiment in many ways. Every time you do something it's an experiment to some extent. You want to go further and further. It was a style suited for what I was trying to do—to get into the reality where you wouldn't impose your values on it. To try to make it look as documentary-like as possible. I just set up the camera and caught the people doing their thing. It was very manipulative in that sense.

JP: What were your expectations for *Killer of Sheep* if you made it just as a thesis for UCLA?

CB: It was a time in the seventies when there wasn't distribution like there is now. This was made as a demonstration to show the working class who they were. There were a lot of student films about the working class and the poor that had no connection. A lot of people were making films where they said if you do ABC, then D will happen; there will be some sort of resolution. But life just isn't like that. [*Killer of Sheep*] was an attempt to make a film about the people I grew up with and their concerns. I hoped it would be shown in a context where there would be a conversation about the working class, where it could be used as a visual aid. There's obviously no simple solutions to the problems, and that's what I was addressing and reacting to.

JP: You talked about how the community where you filmed has changed. Do you think *Killer of Sheep* functions as a time capsule? Do you think it's—

CB: Relevant?

JP: No, I absolutely think it's relevant. But how do you think the film relates to the world in 2007 versus the world in 1977?

CB: I think you can see the seeds of some of the future in the film. The Watts riots were in '65, and we filmed in the early seventies, and you can see that little was done to help the community. In a way, you look back and it's even worse now in many ways. Then, to some degree, you could get a job doing manual labor, but now everything is so technical. Then you could at least pick up a trade from your family, who were carpenters, or plumbers, and now you have to go to school for it. In the film there's an anti-southern thing, like the son calling his mother "my dear," which is like a country code-word, and she tells him not to say that. There was a rejection of certain values, but you sort of need those foundations.

JP: Do you think you were trying to explore how rural, or southern values, can exist within a more metropolitan environment like Los Angeles?

CB: More so in [my subsequent features] *To Sleep with Anger* and *My Brother's Wedding*. Growing up, it was a constant clash. If you were from the South, people called you "country." It was a negative more than a positive. But if somehow you let those [southern] values seep in, through osmosis or whatever, you look at your life and realize [they are] relevant. You find people who don't have those values, and it's like they're missing something. I feel sorry for people who didn't come up with any value system. In the neighborhood where I grew up, the neighbors were like extended family. That's all missing now—most of it. Los Angeles is so urban now, but it used to be full of vast, open spaces. It was rural—like Tom Sawyer and Huckleberry Finn! You could see for miles. City Hall was the biggest building. You could see the mountains every day. You could have chickens, rabbits, ducks—anything—in your backyard. It was a great place to be at that time. It felt country. There was a sense of community. Now it's really dirty. If you go to Africa, in some parts it's like it's brand-new—there you can see for miles and it's not polluted. You go through Namibia and there are elephants on the road. There's a sense of newness. It's not totally exploited.

JP: I read that you wanted to make a film during your UCLA days about the black revolution, and you told this to some older men, and they laughed at you. I find your films both incredibly human and political. Do you feel like your films are an attempt to reconcile anger, political anger, with telling gentle stories about human behavior?

CB: I didn't want to make a revolutionary film about taking over the city or the world, necessarily. What happened was that I was thinking about how to make a film that reflected the reality of the situation. I used to get my hair cut in Watts at a particular barbershop, and there was always some conversation or argument with these older guys inside. I went in there one time, and it was Paul Robeson's birthday or something. I was excited, but their attitude was against Robeson because they felt he'd turned against his country. They were talking about a guy who was a spokesperson for injustice all over the world! So we got into a big debate, and they were saying things like, "I'll give you a plane ticket to Russia if you promise not to come back." Then I realized that they'd lived through the war, they were from the South, they'd been through segregation, and yet they still had a profound patriotism and love of America. It was hard for me to reconcile. They weren't a part of the Watts rebellion; they were responsible people who were into supporting America. They believed in the system. It made me look closely at people who were, say, economically at the lower end but who still believed politically that they had opportunities and who never thought of themselves as poor because they were working and making a living. It was an eye-opener in many ways.

JP: At what age did you first think that you'd like to hold a camera, or perhaps make a film?

CB: I grew up watching films on an old black-and-white television. I always wanted to do still photography but never had a chance. This guy I knew in high school had an 8mm camera, and it was the first time I'd seen or touched one, and I [filmed] an airplane. It was a really interesting thrill. Then I forgot about it, and I was into electronics and thinking I'd be drafted. Then I discovered the student deferment program. [My] reason for going to school was to stay out of the draft. I was going to get a degree in electronics, and I started taking creative writing classes. I was also working at the library and started going to movies before my job would start. Then I decided I wanted to do cinematography and checked out schools. USC was too expensive, but UCLA said, "Come on over," so that's what I did. So I never made a distinction. In my mind, a filmmaker wrote, directed, edited, shot—whatever it takes to get the film done.

JP: With all its accolades, is it hard to consider *Killer of Sheep* a student film?

CB: It was done as a student film—as a thesis film. So it is.

JP: Do you think there was freedom in that? I mean, if someone else put up the money and you knew it would be theatrically released, do you think you would have done things differently?

CB: I wouldn't have done that film any other way, because that was the whole point: doing it the way I made it, doing it anti-Hollywood. It wasn't going to be a commercial film.

JP: Has your writing process changed since you made *Killer of Sheep*?

CB: It changes all the time.

JP: How so?

CB: Each time you look at a blank piece of paper, you wonder how you're going to do it, starting from scratch. Your stories just take a different form. You can try to impose a structure, but that doesn't always work. One of the criticisms I've received is that people will say something like, "You didn't make another *Killer of Sheep*." Folks want you to keep making the same movie over and over. But I've done that. There're other issues, other interpretations. You want to do something that's new and interesting and challenging. And each one is like starting all over again.

JP: When I read about you, the two people whose names are often mentioned are Chekhov and Jean Renoir. I'm sure you get that a lot.

CB: No, I haven't. Or, not enough, maybe! I think Renoir gets mentioned because I refer to him a lot. One of the first films about the South that really moved me was one of his films, *The Southerner*. One of the things I liked about *The Southerner* was the humanity and the broad spectrum of life in it. It wasn't just about whites patronizing blacks. You saw people on an equal scale. It's a rarity to see blacks given the same type of justice and humanity—I think that's what attracted me to the film. In *La Grande Illusion* you see blacks in the background while World War I was going on. You wouldn't see that in an American film. It's amazing that Hollywood could look at reality and then distort it out of prejudice, and it's really painful when you see that continuing in American films. When I was coming up in school, there weren't any positive images of black people, and that affected the children in the community who needed nurturing and support and who weren't getting it from the institutions in this society. Denigrating black people has always been a part of Hollywood. I've had teachers say that blacks are too close to the subject matter to make a film about the black experience! You can imagine how ridiculous that is. You have to fight against beliefs like that. It made Renoir and other European directors even more important to me.

JP: I heard you speak once at the University of Georgia, where they were screening some of your films, and you repeated something that one of your teachers—the British documentarian Basil Wright—once told you, which was something along the lines of "Don't ever judge your subject." Could you talk about that?

CB: Well, at UCLA I was at a crossroads. They had these "end of the quarter" screenings—the best of UCLA films. This was during the time of the hippie movement. And I couldn't identify with any of them. I came from an all-black community with different conflicts and issues. And these other directors had all this freedom to explore things like nudity. There were many good films, but they were often about the internal conflict and problems of the filmmaker. I didn't have a problem, so I couldn't make a film like that that would relate to what I was doing. And people would smoke weed everywhere on campus—it would just come out of vents. I was always paranoid, but the campus police would walk through the hallway and ignore it all. Where I came from, police would stop you and harass you, go through your pockets—it was like apartheid. But in film school, all of these folks had a lot of luxuries and freedoms. So I was lucky to be taking Basil Wright's documentary class at the time. He was a gentleman, very sensitive, and he made a beautiful documentary, *Song of Ceylon*. I felt like I had a connection with him in terms of what I was trying to do. I told him that I felt like I didn't fit in. He told me that the most important thing is respect—for the people you work with and the subject of the film. They're human beings, and you don't exploit them. There's never a justification for exploiting the subject. There was a focus on working with your subject as a living thing that's already been hurt—you don't need to exploit them any more. It's not about you, the director; it's about the people you're focusing on—their needs, their interests. That's the purpose of documentary.

JP: Is *Killer of Sheep* not, to some degree, about an inner conflict for you?

CB: I was only trying to be objective—that was my conflict. Not imposing. I wanted to do something that reflected the way people in the community would see themselves. Coming from another place, you can see a much larger picture. But when you're in a well, you can only see the narrow light above. If you've been living like that for a long time, it can have an unproductive effect on you in many ways. So it wasn't my personal conflicts. It was the conflict of the community.

JP: Do you feel that in most films you see, some individual or group is being exploited?

CB: I feel like in the majority of black films there's exploitation. The black characters are exploited. People of color are. That's a reason why a lot of us got into film—because there were these distorted images of black people. You see the same things: gang movies, kids who are violent, a teacher who has to straighten out the situation—usually a white teacher, who teaches [the students] how to dance, or whatever. And it's superficial. There's one person who's dedicated, but I've seen dedicated teachers eaten up by the system. The problem is systematic, it's systemic, it's in the culture, it's in the school system itself, it's in the political system, it's in this country. It's inherent in this country's policies on education. And these films don't address this. They focus on an individual, like, "Oh, we just need one dedicated teacher, or one parent." And that's just one-millionth of the problem. First, we need to figure out where all the money that [was allocated to] public schools has gone, why it isn't showing up in the classroom, in terms of books, or quality teachers, or after-school programs, or smaller classrooms. And then you take a movie like *Hustle and Flow* where they're saying, "It's hard out here for a pimp." That's the biggest slap in the face! I argue with people who say the main character wants to make it, he's working hard, and you can't knock him for that. You can't? He pimped his girlfriend! He could've gotten a job at McDonald's. And he's supposed to be a hero? The ends justify the means? That logic justifies selling drugs, doing almost anything. And that's what gets promoted? That's the last thing we need in the community. Why not make something that would uplift? It doesn't necessarily have to be overly positive, but [it should at least be] realistic and not trying to denigrate. You can't do that with any other culture except for black culture. And that's the thing that troubles me. Box office receipts don't justify that. It almost seems like a conscious attempt to continue this program of dehumanization.

JP: How do you feel when you're labeled a "black filmmaker" or an "African American" filmmaker? Would you prefer just to be called a filmmaker?

CB: This country is like that. It's divided. It segregates people. When I started film school, I was just a filmmaker. Then I was grouped with African American film, black film. It became a way of categorizing. I think it's an indication that this country isn't a melting pot. Even in terms of just trying to produce a script, if it's a black story, you're told that it won't make money, it won't sell in Europe.

JP: As a filmmaker, how do you describe your work?

CB: I see myself as a person who makes films about people, their conflicts, their condition, their failures and successes, the things that resonate—things that seem simple, but have universal meaning. To share experiences—that's what art is for. I see film as more of an art form than a commercial thing. I think because I come from a segregated experience, there's a need to tell stories other than mainstream stories. You could say, "The stories you're doing are about predominately black subject matter," but they are still about the American experience.

JP: How does it feel to have a film you've made be declared a "national treasure"?

CB: This is the irony of it: I went to Zimbabwe and bought a pair of shoes for something like six million dollars. And I thought, if you can buy a pair of shoes for six million dollars, you've arrived! Of course, inflation is such that it costs almost half that to buy a doughnut. But in terms of getting another job, it hasn't really had an effect. In some ways, it's made it worse. People think I'm an artist. They might not consider me for a job, like I'm not going to be part of the team. When *Killer of Sheep* won the Critics Award at the Berlin Film Festival, it was in all the European newspapers, but when I came back to the U.S., there was no press. So the "national treasure" thing is nice for my friends and me, and we enjoy it, but it has no effect on getting another film made. You just start over from a blank page. I guess it's had its blessings. At least I haven't gotten a big head. Honestly, I can't complain.

JP: What are you working on now?

CB: I'm finishing up a film shot in southwest Africa, in Namibia. It's an epic drama. Takes place from around 1930 to about 1990, when they finally got their independence. It's about the history of the People's Organization and Sam Nujoma, the first president of Namibia.

A Conversation with Charles Burnett

David Lowery/2007

From www.road-dog-productions.com, June 2, 2007. Reprinted by permission.

Charles Burnett's *Killer of Sheep* was one of those films I'd always heard mentioned here and there during my cinematic matriculation; most of what I knew about it was that I couldn't see it, due to soundtrack rights issues that had kept it unreleased ever since it was made in 1977. But then, earlier this year, a trailer for the film began to show up in theaters. UCLA had restored the film, the soundtrack had been cleared and Milestone was going to put it out into theaters for the very first time.

Killer of Sheep is, suffice to say, more than deserving of its enduring legacy. It's a great film, and an important one—not just as a piece of film history, not just as a document of social unrest, but as an example of cinematic form so strong and assured that it's difficult to believe that it was Burnett's first picture, or that he made it under the circumstances it was (a ten thousand dollar budget and shooting schedule made up of a year of weekends).

I was lucky enough to have the chance to sit down and discuss the film with Burnett last week. This is what he had to say.

David Lowery: I finally saw *Killer of Sheep* for the first time the other day. I loved it, and was also struck by how familiar certain elements were; you can see the influence the film had on everything from early Jim Jarmusch to *Barbershop*. Do you ever go to the movies and see your own influence up on the screen?

Charles Burnett: Sometimes. Sometimes people call me and say "I want you to see my film because I was impacted by your film, and I want to see what you think of it." I've had that on occasion.

DL: Did David Gordon Green call you when he made *George Washington*?

CB: Yes, everyone brings that up! He sent me a tape of it. He's doing very well now.

DL: You started this film when you were at UCLA. Was it actually a student film, or was it produced outside the curriculum?

CB: No, it was a student film. It was my thesis film, and it was a part of an ongoing discussion and debate about how film can aid in changing society. A lot of people were very much interested in that, and were making films about the working class, but they had no relationship with the working class. They were making the same film over and over again, with the same solution over and over again, about the factories being exploited by management, getting the unions started and everything.

Where I came from, people were in totally different situations. I said I wanted to make a film, without imposing my values, and say, "Look, here's a situation. How can we help Stan [the central character in the film]? How can we help the community? What can we do to change it?" And that was the point of the film. To create a debate and not just say here's a solution, here's a filmmaker's point of view. So that was the idea behind the film, and also to make it so anti-Hollywood that it appeared to be something captured in the moment. To form the narrative by having these events that, in the way they're tied together, lead to insight and story.

DL: Did you go to film school with the goal of making this sort of film, or was it something that evolved over the course of your studies and making short films and such?

CB: No, I wanted to tell a story, I wanted to tell what happened to people in the community. When I was in high school, I saw how the system was crippling the kids. The whole idea of encouraging kids to go to prison, like it was a rite of passage. Our school did nothing to help. I mentioned in some other interviews that when I was in class, one of our teachers just went down the aisle, pointing and going, "You're not going to be anything, you're not going to be anything." There was always this antagonism between teacher and student. Most of these kids, no one in their family had a college education. What they used to tell us coming up was to just get a high school diploma. Because then, before the sixties, you could make a living with a high school diploma. You could get a manual labor job and do quite well. No one ever told us what the reasons were. School's supposed to be a nurturing place where you could take a kid and inspire them. You've seen teachers who come

in and change students, because they have that dedication. I wanted to do something about that.
DL: To capture the results of this sort of conditioning?
CB: Yeah, the whole thing of who's responsible. Stan's responsible, society is definitely responsible, and I think that if you realize that it's a complex issue, who the good guys and bad guys are is not always clear.
DL: I felt that, precisely because you don't point fingers in the film, there's a general sense of social malaise but also a great deal of hope and opportunity shining through the cracks. There wasn't necessarily any one thing keeping anyone down.
CB: I think back then it was more optimistic. The thing about it was that when we were coming up, the idea of a man was to provide for your family, to keep a job no matter what. The positive thing about Stan is that he endured. He didn't fail or drop out. He was determined to do things to make sure his family was going to survive, and so that in itself is very positive. It's not the kind of thing where he wins the lottery and his kids go to Harvard or whatever. His kids are going to have a rough time just like he did. All those kids in the community are going to have a rough time. They're being trained and conditioned to be able to survive and endure.
DL: The film's been widely cited for its almost documentarian approach, but I understand that it was completely scripted, and even storyboarded.
CB: It's scripted, yeah. There's a few places where we ad libbed. It was made to look like a loosely shot film, where the narrative sort of evolves, but it was scripted. A lot of the images were drawn. I was looking for specific things in the scenes, but the idea was not to have perfect lighting and stuff like that. Also, the idea was to bring filmmaking into the community and demystify it, to encourage kids that, look, if you can turn a HiFi on, you can turn a Nagra on and do sound. Just watch the button and keep it level. And they would do it. Five-year-old, six-year-old kids. The kids you see running around, they'd drag the lights, do the slate. The only thing they didn't do was change the magazine and load the camera, but everything else they had their hands on.
DL: That's fantastic!
CB: We had a crew from the film school, but they got sort of impatient about waiting. So it was just myself and Charles Bracy, a friend of mine who was an actor. When he wasn't in front of the camera, he was also

helping behind the scenes. He was probably the most consistent adult we had.

DL: Do you think you could get away with something like that now? Film school has become so institutionalized . . .

CB: It has, it has. The attitude has changed. When we went to film school, we didn't think about getting into Hollywood. At the time, you could just get in as a technician. Become a cameraman. You had to go through the union, go through all these steps, and you accepted it. I wanted to be a cameraman, and I knew that in order to be one it was going to take fifteen or twenty years. It was hard to get into the unions then. Sundance didn't exist then. We weren't under any illusions about three-picture deals. We made films because we liked making films, and the best place to do what we were doing was in film school. Today it's not like that. The studios are right there looking at these kids coming up, and they're picking them off the tree before they're ripe, because they figure these kids know what the audience wants.

DL: Was it surprising to you that *Killer of Sheep* developed such a tremendous legacy? And, considering that you didn't have any expectations when you made it, is this theatrical release thirty year later just icing on the cake?

CB: It's not icing on the cake. If I made the film yesterday, it would have had a different effect. A totally different effect. My new film has a lot of commercial elements, totally different from *Killer of Sheep*. You can't sell the concept; you sell stars, and how much money it's going to make at the box office and what audience it's for, and it really affects your approach to the subject. You're already compromising, thinking that you have to have this commercial appeal. When I was doing *Killer of Sheep*, I didn't care one way or another. It wasn't made to appeal to people in that sense. If I had been thinking about it, I would have been conscious of a lot of different things.

DL: But I imagine you were able to make a much stronger film as a result of being liberated from any sort of mainstream expectations.

CB: Unfortunately, I think we have to consider that if you're going to make a living in this business. You're up and down; you have success and disappointments, success and disappointments, and so it sort of balances out a certain way. You take it knowing that tomorrow's another day, and you have to wake up in the morning and look at an empty page all over again and hopefully get something done, and fight again to try and get a film made. What you've done in the past gets your foot in the door, but that's all it does.

DL: Did *Killer of Sheep* open any doors in Hollywood for you?

CB: No. It didn't open any doors at all, actually. When I was at Berlin, I got some money to do *My Brother's Wedding* after they saw the film, so in that sense, yeah, but it wasn't from Hollywood. It was local European television. Then I wrote this script, *To Sleep with Anger*, and I was really lucky to find the right people who had the money and the interest to look for money to put the film together. I think that's the film that's helped me more than anything.

DL: I read that when you finished *Killer of Sheep*, you took it to black communities around the country . . .

CB: To a certain number of cities. Oliver Franklin in Philadelphia and Pearl Bowser each had this program, this tour of black film that they created. So we were a part of that and we took our film around to different communities, and screened it and talked to the neighbors, to the people. And that was a very, very important thing.

DL: That reminds me of how John Cassavetes wanted to show his pictures to working class audiences; he always thought they would be his most appreciative audience, that they would intrinsically understand his films, and he was always disappointed when they didn't respond. Did you find that people got what you were trying to do with *Killer of Sheep*?

CB: No, no, no. They normally don't, and that's not important. Everyone has their own reality, their own perception of what life is, and someone living two or three houses down sees things differently. The film never claimed to be a total representation of black community. I didn't expect anyone to understand the film. And particularly now, when people are so used to seeing these really commercial action-oriented films . . . I look at *To Sleep with Anger* and see how slow it is. It just plods along. Things have changed. Just looking at the image used to be really exciting in and of itself. It had a story to tell.

DL: Are there any films that excite you these days?

CB: I can think of a lot of filmmakers working now that I admire greatly, and from the past as well. I don't want to name any names because tomorrow I'll be like, "Oh, I wish I had said this, I wish I'd said that." But there's a lot of good work.

DL: When you watch *Killer of Sheep* now, how do you feel about it?

CB: I don't really look at it. I saw it so many times while editing it. The mistakes you see get magnified instead of atrophied. It's not a perfect film. A lot of filmmakers go back and re-edit their stuff. But it's never going to change. You have to live with it.

DL: I read that, in the scene where Stan dances with his wife to Dinah Washington's "This Bitter Earth," you had a different song in mind . . .

CB: Yeah, I had Luis Russell's "Sad Lover's Blues." I took it to school, the 78, and the thing was so brittle that it cracked and broke.

DL: Did you ever consider going back and putting it back in?

CB: Yeah, actually, we found a copy of it, and we played it. It's a different melody, it's just as haunting, but when you're used to the Dinah Washington, it's kind of hard to change. I don't know if I'd have lost anything if I went back to it, but it's still hard to get used to. But we used it in the trailer, and it goes very nicely there.

DL: One thing I meant to ask earlier was whether, when you were shooting, you had difficulty getting access to film in a slaughterhouse?

CB: I had difficulty getting into a slaughterhouse in the L.A. area, because at the time I was making the film, there was an upsurge of vegetarianism. A lot of the vegetarians were also making movies, and they went to slaughterhouses and exposed a lot of the cruelty to animals. So they were hesitant about letting me use it. So I went up to another meatpacking place near Vallejo. They were this real meatpacking company owned by this guy who said, "I want to help someone who's trying to help himself. If you come in and don't interrupt the assembly process, you're okay to do this." People were very helpful. This is why I tried to shoot in the community, because businesses were very helpful about letting me use their facilities if I was doing something positive.

DL: The effect the title has on the film itself, the weight that it gives to Stan as a character, is tremendous. Was that always going to be the title, or did you come up with it later?

CB: That was pretty much the title as long as I can remember. I was working on this story about this guy who had problems sleeping and had these nightmares, and all the things that had an impact on him. I was going to college at the time, and I always saw this one guy on the bus. One day he happened to sit by me, and I had the opportunity to ask him what he did. He told me he worked at the slaughterhouse, and what he did was kill sheep. What they did then was they had a sledgehammer, and they would hit the animal in the head with the sledgehammer and crush the skull. And I just couldn't imagine someone doing that every day, day in and day out, without it creating some nightmarish effect. I never looked at him the same after that. So that's where I got that the idea that this was what Stan ought to do. Something as horrible as that.

Charles Burnett's *Namibia* Premieres at the 2007 LAFF

Diane Sippl/2007

From *Cinema Without Borders* (www.cinemawithoutborders.com), July 4, 2007. Reprinted by permission.

Lauded as one of America's most gifted filmmakers, Charles Burnett has just completed his largest film ever, *Namibia: The Struggle for Liberation*. While earning his MFA in filmmaking at UCLA, Burnett made the now classic *Killer of Sheep*, and on that basis he was awarded the prestigious John D. and Catherine T. MacArthur Fellowship (also known as the "genius grant") with others to follow from the Guggenheim Foundation, the Rockefeller Foundation, the National Endowment for the Arts, and the J. P. Getty Foundation. He is also the winner of the American Film Institute's Maya Deren Award and Howard University's Paul Robeson Award for achievement in cinema. *To Sleep with Anger* won the 1991 Independent Spirit Award for Best Director and Best Screenplay for Burnett and Best Actor for Danny Glover, and the Library of Congress has entered it along with *Killer of Sheep* in the National Film Registry. Among his numerous films since then, Burnett has written and directed *Nat Turner: A Troublesome Property*, a splendidly mind-boggling work about history as interpretation, and also *Warming by the Devil's Fire*, a sensual, quasi-autobiographical tale of an L.A. boy getting religion and the blues in the same visit back home to Mississippi.

    A starkly different venture nearly three hours long, *Namibia: The Struggle for Liberation* is an epic that spans sixty years of history with 150 speaking roles in multiple languages and dialects, dramatizing Namibia's fight for liberation from South African occupation that culminated in Namibia's independence in 1990. The cast includes Carl Lumbly and Danny Glover as well as local African actors, and the crew used former soldiers from both Namibia and South Africa who had fought against each other. I interviewed Charles Burnett in Westwood just following the film's world premiere at the 2007 Los Angeles Film Festival.

Diane Sippl: Can you explain the genesis of the project?
Charles Burnett: It started with the government's formation of PACON, the Pan-African Centre of Namibia, and their mandate was to do stories and themes in art works that dealt with Pan-Africanism. At the same time Sam Nujoma, the first president of Namibia and the former president of SWAPO (South West Africa People's Organization), had just finished his autobiography called *Nujoma: Where Others Wavered.* Uazuva Kaumbi, the executive producer of the film, *Namibia: The Struggle for Liberation,* was on the board of PACON and suggested that they make a movie from the book.

They hired a Namibian first-time writer for the first screenplay and brought in a Nigerian to do a polish. Then they took the script around looking for a director—Raul Peck was one—and they were looking for actors at the same time, believe it or not. They finally came around to me, and I read the script and thought it was feasible. When I was going to school I was aware of SWAPO, so I was very excited about doing it.

But the script had limitations; it was more or less a TV movie. It didn't cover the whole movement of SWAPO. It was just based on the book and needed to be expanded. It was all about Nujoma and they wanted it to be more about the people of Namibia. So we expanded it into an epic story of the human struggle of people wanting to get out from under the yoke of colonialism and free of South Africa's apartheid system.

The producers were supposed to find matching funds to support the production, but they never managed to do this, so the Film Commission, which is sponsored by the government, ended up financing the whole film. This cost about $10 million.
Diane: How did you research the rest of the fighters and the military operations?
Charles: I used the book only chronologically and for details about Nujoma's family that he knew a lot about. But historically, I wanted to find the real facts and not rely on his perspective. So I read a lot of books, and Isaac !karuchab, who was a member of one of the military arms of SWAPO, a PLAN (People's Liberation Army of Namibia) fighter, gave me a lot of information about the war, the battles, the songs they

sang, who was who, and he corrected some of the errors that were going around about what was true. We talked about the young people who were in exile, some in foreign countries going to schools, and some others who ended up in dungeons. It surprised me—some of their friends and family members were also in exile. It's a part of history that isn't talked about, and we just mention it in the film. And there were other stories like that, that were too complicated to get involved with due to the limits of the project.

Diane: This is the first film of yours that at times uses lots of action and involves spectacle. It opens with a very long, wide shot of the man in the vastness of the land, and you keep it for awhile and return to it later. Is it related to your way of making an epic?

Charles: Well I wouldn't call this an "action film" as such because it's not about that. It's about a country, a people in conflict, trying to establish their rights as human beings, and it took a war to do so. It took an armed struggle, so there was action in that sense.

And this is living history, so it had to be exact, very accurate. There was no room for interpretation. Even though it's a film, and there are some dramatic liberties, chronologically there are none. Everything had to be in place.

And it *was* a big picture. There were many battles and atrocities. The first one happened when women argued in front of a priest in his office about being forcefully moved, and a confrontation broke out and eleven people were killed. That led to the whole exile movement.

And then in Omugulu-gOmbashe insurgents fought South Africans for the first time in battle. And then came Kassinga and Cuito-Cuanavale—they're all important battles, a lot of fight scenes, and they're significant in terms of the outcome of this whole struggle. They're not in there just for commercial appeal; they're the key moments, and they are absolutely essential. And there are people who were there at the time, from the first massacre to Omugulu-gOmbashe to Kassinga and then to Cuito-Cuanavale. These people are still alive and they are very guarded about how you portray these scenes.

The character Danny Glover plays, Father Elias, is a composite of a number of Christian people who were very instrumental in helping the indigenous people of Namibia to sustain themselves. Namibia has been a very Christian country with a lot of Lutheran churches, and they played a big role in the struggle—something like the abolitionist movement in the United States. But people like Reverend Michael Scott were deported and not allowed back in South Africa. You see at the end of the film that he was a really important figure in terms of the United Nations. Father Elias is one of the reverends whose son is marching in the funeral. There were a lot of issues with priests who took a political stance and the government forcefully moved them to different areas like Ovamboland.

Diane: Isn't spectacle powerful in making a film of this nature?

Charles: Well, I think so—when you know the history, when you *are* the people, here the Namibian people. They know about a massacre, so then they cry at it, and they know about Omugulu-gOmbashe and particularly Kassinga. It's the way someone of the Jewish faith would look at the Holocaust, at Auschwitz and other places; they have particular meaning.

It's not like an "action film" action film; it's an historical event that has to be told. It's part of their story, their history. And these events are very critical battle scenes, not just any battle scenes. There are others we could have used, but these were the most meaningful ones, the turning points.

Diane: In how many countries did you end up shooting?

Charles: We shot only in Namibia, but we shot all over Namibia. We were going to shoot in Cuba, in South Africa, Robben Island, and in New York. Well, we have New York in the film, but it was shot in Namibia. We took some stock footage, and for the U.N. we shot in Namibia's Parliament, its government building.

Diane: Was it difficult working with the various languages? How does a filmmaker approach that situation? Not so many bother to take it on.

Charles: A lot of people in Namibia speak multiple languages, various tribal languages, or they speak Oshivambo, for example, but maybe not perfectly. Now this presents a problem in casting, because you ask the actor, "Can you speak Oshivambo?" and he says, "Yes." But then you find out he can't. Or he speaks it, but he's from the city, and in the countryside there's a dialect, and it becomes an issue. We had a crew member who speaks Oshivambo who never caught that, but then people who watched the film did. We'd like to change it, but we can't—it's locked in.

You know we invited people to come in and see the dailies and make comments, and no one did. There's a word or two in a song in the film that might sound derogatory about an Angolan child. They heard this song every day, and all of a sudden, to avoid conflict with their neighbors, they want it changed. This is after we mixed the film. Well, the train is at the station, you know . . .

But also with languages, there are certain words you can't translate. Even in Afrikaans, we had this problem. For example, the language has no word for "humanitarian." They have the word "philanthropical," but not "humanitarian."

Then there's the slang. We wrote in the script that a soldier's sister was "pissed" because her husband joined the service, right? Well this meant "drunk" to the South Africans, so we needed to change it to "pissed *off*."

Diane: You've worked with Carl Lumbly (who plays Sam Nujoma) and Danny Glover (who plays Father Elias) before, and you're also working here with people who've maybe never acted in the cinema prior to this film. What was the give-and-take between the local actors and the international figures?

Charles: First of all, every person in Namibia wanted to be in the film, to play a part, no matter what part, because they felt it was important. But during casting I was kind of worried, because they had the wrong idea of what it was about. The other thing is we had 150 roles or more that people were coming in for, and I couldn't remember their names—they were really complicated for me, and some people were coming back a second time and others were trying out for multiple roles. Hundreds of people were coming for these 150 roles—it drove me crazy. It must have taken at least a month. It was just a nightmare.

Diane: Had they acted before?

Charles: The South Africans had more experience, I must admit. The Namibians had some stage experience. But they were really wonderful, once I got over that fear, because they didn't do well in the reading. But once they got on the set it was like, whoa! They were really into every role, and naturalistic, and you know, we didn't have a lot of time. It was a low-budget film. But they were just amazing. They had the dedication, the discipline—it wasn't a problem. They were on the job and doing their thing, overly so, and they didn't get paid on time . . .

Diane: Was your crew international?

Charles: We got the camera, John Demps as D. P., and the focus puller from Los Angeles, and a loader and a line producer from New Jersey, and Ed Santiago as editor and myself from Los Angeles. And everybody else was from Namibia, South Africa, and the African continent—we had people from Zimbabwe. We edited in L.A. and we did the rest of the post-production in South Africa—the mixing, the sound, the color, the print.

Diane: In what ways is the finished film Pan-African?

Charles: We have actors from Ghana, Zimbabwe, Zambia, South Africa, people from the States, the diaspora—we brought them all down there to work on the film. So this is actually Pan-Africanism *working*, in the casting and in the whole idea of the film.

It isn't done often. You know there's nationalism and tribalism in the country, and there are job scares and fighting over jobs. But the film itself talks about aid from other African countries supporting everyone fighting in the liberation struggle—so you have the Pan-African theme there. And a lot came out of that. The commitment came because Nujoma and the fighters got aid from these other independent countries, and the idea was to carry on this theme of support from the different countries and peoples of Africa—all of Africa—and in a sense the film celebrates that as well.

For me it was a chance not only to play a supportive role but also, concretely, to have a hand in getting a piece of work out that responds to a need. Namibians need to see themselves as members of a Pan-African culture and history. And it's also important for other African countries—Botswana, Zimbabwe, Angola when gaining independence from Portugal—to see the film and recognize the support that they and their leaders gave to the struggle for liberation throughout Africa.

Charles Burnett Celebrates a Milestone

Susan Gerhard/2007

From *GreenCine* (www.greencine.com), November 12, 2007. Reprinted by permission.

Though its film stock had nearly turned to vinegar by the time UCLA stepped in with a timely restoration, Charles Burnett's *Killer of Sheep* is of a vintage that only gets better with age. Its neorealist approach to the life of a neighborhood is rich, but the surprise is that it's also as fresh as the day it was made thirty years ago. It's difficult to locate a single visual or narrative cliché in the story of a slaughterhouse worker's alienation amongst a family and neighborhood bustling with hopes and hijinks. That may be because the daily lives of African Americans have rarely been treated with the low-fi soulfulness of the cinema vérité–style lens.

The humor in *Killer of Sheep*—including the physical comedy of falling objects and children in motion—is never box-office laugh-out-loud funny, the way mainstream films cut with demographics in mind tend to be. Though never precious or faux sophisticated, the camera in this debut feature film settles peacefully into the morose ennui of an international festival circuit film.

Strange, then, that it wasn't discovered in that circuit. As Burnett recalls, it opened to some ten African American community centers and at least one church in the late seventies, played via PBS a couple of times, and hit mostly campus movie theaters intermittently. It may be the most auspicious first film to never quite reach its larger audiences. Of course, by now, Burnett doesn't have to worry about popular opinion: His awards include a MacArthur "genius" grant, a listing of *Killer of Sheep* in the Library of Congress National Film Registry, a Grand Jury Prize at Sundance, and a couple of Independent Spirit Awards. But what really separates Burnett from other film auteurs is the true eclecticism in his catalogue.

Milestone Film and Video—the company that secured the music rights for the film (with the help of Steven Soderbergh) and encouraged the UCLA restoration of the work, and who's releasing it theatrically this spring and on DVD along with *My Brother's Wedding* (1983) this fall—lists a few other lesser-known Burnett classics as well: *The Horse* (1973), a startling film short with animals at the altar, the South Central–based *Killer of Sheep* precursor *Several Friends* (1969), and a piece of whimsical community-based fiction that feels more like an agitdoc, *When It Rains* (1995). To take a trip through the more crossover-appealing works in Burnett's filmography is a dizzying experience in topical shifts, with the folklore-enhanced *To Sleep with Anger* (1990), the interracial police drama *The Glass Shield* (1994), and a Disney-made project on literacy and slavery, *Nightjohn* (1996), among them.

I got a chance to speak with Burnett over the phone from Los Angeles, a few weeks before *Killer of Sheep* itself celebrates a milestone with the help of a film company that goes by the same name. I took the opportunity to grill Burnett not so much on the films that made it to major festivals and television in the past few decades, but the more personal collection housed at Milestone and recently saved by UCLA.

Susan Gerhard: What's brought about the restoration and recent re-release of *Killer of Sheep*? It's been thirty years.
Charles Burnett: Ross Lipman at UCLA archives is largely responsible for getting it restored. He caught it just in time, because [the original print] was smelling like vinegar. They spent a lot of time; he went back to the original 35mm track for the sound. He and Dennis Doros (Milestone Film and Video) knew each other. Dennis was interested in distributing and releasing the film. Everything came at the right moment. The problem was the releasing of the film—it could have been six years earlier or more—but the musical rights were never cleared. It wasn't a problem when I made the film. It wasn't made to be distributed, so the music wasn't an issue.

He spent a good portion of the time trying to secure all the musical rights to the film. There was one holdout—he worked night and day to get the rights to "Unforgettable," and it didn't happen. "Unforgettable" is at the end of the film, the very end piece. We used another Dinah Washington song ["This Bitter Earth"] that sounded very similar; the lyrics were a bit different. One was about love, another about the loss of love.

SG: Nelson Kim at *Senses of Cinema* called *Killer of Sheep* one of the saddest happiest movies imaginable, and as I watched it again recently, it occurred to me that music contributes so much to the film's wistful tone. Can you talk more about some of the other selections and why you chose them? Let's start with Paul Robeson's "The House I Live In."

CB: Most of the music in there I heard as a kid growing up. In listening to them, they conjured up images. When I was thinking of each scene, I'd have a song in mind for it. Paul Robeson's song—he talks about "What is America to me"—lists this happy life, Norman Rockwell kind of painting situation; what you see on the screen is the opposite: Kids living in places where things are torn down, yet still being kids and not really realizing it. It's a contrast between the lyrics and what's going on in the screen. This mean old world comes into play. You see the slaughterhouse and reflect on what's going . . .

SG: Has time changed the way audiences receive the film? How was it first released?

CB: Pearl Bowser and Oliver Franklin had this tour of black independent films in the late seventies. We toured ten communities—Philadelphia, Milwaukee [among others]—and screened at community centers in these places. I vaguely remember that. It was shown to the black communities; we screened it at a church. The response was favorable. A lot of questions. Most of those things are about the questions, the director explaining the film. It's more of an educational thing than purely entertainment. Other than that, it hasn't really been screened that often. It's been over the years on campuses more than anything. PBS had a screening of it once or twice. Third World Newsreel has rented the film out.

SG: *Killer of Sheep* has such a wonderful pace that I associate with film, as opposed to digital. By now, you've worked in so many media, for so many reasons: I'm curious about your thoughts on film technology versus video technology, pros and cons.

CB: We're in a process of grading the film now; doing color correction. The color sees a difference between film and digital. I prefer film any day. There's more information, more latitude, you can do more things with it. Technically, film is sharper. Shooting with digital, in terms of hi-def, you need a large monitor to see what you got. With film, you kind of know. You've grown up intuitively. Digital, you need a monitor to see what you're doing. There's discipline: One of the things about film, it teaches you discipline. You can't just shoot continuously. Docs in digital I've shot—you get tons and tons of footage. You're able to have all this footage—it's good and bad, but you may not be able to, by yourself, look at all that stuff.

We did a film once in the desert for a TV show. We had a number of hi-def cameras going and didn't want to stop. We didn't even slate a lot of stuff. Just told the actors to repeat it. But at the end of the day, the editors didn't want to look at all that stuff. But it's cheaper, accessible—you can do everything basically on your home computer once you've shot it.

SG: The films of yours that Milestone offers span so much time. Watching *Several Friends*, from 1969, I was struck with how thickly it captures the very local, very colloquial. How did this story come about?

CB: I always wanted to do films about my neighborhood and the community of people, for some reason. I saw how the system created more problems than it solved—schools, police. I was really angry about that. That's the reason I got into film. When I had the opportunity to make this film about the people I grew up with, it was partly in opposition to the kinds of films that were being made about the working class and the working poor, and how these issues were resolved by joining the union, some easy alternative.

I was always interested in showing a slice of life and recording an experience that had a narrative inherent in it. That's how *Killer of Sheep* came about, telling a story without me imposing; telling the people's story as opposed to my story. Having grown up there, you know your solutions don't really work [and are] far from appropriate in many ways in solving problems. The only thing you can do is present scenes that you've witnessed, put them in some sort of order that creates a narrative, and give the impression that you're looking at what's real.

SG: Can you talk more about the times at UCLA, which produced you, Julie Dash, and a few other important figures? What were you reacting against?

CB: What happened was, Elyseo Taylor, a teacher who helped politicize the department, one of the first black teachers at UCLA, brought in Third World Cinema, and got the school to establish a program where they brought in Native Americans, Blacks, Latinos/Chicanos—and Third World Cinema got started. A lot of interesting people came at that point: Julie Dash, Haile Gerima.

SG: *Horse* (1973) is a fascinating film, and, like *Killer of Sheep*, uses the animal world as more than a metaphor. I'm wondering if you can talk about working with animals, and why.

CB: I was experimenting more or less. I started with the actor—very funny—[who was] just right for the part. But he was so stereotypical, on the one hand. The other guy was from Canada; he was so different. I thought that "different" would add to the character. We didn't have much time to work; it wasn't very fair to him. We were way out there—two hundred miles or so from Los Angeles—and for some reason, he had to get home every night, and so that was not a very good thing. We managed to live through that. The horse we had—it was only supposed to be a couple days' shoot—he was an old horse initially. When we came to finish shooting, they had taken that horse to the glue factory. There's a young colt that takes his place. For some reason people don't notice the switch of horses: It's day and night; one is jet black, the other a well-shaped, well-fed young horse. It was interesting. It was a lot of fun making the film.

After making the film, it was screened on campus somewhere. I was walking there, and a student ran into me and asked me to tell him about the symbolism of it. "The boy with blood on his shirt." They counted the number of drops of blood on his shirt, and it was the same number as the Wise Men. There was an old clothesline in the shot—you can see it when the car comes in the evening. He looked at that as a religious symbol, and found all this story behind it. I was like, "No, not exactly." The blood: we couldn't make it visible enough to register on film, and the clothesline, it was just there. I think I spoiled the film for him. I told the professor. He said, "It's there, but you don't know. You made the film but it's not yours anymore." That's scholars for you. I said, "What the heck."

SG: *My Brother's Wedding* (1984) feels like a real departure. Its humor, particularly the family dining scenes, feels very John Waters. Can you talk about where this film came from? I know it also had some drama in the making, if you'd like to recall that.

CB: It was difficult shoot in many ways. I never finished. I keep saying I'm going to go back and re-edit it. It was a first assembly, in a sense. I had to get it to Germany, because we had a deadline. I could have pushed it for later. I started late shooting the film, because the weather was bad for awhile, then the actor I had disappeared for God knows how long. It was a real big problem. When I finally found him in some southern state, he claimed to have been ordained as a preacher. I paid for him to come back to L.A., and he came out [of the plane] in a Dracula cape—the most ridiculous guy I ever met in my life. There were delays; he wanted more money. We managed to get the film finished, in a rush job, because I didn't have time to edit it. It means well.

[In terms of the story,] I was in a situation very similar. This girl I know was getting married. She didn't have many friends. I said I'd be there, but just as she was getting married, a friend of mine died, and I'm thinking, "I gotta go to that one, that's more emotional." I went to tell the person, the young lady getting married, "I can't make it," but as soon as she saw me, she said, "You're not gonna tell me you can't make it." I thought I could do both the wedding and the funeral, but of course, the wedding started so late. It was just a disaster. What can you do?

SG: By the time you got to *When It Rains* (1995), another Milestone short, you'd already done *The Glass Shield* (about police) and were about to complete *Nightjohn* (slavery and literacy). You'd covered so many political issues, can you talk about this particular film's politics?

CB: I'd just finished a big film (*Nightjohn*). [With a film like that], there's always a discussion about the content of the film, the editing of the film. When I did *Nightjohn*, there were some things I could have done differently. Disney was very good, but they had their way of making movies. I would have made it more naturalistic. We had just gotten through discussing things—their standards and practices; they have an audience. Everything we shot was in the script. We started a day ahead. We'd spent the day at an Air Force base, which we didn't know until planes were screeching over.

We had this rabbit scene, rabbits running in a straight line, kids chasing them. We finally got one rabbit to go halfway straight. That scene precedes a scene where a rabbit is being cooked. When Disney saw the film, they said "You can't put that scene in, because the rabbit—you see it cooked. People wouldn't like that." But we had spent that whole day! Another scene they didn't want was the old man holding Outlaw's hand while Beau Bridges whips him.

When you finish a film [like that], you want to do something that's yours. We had the use of a camera, and a group of us just shot this film [*When It Rains*] over a couple of days. It was kind of therapeutic and refreshing.

SG: Many of your films have been filmed in L.A.—and the South. Where did your film-in-progress *Nujoma* take you?

CB: We shot it in Namibia. We're trying to finish mixing it soon. We're going back to South Africa. It was really great in terms of being in a country where you can run into elephants night or day. It's just a beautiful country and the people are great. The film is about the liberation of southwest Africa, based on a true story, except for two characters we created to give it meaning and balance. Actors there are really interesting, in terms of casting.

The Namibians don't have a film industry; they don't get much exposure—don't have much of an opportunity to work in films. People use them for extra parts. The crew doesn't generally get to be keys, but we changed all that. We gave them responsible jobs. But for acting, they were at a handicap, because they had never done it before. They sort of overdid it [in casting]. When they got to the set and went to do their thing, it was natural and great, a surprise turnaround.

We shot in Etosha, a big game park, with elephants and lions—just wonderful. You see people living in these old kraals, homesteads, and it's like living a hundred years ago. People walk for miles. It's nothing for them to walk for hours, not a problem.

SG: Do you have any advice to filmmakers starting out?

CB: Make as many films as you can, experiment as much as you can with a camera. I suppose most people want to get to Hollywood. If you don't know what you're going to do before then, you're going to be totally confused. You're going to have to learn how to say "No." Get as much experience working with actors and blocking a scene as possible. You have to know where to put the camera; there's no stopping at that point. Any delay costs you a scene.

Blues People

James Bell /2008

Published in *Sight & Sound*, July 2008. Reprinted by permission of the British Film Institute.

Writing in *Sight & Sound* in 2002, the American critic Armond White called Charles Burnett's 1977 debut feature *Killer of Sheep* "the least-known great modern movie from the United States." But over the past year awareness of the film has grown, at least in the U.S., where its rerelease last year had critics rushing to acclaim it as a rediscovered masterpiece—something White greeted with suspicion. "Words like 'masterpiece' fall too easily upon the thorny history of Burnett's debut," he has written, arguing that it is too tidily convenient to slot the film retrospectively into the canon, leaving its champions feeling safe and satisfied.

Burnett's debut remains one of the most startling films in American cinema precisely because of the challenges it presents. More a series of poetic vignettes than conventional narrative, the film centers on a working-class black man named Stan who works in a slaughterhouse to support his wife and two children. Made as his thesis film while he was a student at UCLA, *Killer of Sheep* was shot over a year at weekends with non-professional actors from his home district of Watts. It portrays an economically deprived black community that simply hadn't been seen on screen before—and rarely since. The challenges of *Killer of Sheep* also come from its subtly original form, which owes an obvious cinematic debt to Italian neorealism and documentary, but with an inspired improvisatory feel that's unique in cinema—something closer to the feel of blues or jazz.

L.A. Rebellion

After abandoning early ambitions to become a stills photographer, Burnett enrolled at UCLA's celebrated film course in the late 1960s, partly to avoid the draft, but also through a need to do "something." "It was a period when there was a lot of social activism," he recalls. "People were really using arts as a means to social change. Film was there, and I gravitated towards it."

At UCLA Burnett formed friendships with like-minded black filmmakers such as Julie Dash and Haile Gerima, a group sometimes referred to as the "L.A. Rebellion" for the political and socially aware films they sought to make. "I just didn't identify with the films the majority of students at UCLA were making, which were coming out of the flower-child, hippy movement," says Burnett. "I was more interested in films about what I saw as the real issues. The other stuff was a luxury." Instead, he took inspiration from the Italian neorealists, Jean Renoir, and the British documentary movement.

But although he had got into filmmaking to make socially aware films, Burnett saw a dishonesty in many of the more dogmatic films of the time. "At UCLA there was a small group of people who were making political films," he recalls, "but they were romanticizing poverty and creating scenarios that just didn't apply to reality. Making a film about the black community, you had to be very aware of who you are. I wanted it to feel like I'd just taken a camera into the community and recorded what happened." It's this sense of an honest capturing of small incidents that makes *Killer of Sheep* so rich. Although every shot is carefully composed, the film has a documentary immediacy that feels spontaneous. There's also an indefinable poetry to many of the film's images, which display flashes of humor and beauty, underpinned by a deep sense of melancholy—much like the blues. In one scene Stan's daughter stands by a wire-mesh fence wearing a dog mask; like so many others in the film, the image is striking, humorous, unforgettable, and yet also somehow unsettling.

Such images are made more forceful still by Burnett's use of music. Rarely have songs and images been combined so resonantly and beautifully as in *Killer of Sheep*, whose soundtrack boasts Scott Joplin, Louis Armstrong, and blues singers like Little Walter, Elmore James, Faye Adams, and Dinah Washington. "The music was mainly pieces that my mother used to play," recalls Burnett. "I had decided on them before filming and they helped me to think of certain images for the film. For example Luis Russell's 'Sad Lover Blues' inspired the scene of Stan and his wife dancing together though in the end I broke the record so

I didn't get to use it, and used Dinah Washington's 'This Bitter Earth' instead." The music featured in the film was, in fact, one of the reasons why the film was screened so infrequently for so many years, as the rights to use the songs hadn't been cleared.

Song of the South

Burnett's distinctive voice is apparent even from his first short, *Several Friends* (1969), which feels like a dry run for *Killer of Sheep* both in its grainy black-and-white photography and its documentary-like focus. In the supportive enclave of the UCLA film department, as he worked towards getting *Killer of Sheep* made, he also found the time to make *The Horse*, a hauntingly poetic short set in the rural South. It follows three white men sitting on the creaking wooden veranda of an abandoned farmhouse watching a young black boy tenderly stroking an ailing horse they have decided must be killed. Unwilling to shoot it themselves, they wait until dusk for the boy's father to arrive and do it for them. "That film really came through a lot of the short stories I was reading at the time," Burnett recalls. "I was very much into William Faulkner, and *The Horse* was an attempt to do something in that vein: an allegory about southern power and its decline."

In fact the South's enduring and complex legacy in the American consciousness—at once terrible and romantic—is a theme that runs throughout Burnett's films. He was born in Mississippi in 1944, but like many other black families at the time, his parents moved to Los Angeles in search of opportunity when he was an infant. In *Killer of Sheep* the strong sense of community is a legacy of the social ties forged back in the rural South, but it's a legacy that's inevitably fraying: "country ways" are scorned by Stan, and when he hears his son address his mother as "muh'deah" he angrily scolds him.

Made ten years after *Killer of Sheep*, Burnett's second feature *My Brother's Wedding* looked at the further erosion of such ties. The film centers on a thirty-year-old man named Pierce who lives at home with his parents and works at the family's dry-cleaning business. He's resentful towards his brother, who's about to marry into a middle-class family. When an old friend is released from prison, Pierce finds his loyalty to his family tested.

Though it's more driven by narrative than *Killer of Sheep*, the joy of the film similarly lies in the details it captures about even marginal characters' lives. The teenage girl with the crush on Pierce who flirts with him as he's working is a wonderfully honest observation of the nature of emerging sexuality, while Pierce's mother's eagerness to impress her wealthy new in-laws reveals acute insights into class relations within the black community of the time.

Hanging over the film, too, is the sense that the L.A. neighborhood is becoming a more menacing one. As Burnett recalls: "Comparatively speaking, the 1960s and 1970s had been somewhat innocent, but at the beginning of the 1980s drugs and guns became rampant. I shot *My Brother's Wedding* in 1983, and I think what you see in the film is the time just before that happens."

The film is a more uneven work than *Killer of Sheep*, a reflection perhaps of its troubled production. Burnett had promised his financiers he would deliver the film by a set date, but the unreliability of Everette Silas, who played Pierce, extended the shoot and left little time for editing. The rushed cut was dismissed by critics and the film all but disappeared until last year, when a new, re-edited version was released.

"It was difficult going back to it because I didn't have all the material I had shot," admits Burnett. "It was a matter of trimming rather than being able to take scenes and make them work by using other material. I was able to cut out a lot of the bad performances, but if I'd had all the original material it would have been a lot better. It's not what I had originally envisaged."

His next move was to write and act as cinematographer on *Bless Their Little Hearts*, a black-and-white, documentary-style drama set in South Central L.A., directed by Billy Woodberry, a fellow member of the L.A. Rebellion group. Little seen since its first release, the film is almost a companion to *Killer of Sheep*, sharing its implicit anger at the predicament faced by its characters.

Burnett developed his third film *To Sleep with Anger* after receiving a grant in 1988, but the film only really came together once Danny Glover, hot off *Lethal Weapon*, joined the cast as charismatic trickster Harry Mention. The film again explored the legacy of the South, and in particular the folklore of an earlier age that creeps into the lives of a middle-class black family and disrupts their fragile stability. Arriving in L.A. from the South, Harry brings with him the old-time ways, reminding the family of their not-too-distant rural origins. It's a true ensemble piece with a uniformly impressive cast, but Glover is mesmerizing as Harry—a conman apparently possessed of hoodoo powers.

Despite Glover's presence, *To Sleep with Anger* again had a troubled gestation: the original financiers demanded that Burnett tone down the emphasis on folklore, a request he refused, forcing him to shop the film around to raise finance to complete it. Poorly marketed by its distributor, the film failed to attract the audience it deserved.

Towards the mainstream

It could be that Burnett was just out of step with Hollywood's narrow view of a black audience's expectations. *To Sleep with Anger* was released just as a new era of films about the blight of drugs and gang violence was emerging with the likes of *New Jack City* and *Boyz n the Hood*. Burnett doesn't refer to either of those films, but of some of the bandwagon-jumping titles that followed he says: "I just didn't find it interesting. They seemed to me to be a continuation of 1970s black exploitation films to some extent, which I was really opposed to."

Instead he directed a documentary about immigration to the U.S., *America Becoming* (1991), before making his fourth feature in 1994. Produced in the aftermath of the Rodney King case, *The Glass Shield* marked a departure in that it wasn't set in Burnett's immediate local community or focused on the family. Centering on the true-life case of an idealistic black rookie policeman's disillusionment when he realizes that corrupt officers at his station have fitted up a black man for murder, it's arguably Burnett's most generically conventional feature. But looking back at the film today, he doesn't see it as such a change of direction: "It was another issue that people in the community were facing. It wasn't a philosophical departure, though it may look like one stylistically."

Viewed today after the kinetic, naturalistic approach of *The Wire* has become the norm for dramatic depictions of police work, *The Glass Shield* seems at times too tidily plotted, and some of its peripheral characters in particular feel uncommonly stereotypical. It's a lesser work than his first three features, but Burnett's distinctive voice is nevertheless felt: scenes of the rookie J. J. with his family have a convincing honesty absent in similar police dramas.

A Miramax production, *The Glass Shield* typically involved lengthy tussles between director and producers. Reacting to the experience, Burnett next returned to a small-scale, local subject in the deceptively simple short film *When It Rains*, a story about a man's attempt to help out a female friend facing eviction by asking around the community for donations. In its thirteen minutes, the film manages to say volumes about the importance of community ties and values, and also about the role of music: despite not raising the money, the landlord agrees to let the woman off in exchange for a coveted jazz album her helper happens to have under his arm. "*When It Rains* was such a fun experience," Burnett remembers. "It was really just made with a bunch of friends. I'd just been fighting tooth and nail with the producers of *The Glass Shield*, and *When It Rains* came as a relief. It reminded me of how important it is to have full control."

Burnett's work since the mid-1990s has trodden a similarly alternating path between small-scale, resolutely independent films such as *The Final Insult* (1997), an experimental digital-video film about homelessness, or 2007's *Quiet as Kept*, a response to the Hurricane Katrina disaster, and larger-scale features such as 1997's *Nightjohn*, an affecting period film about a slave who defies the law of his plantation to teach a twelve-year-old girl to read. *Nightjohn* was produced for the Disney Channel, as was his 1999 film *Selma, Lord, Selma*. But, as critic Jonathan Rosenbaum has noted, moving in such mainstream areas somehow only served to increase Burnett's anonymity.

More recently Burnett contributed a film to the Scorsese-produced series on the blues, *Warming by the Devil's Fire*, which charted the 1920s to the 1950s. "I wanted to do a film that looked at the role blues music had played in my growing up, its role in the family and community," he explains, "the way my grandmother didn't want my mother to play the blues for what she saw as its anti-religious elements—how it exposed tensions like that."

It seems likely that Burnett will remain in the margins, his strongest artistic successes too rooted in the black experience for a wider audience, while his refusal to sell out and produce populist fare aimed at a black audience—be it blaxploitation or comedy hip-hop tie-ins—means his vision will always need to be twinned with a doggedly independent spirit. "Hollywood has been injurious to images of black people from *Birth of a Nation* on," he insists. "We have more people of color having access to studio facilities to make films now, but they're making the same film. The comedies may make you laugh, but can perpetuate the same myths. As they say: 'The more things change, the more they stay the same.' I think that's still the case."

Index

Actors, Burnett's direction of, 61
Adams, Faye, 182
Adams Heights (Los Angeles neighborhood), 59
Addams Family Values, 84
Africa: Burnett's feelings about, 21–22; struggle for liberation, 173
Agee, James, 4, 52, 132
Allamehzadeh, Reza, 43
America Becoming, xviii, 40, 60, 62, 69, 85–86, 123, 185
American Film Institute, xiii, xxviii, 28, 35, 65, 168
American Museum of the Moving Image, xix, 95, 101
Andersen, Thom, 138
Annihilation of Fish, The, 108, 124, 140
Anti–Vietnam War movement, 47
Apartheid, 78–79, 157, 169
Armstrong, Louis, 150, 182
Arnaud, Catherine, 49
Art house director, Burnett as, xix, 95–96
Atalante, L', 66

Baldwin, James, 126
Barbershop, 161
"Bear, The" (Faulkner), 48
Becket, 98
Bell, Willie, 51

Berlin International Film Festival, xxvii, 10, 28, 42, 65, 82, 83, 119, 151, 159
Bible, 113
Bicycle Thief, The (*Ladri di biciclette*), 151
Birth of a Nation, The, 82, 100
Black actors, 49
Black community, 38, 60, 76, 80, 81, 93, 122, 130, 135, 148; in Boston, 74; in Burnett's films, 77, 116; class differences, 56, 82, 100, 184; in *Killer of Sheep*, 6–7, 19, 120–21, 162, 165, 182; in Los Angeles, 11; in *My Brother's Wedding*, 56; in *To Sleep with Anger*, 45, 56
Black filmmakers, 3, 51, 72, 122, 186
Black Independent American Cinema (retrospective in Paris, 1980), 3, 65
Black independent cinema, 3, 28, 81, 82, 142
Black independent film tour (Berlin, Amsterdam, Paris, 1981), 49
Black independent film tour (U.S., 1979), 48, 165, 176
Black middle class, 13, 30, 45, 85
Black Muslims, 17, 31
Black Panthers, 17–18, 29, 31
Black women in film, 73
Blackwell, Don, 18, 57
Blakey, Art, 50
Bland, Bobby, 51

Blaxploitation, 31, 58, 82, 143, 145, 185, 186
Bless Their Little Hearts, 5, 34, 52, 92, 138, 184
Blockbuster Video, 136
Blues, 40, 50, 113, 123, 130–33, 186; sexually explicit lyrics, 130, 132–33; women's issues in, 132–33
Blues, The (miniseries), xxiii, 186
Boatman, Michael, 95
Bogan, Lucille, 132–33
Bowser, Pearl, 165, 176
Boyz n the Hood, 103, 185
Bracy, Charles, 163–64
Bradshaw, John, 46
Breckman, Andy, 68
Brer Rabbit, 47
Bresson, Robert, 6
Bridges, Beau, 179
Brokeback Mountain, 147
Brooks, Richard, 39, 54
Burnett, Angela (niece), 143
Burnett, Charles: advice to young filmmakers, 180; awards and honors, xix, xxviii, xxix, 168; brother, 39, 45, 46; character, xv, 118–19; childhood and youth, xi–xii, 10–18, 29–30, 97; as cinematographer, 5, 43, 61–62, 92, 184; education, Fremont High School, 30; education, Los Angeles City College, xxvii, 12–13, 16, 18, 30, 40, 84, 97–98, 119, 138; education, UCLA, ix–x, xxvii, 5–6, 18–19, 31, 40, 49, 57–58, 84, 98, 109, 119–20, 138, 142, 156, 157, 162, 177, 181–82; family, xxvii, 13, 15, 97, 99; father, 15, 39, 97; favorite films, 51–52, 66, 97; grandmother, 15, 26, 97, 186; influence, 161; interest in photography, 5, 16, 30, 155; mistakenly arrested, 99; mother, 15, 40, 50, 80, 97, 186; as screenwriter, 43, 88, 92, 99, 156, 184; as script reader for talent agency, 22, 31, 83–84, 99; southern roots, xiv–xv, xxiv, 5, 40–41, 47, 76, 80, 97, 183; speech impediment, 56; as storyteller, 26, 29, 35, 146; style as filmmaker, 62; as teacher, 31, 57, 83; as theatrical director, xxix; trumpet playing, 30, 118, 132

Burnett, Jonathan (son), 99
Burnett, Steven (son), 99
Butler, Paul, 25, 39, 53, 61, 122

Cabin in the Sky, 51
Cahiers du cinéma, xvi, 35
Cain, Bill, 124
Caldwell, Ben, 3, 31, 32, 42, 81
Caltech, 134
Camus, Albert, 98
Canby, Vincent, 97
Cannes International Film Festival, xxviii, 43, 55, 99
Cassavetes, John, 165
Chaplin, Charlie, 66
Charles, Ray, 29
Chekhov, Anton, 51, 100, 156
Cherry, Eugene, 151
Chicano Coalition, 57
Children: in Burnett's films, xi, 8, 63, 120, 124, 151–52; as crew, 8–9, 163
Christopher, Frank, 127
Chubb, Caldecot (Cotty), 23, 44, 53, 55, 59, 85
CIA, 148
CiBy 2000, xx, 89, 90, 101, 104, 123

Cinematographer, Burnett as, 5, 43, 61–62, 92, 184
Cinematography, 44–45, 61–62; close-ups, 35, 54, 62
Clark, Larry, 3, 31, 57, 134
Class differences in the black community, 45, 53, 56, 82, 100
Cocksucker Blues, 150
Confessions of Nat Turner, The (Gray, 1832), 135
Confessions of Nat Turner, The (Styron, 1967), 126, 128, 135
CPB (Corporation for Public Broadcasting), 23, 27, 43, 55, 85; unrealized project for, 22, 43, 55
Craft, Ellen and William, xxv
Crash, 139
Crazy Kill, The (Himes), 125
Crazy Kill, The (*Man in a Basket*) (unrealized project), xxv, 125
Creative writing, 5, 40, 51, 98, 155
Critics Prize. *See* FIPRESCI (International Federation of Film Critics) Prize
Cuito-Cuanavale (battle, 1987–88), 170

Dad (1989 movie), 46
Dances with Wolves, 66, 74
Dash, Julie, 24, 28, 31, 42, 57, 59, 81, 85, 92, 104, 177, 182
Daughters of the Dust, 57, 85, 104
Daves, Delmer, 97
Davis, Miles, 50
Davis, Reverend Gary, 130
Day of the Jackal, The, 57
Daytime Emmy Awards, xxix
De Sica, Vittorio, 29
Demps, John, 172
Devil's Dip (Los Angeles swamp), 14–15, 30, 97

Digital video versus film, 176–77
Disney Channel, 106–7, 124, 140, 179, 186
Distorted images of blacks in film, 31, 71–72, 81, 158, 186
Do the Right Thing, 103
D.O.A., 51
Documentaries, xi, 6, 52, 57–58, 86–87, 157, 182
Doros, Dennis, 142, 146, 153, 175
Dorsey, Thomas A. ("Georgia Tom"), 130
Dostoyevsky, Fyodor, 46
Double Indemnity, 30
Douglass, Frederick, 81, 90–91, 93, 96, 107, 136; unrealized project on, xxv, 91
Draft board, 11
Dred (Stowe), 127, 135
Drummond, Jack, 143
Du Bois, W. E. B., unrealized project on, xxv

Earth, Wind & Fire, 150–51
Ebonics, 107
Editing, 62
Edmonds, Randoph, 127, 135
Education, importance of, 107
Ethnic diversity in the U.S., 60
Etosha National Park, Namibia, 180
European reception of Burnett's films, x, xv–xvi, 64, 83
Evans, Walker, 132

Fairley, Juliette, xxix
Family, importance of, 34, 38–39, 56, 111
Fanaka, Jamaa, 31, 58
Faulkner, William, 48, 95, 96, 97, 98, 183

190 INDEX

Festival of Three Continents (Nantes, France), xxvii, 3
Field, Gwen, 104
Film Society of Lincoln Center, xxi, xxvii, xxviii, 106
Film versus digital video, 176–77
Final Insult, The, 186
Finding Buck McHenry, xxii, 124
FIPRESCI (International Federation of Film Critics) Prize, xxvii, 10, 82, 83, 159
Folklore, black, 22, 23, 25–26, 34, 40, 43–44, 47, 54, 110, 184
Folkways, 109, 113, 116
For Whom the Bell Tolls (Hemingway), 95
Ford Foundation, 40, 60, 69
Frank, Robert, 150
Franklin, Oliver, 48, 165, 176
Fremont High School, 30
Frye, Marquette, 12

Gallacher, Megan, 128
"Genius grant." *See* MacArthur (John D. and Catherine T.) Foundation Fellowship
George Washington, 143, 150, 161–62
"Georgia Tom," 130
Gerima, Haile, 21, 24, 31, 42, 48, 49, 57, 81, 92, 136, 138, 177, 182
Glass Shield, The, xx, 77, 89–90, 95–96, 99, 101, 103–5, 106, 109, 123, 140, 146, 175, 179, 185; budget, 104; conflicts with producers, xx, 104–5, 186; credits sequence, 101; ending, xx–xxi, 101–2, 104; festival screenings, 99, 101; financing, 89, 101, 104; marketing, 123; prizes and awards, xxviii; test screening, xx, 104; trailer, 103
Glover, Danny, 26, 36, 53, 61, 97, 100, 122, 128, 139, 168, 170, 172, 184–85; on Burnett, 147–48; preparation for role, 47–48
Golden Leopard Award, xxviii
Gordon, Walter. *See* Fanaka, Jamaa
Grande Illusion, La, 156
Grant, Bob, 18, 57
Gray, Thomas R., 127, 135
Greaves, William, 3, 18
Greek tragedy, 21
Green, David Gordon, 143, 150, 161–62
Green Pastures, The, 51
Greenberg, Kenneth S., 127
Gregor, Ulrich, 49
Guess Who's Coming to Dinner, 50
Guests of Hotel Astoria, 43
Guggenheim Foundation, xxviii, 28, 168

Hairy Man (folk character), 23, 44, 47, 80, 111, 116–17n3
Hall, Arsenio, 79
Hallelujah!, 51
Hamilton, Charles V., 126–27
Handy, John, 123–24
Handy, W. C., 132
Harlem Renaissance, 96
Harris, Wendell B., Jr., 28
Harvard Film Archive, xxix
Haynes, Todd, 150
Hearts and Minds, 16
Heller, Amy, 142
Henry, John, 18, 57
Hesselink, Ard, 49
Hicks, Tommy, 131
Higgins, Colin, 31
Himes, Chester, xxv, 54, 125
Hitchcock, Alfred, 66
Holiday, Billie, 133
Holocaust, 136–37
Holzman, Michael, 44

Homelessness, 78
hooks, bell, xxii
Hope, Kenneth, 29
Horse, The, 3, 5, 31, 48, 49, 175, 177–78, 183; prize winner at Oberhausen, 5
House, Son, 130
"House I Live In, The," 76, 139, 176
House Party, 38
Howard University, 48, 92, 168
Hudlin, Reginald, 38, 40
Hudlin, Warrington, 28, 38, 40
Human Rights Watch International Film Festival, xxi, xxviii
Humor: in Burnett's films, 67; in *Killer of Sheep*, 174; in *My Brother's Wedding*, 178; in *To Sleep with Anger*, 47, 54
Hurston, Zora Neale, 34
Hustle & Flow, 139, 158

Ice Cube, xx, 99, 101, 123
IFP (Independent Feature Project), 70
Immigration, 60–61, 85–86
Improvisation, 45
Independent filmmaker, Burnett as, 24, 31, 55, 69–70, 82, 88, 100, 121, 186
Independent Spirit Awards, xiii, xxviii, 168, 174
Ivens, Joris, 52, 57

J. P. Getty Foundation, 168
Jackson, Mississippi, 47
James, Elmore, 182
Jarmusch, Jim, 161
jazz, 50, 103, 123, 186
Jefferson, Blind Lemon, 132
Johnson, John Eddie, 89, 104
Johnson, Robert, 132, 133
Jones, Allison, 124
Jones, James Earl, 124, 126
Joplin, Scott, 150, 182

Joyce, James, 151
"Junior," 7, 46

!karuchab, Isaac, 169–70
Kassinga (battle, 1978), 170, 171
Kaumbi, Uazuva, 169
Killer of Sheep, x, xii, 8–9, 19–21, 24, 30, 33–34, 35, 39–40, 41, 44, 48, 49–50, 56, 75, 77, 96, 98–99, 100, 114–16, 119–21, 139, 141–44, 145–47, 150–54, 156, 158, 161–67, 174–77, 181–83; audience reaction, 75–76; black community in, 6–7, 19, 120–21, 162, 165, 182; black independent film tours, 48–49, 165; budget, 10, 26; children as crew, 8–9, 163; children in, xi, 8, 76, 151–52; distribution problems, 48, 119; DVD release, 140, 141; festival screenings, xxvii, 3, 28, 42, 65, 82, 83, 119, 151; filming conditions, 8–9; financing, 49; first commercial release, xxiv, xxix, 143, 145, 151, 161, 175; humor in, 174; music clearances for, 142–43, 146–47, 150–51, 153, 175; music in, 33, 50, 142, 150–51, 175–76, 182–83; National Film Registry, selection for, 75, 96, 100, 104, 109, 119, 128, 134, 138, 142, 146, 159, 174; non-professionals in, xi, 8–9, 142, 145, 181; opening scene, 8, 19, 39, 151; prizes and awards, x, xxvii, 10, 28, 75, 82, 83, 119, 146, 151, 159; restoration of, xxix, 142, 146, 174, 175; reviews, 75, 83; style, 4, 20, 106, 114–15, 121, 153; themes, 19, 115; as tragedy, 21; video transfer, 141
Kim, Nelson, ix, 134, 176
Kim-Gibson, Dai Sil, xviii, 60, 77
King, B. B., 50

King, Martin Luther, 17, 21, 58
King, Rodney, 74, 99, 185
KJM3 Entertainment Group, 104
Korea Times, xviii
Krantz, Steve, 32

L.A. Rebellion, ix–x, 56–57, 182. *See also* Los Angeles School of Black Filmmakers/L.A. Rebellion
Lane, Charles, vi, xvii, 49, 59, 65–74
Lanzmann, Claude, 136
Larkin, Alile Sharon, 5, 42, 62, 81, 92
Lawrence, Carol Munday, 35
Lee, Bill, 39
Lee, Spike, 29, 38, 42, 49, 51, 59, 72, 79, 96, 100, 122, 128, 134, 146, 148
Leonardo da Vinci, 35
Let Us Now Praise Famous Men (Agee and Evans), 4, 52, 132
Light in August (Faulkner), 96
Lipman, Ross, 142, 146, 175
Little Miss Sunshine, 147
Little Walter, 182
Lloyd, Walt, 27, 44, 62
Locarno International Film Festival, xxviii
Los Angeles, 109, 154; in film, 138–39; segregation in, 13, 77–79; violence in, 79, 148. *See also* South Central Los Angeles; Watts
Los Angeles City College, 12–13, 16, 18, 30, 40, 84, 97–98, 119, 138
Los Angeles Film Critics Association, xiii, xxviii
Los Angeles Film Festival, xxix, 169
Los Angeles Plays Itself, 138
Los Angeles Police Department, 17–18, 146
Los Angeles riots (1992), 78

Los Angeles School of Black Filmmakers/L.A. Rebellion, ix–x, xxvii, 31–32, 56–57, 92, 182
Lukács, Georg, 4
Lumbly, Carl, 36, 54, 95, 107, 124, 168, 172

MacArthur (John D. and Catherine T.) Foundation Fellowship ("genius grant"), xix, xxviii, 10, 29, 53, 63, 75, 96, 104, 109, 123, 134, 139, 142, 168, 174
Mala Noche, 100
Malcolm X, 16–17, 21
Man for All Seasons, A, 98
Man in a Basket (*The Crazy Kill*) (unrealized project), xxv, 125
Marxism, 32
Mary Alice, 53, 61, 122
Maslin, Janet, 75
Maya Deren Award, xxviii, 168
McCarthy, Todd, 99
McGee, Vonetta, 27
Menace II Society, 103
Micheaux, Oscar, 3, 16, 33, 82
Midnight Cowboy, 66
Milestone Film & Video, 140, 142–43, 146, 151, 152, 161, 175
Miramax, xx, xxi, 95, 101, 103, 104–5, 118, 123, 140, 185
Mississippi, xiv, 13, 41, 80, 130, 131, 183
Mo' Better Blues, 38
Modern Videofilm, 141
Monterey Park, 86
Moore, Kaycee, 141, 143, 151
Morrison, Toni, 40
Moss, Carlton, 18
Moynihan, Daniel Patrick, 38

Mulatto: A Never Ending Saga (Fairley), xxix
Murphy, Eddie, 42, 68
Museum of Modern Art (New York), xxvii, xxix
Museum of the Moving Image, xxviii
Music, 50; in *Killer of Sheep*, 50, 142, 150–51, 175–76, 182–83; in *To Sleep with Anger*, 50–51, 63
My Brother's Wedding, xii, 10, 19–21, 34, 42–43, 53, 56, 96, 139, 178–79, 183–84; black community in, 56; budget, 10; director's cut, xxix, 184; distribution problems, 43, 100, 119; DVD release, 140, 175; festival screenings, xxvii; filming conditions, 50; financing, 10, 89, 165; first commercial release, xxix; humor in, 178; restoration of, xxix; southern values in, 154; style, 19–20; themes, 100; unavailability, 138; unfinished, 122
My Father's House (unrealized Billy Woodberry project), 35, 62
Myers, Walter Dean, xxv

Namibia, 155, 159–60, 168–73, 179–80
Namibia: The Struggle for Liberation, 147, 168–73, 179–80; actors, 172; budget, 169; crew, 172–73; locations, 171; Pan-Africanism in, 173
Namibia Film Commission, 147, 169
Nat Turner (Edmonds), 127, 135
Nat Turner: A Troublesome Property, xxii–xxiii, 126–29, 134–37, 140, 168
Nat Turner's insurrection (1831), 126, 134–36
National Association of Black Social Workers, 104

National Endowment for the Arts (NEA), xxviii, 28, 168
National Film Registry, Library of Congress, 75, 96, 100, 104, 109, 119, 128, 134, 138, 142, 146, 159, 168, 174
National Society of Film Critics, xxi, xxviii, 146, 151
Neorealism, 10, 66, 106, 138, 174, 181, 182
New Directors/New Films, xxvii, 100
New Jack City, 185
New York Amsterdam News, xvii
New York Film Critics Circle, xxix
New York Film Festival, xxviii
New York Times, xvii, xix, xxi, 75, 97
Nightjohn, xxi–xxii, 106–7, 124, 128, 140, 175, 179, 186
Non-professionals in Burnett's films, xi, 8–9, 142, 145, 181
North by Northwest, 66
North Philadelphia, 60
Nothing but a Man, 4
Nouveau roman, 51
Nujoma, Sam, 140, 160, 169, 172, 173
Nujoma: Where Others Wavered (film). See *Namibia: The Struggle for Liberation*
Nujoma: Where Others Wavered (Nujoma), 169
Nuñez, Victor, 24, 82

Oberhausen International Short Film Festival, 5
Omugulu-gOmbashe (battle, 1966), 170, 171
145th Street (unrealized project), xxv
Opher, James, 127
Orr, Tim, 150
Oshivambo language, 171
Ovamboland, 171

Pacific Film Archive (University of California, Berkeley), xxix
PACON (Pan-African Centre of Namibia), 169
Pan African Film & Arts Festival, 147
Pan-Africanism, 32, 173
Paul Robeson Award (Howard University), 168
Paulsen, Gary, 124
PBS (Public Broadcasting Service), 85, 100, 108, 123, 174, 176
Penitentiary films, 58
Peterson, Louis, 128
Petty, Lori, 95
Philadelphia, poverty in, 60, 86
Photography, Burnett's interest in, 5, 16, 30, 155
Place in Time, A, 65, 66
PLAN (People's Liberation Army of Namibia), 169–70
Poitier, Sidney, 50
Poverty, 59, 60; in Philadelphia, 60, 86
Pratt, Elmer "Geronimo" (unrealized project), 29
Preproduction, 87–88
Pressman, Ed, 26, 53, 55, 59, 70, 85, 100
Proverbs, 114, 117n4

Quiet as Kept, 186

Race movies, 16, 51, 82
Racism, xx, 11, 23, 69, 89, 95, 121, 131, 140, 146; in the film industry, xxv, 71, 148
Rainey, Ma, 133
Raleigh Studios, 77, 97
Ralph, Sheryl Lee, 36
Ray, Satyajit, 119
Rebuild L.A., 78

Red House, The, 30, 51–52, 97
Redgrave, Lynn, 124
Rehearsals, 61
Renoir, Jean, 4, 6, 52, 97, 119, 139, 156, 157, 182
Retrospectives of Burnett's films: American Film Institute, xxix; American Museum of the Moving Image, xix, xxviii, 95, 101; Film Society of Lincoln Center, xxi, xxviii, 106; Harvard Film Archive, xxix; Museum of Modern Art, xxix; Pacific Film Archive, xxix
Reynaud, Bérénice, 35
Richardson, Nancy, 62
Ringler, Jeff, 44
Rissient, Pierre, xx
Robbe-Grillet, Alain, 51
Robert Flaherty Seminar, 48
Robeson, Paul, 46, 76, 139, 150, 155, 176; unrealized project on, xxv
Rockefeller Foundation, xxviii, 28, 53, 168
Rosenbaum, Jonathan, xxi, 186
Roth, Bobby, 144
Ruelle, Catherine, 49
Russell, Luis, 166, 182

Samuel Goldwyn Company, 35, 101, 103, 122
San Francisco, 66
Sanders, Henry Gayle, 7, 8, 49, 143–44, 151
Sankofa, 136
Santiago, Ed, 172
Sarraute, Nathalie, 51
Saturday Night Live, 68
Schroeder, Carolyn, 103, 104
Scorsese, Martin, 131

Scott, Darin, 25
Scott, Reverend Michael, 171
Screenwriter, Burnett as, 43, 88, 92, 99, 156, 184
Screenwriting, 5, 88, 99, 156
Segregation, 159; in Los Angeles, 13, 77–79
Selma, Lord, Selma, xxii, 124, 186
Sembène, Ousmane, 57
Several Friends, 42, 48, 175, 177, 183
sex, lies, and videotape, 27, 42, 62
Shannon-Burnett, Gaye, 99
Shooting ratio, 62
Siegel, Allan, 49
Silas, Everette, 184
Singleton, John, 122
Sisyphus, 24
Skin colors, stereotypes of, 45, 82
Skins (unrealized Charles Lane project), 65, 67
Slavery, 21, 38, 107, 124, 129, 135, 137
Smith, Bessie, 130, 133
Smith, Mamie, 133
Sobibor, October 14, 1943, 2 p.m., 136
Social issues in film, x, xvii–xviii, 57, 67, 74, 81, 89, 105, 147, 162, 182
Soderbergh, Steven, 143, 175
Soldier's Story, A, 74
Song of Ceylon, 6, 157
Sony SVS, 26, 44, 103
South (U.S.), 48, 52, 156, 183; antebellum, 107, 124; black attitudes toward, 41, 80; black culture in, 131–32; black migration from, 13, 76, 112, 183
South Africa, 168, 169, 171, 172, 173, 179
South Central Los Angeles, xi, xxvii, 18, 30, 79, 99, 184; in *The Glass Shield*, 104; in *Killer of Sheep*, 41, 75, 96, 100, 120–21, 139; in *Several Friends*, 175; southern migration to, 13, 41, 76, 122; in *To Sleep with Anger*, 25, 97; violence in, 148; and the Watts Riots, 12. *See also* Los Angeles; Watts
Southern values in black culture, 41, 97, 154, 183, 184
Southerner, The, 4, 52, 97, 119–20, 120, 156
Soweto, 78–79
Spalsa, Montezuma, 57
Spheeris, Penelope, 31
Stanley Ann Dunham: A Most Generous Spirit, xxv–xxvi
Stephen Hero (Joyce), 151
Stereotypes, x, 68, 121, 148; of skin colors, 45, 82
Stories and storytelling, 5, 19, 26, 29, 33, 35, 40, 47, 109, 177
Storyboarding, 44, 62, 163
Stowe, Harriet Beecher, 127, 135
Student deferment program, 11, 155
Studios, conflicts with, 70–72
Style as filmmaker, Burnett's, 62
Styron, William, 126–28, 135
Sugar Hill (Los Angeles neighborhood), 59
Sundance Film Festival, xxviii, 28, 33, 119, 151, 174. *See also* U.S. Film Festival
Superfly, 32
Superstar: The Karen Carpenter Story, 150
SWAPO (South West Africa People's Organization), 160, 169

Tarzan movies, 16
Tate, Greg, 101
Taylor, Clyde, 56–57

Taylor, Elyseo, 3, 51, 57, 177
Television work, xxii, 107, 140
Temecula Valley International Film and Music Festival, xxix
Tharpe, Sister Rosetta, 50, 63, 130
Third World cinema, 57, 58, 177
Third World Newsreel, 176
"This Bitter Earth," 33, 144, 150, 166, 175, 183
Thomson, Kathy, 141
To Sleep with Anger, xiii–xiv, 22–23, 38–40, 53–55, 84–85, 100–101, 109–14, 116, 122–23, 128, 139–40, 146, 175, 184–85; actors, 61; audience response, xvii, 34, 96–97; biblical references in, 113; black community in, 45, 56; box office grosses, 103; budget, 45; credit sequence, 55; festival screenings, xiii, xxviii, 43; filming conditions, 25, 27, 36–37, 44–45, 62–63, 148; financing, 53, 55, 85, 165; folklore in, 25–26, 34, 40, 43–44, 54, 80, 110–12; folkways in, 113–14; humor in, 47, 54, 67; location, 36–37, 59, 112; marketing, xvii, 35–36, 103, 122; music in, 50–51, 63; National Film Registry, selection for, 168; pace, 165; prizes and awards, xiii, xxviii, 28, 168; reviews, 97, 103, 119, 122; script, 26, 44, 55–56; southern values in, 80, 154; style, 106; themes, 34, 115
Toronto International Film Festival, xxviii, xxix, 12
Tradition, 112–13
Training Day, 146
Tree of Wooden Clogs, The, 82
Trickster, 26, 54, 111, 184
True Identity, 67–69

Tubman, Harriet, 136
Tulchin, Harris E., 26–27
Turner, Nat, 126–29, 134–36, 140

UCLA, 5–6, 13, 18–19, 31, 40, 49, 57–58, 79, 83, 84, 98, 113, 119–20, 128, 138, 142, 146, 156, 157, 161, 162, 168, 174, 175, 177, 182, 183; and minorities, 57; School of Film and Television, 109, 119; strike against, 47
UCLA Film and Television Archive, xxix, 151, 175
"Unforgettable," 144, 153, 175
Unrealized projects, xxv–xxvi, 22, 29, 43, 55, 64, 91, 108, 125
U.S. Film Festival, 28, 116n1, 151. *See also* Sundance Film Festival

Vallejo, California, 166
Van Gogh, Vincent, 51
Van Sant, Gus, 100
Vancouver Film Festival, 101
Variety, 99
Vicksburg, Mississippi, xxvii, 30, 47, 76, 97
Vietnam War, 57; and the black community, 11–12
View Park (Los Angeles neighborhood), 99
Vigo, Jean, 6, 66
Violence, 14, 79, 148, 153; in the family, 44, 46; in films about blacks, 36, 96, 103, 145, 147, 185
Visual Communications, 57
Visual sense, importance of, 88

Wallace, Dimitria, 55
Walt Disney Company, 69, 70, 118

Warming by the Devil's Fire, xxiii–xxiv, 130–33, 168, 186
Washington, Dinah, 33, 144, 150, 153, 166, 175, 182, 183
Waters, John, 178
Watson, Orson, 76
Watts, xxvii, 3–4, 5, 30, 56, 95, 97, 98–99, 109, 112, 143, 148; barbershop in, 46, 112, 155; in *Killer of Sheep*, x, 7, 96, 145, 150, 181; in *To Sleep with Anger*, 139–40. *See also* Los Angeles; South Central Los Angeles
Watts Riots (1965), 12–13, 77, 154
Watts Writers Workshop, 16
Wayans, Keenen Ivory, 28
Wayans brothers, 40
Wayne's World, 84
Wedding, The, xxii, 124
Wedding, The (West), xxii
Weinstein brothers, 101
Wenders, Wim, 83
West, Dorothy, xxii
"What Is America to Me?," 76, 139, 176
When It Rains, xxi, 118, 123–24, 175, 179, 185–86
White, Armond, xxi, xxii, 106, 181
Whitehead, Margaret, 128
William and Ellen Craft Story, The (unrealized project), xxv
William Styron's Nat Turner: Ten Black Writers Respond, 126
Williams, Spencer, 16, 33
Williamson, Sonny Boy, 133
Wilson, August, 40
Winfrey, Oprah, 124
Wire, The, 185
Wolper, David, 128
Woodberry, Billy, 5, 31, 32, 34, 35, 42, 43, 49, 59, 62, 92, 138, 184

Working class in student films, 6, 19, 98, 153, 162, 177
Wright, Basil, xi, 6, 52, 57–58, 120, 121, 157

Young, Robert, 4
Your Children Come Back to You, 5, 62

ZDF (Zweites Deutsches Fernsehen), 10, 89
Ziegler, Isabelle, 13, 51, 84
Zimbabwe, 159, 173

www.ingramcontent.com/pod-product-compliance
Lightning Source LLC
Chambersburg PA
CBHW021838220426

43663CB00005B/307